TO EVERYTHING THAT MIGHT HAVE BEEN: THE LOST UNIVERSE OF *SPACE 1999*

TO EVERYTHING THAT MIGHT HAVE BEEN: THE LOST UNIVERSE OF *SPACE 1999*

DAVID HIRSCH AND ROBERT E WOOD

WITH CHRISTOPHER PENFOLD

First published in the UK in 2022 by
Telos Publishing Ltd
www.telos.co.uk

Telos Publishing Ltd values feedback. Please e-mail us with any comments
you may have about this book to: feedback@telos.co.uk

ISBN: 978-1-84583-196-7

To Everything That Might Have Been: The Lost Universe of Space: 1999 © 2022
David Hirsch and Robert E Wood

The moral right of the author has been asserted.

Index by Ian Prichard.

British Library Cataloguing in Publication Data.
A catalogue record for this book is available from the British Library.

ACKNOWLEDGEMENTS

The authors would like to extend our deepest thanks to the following people and companies:

Christopher Penfold, whose generous assistance and input has been invaluable!
Jamie Anderson
Dee Anderson
Susie Landau
Hayward Morse
Cathy Arden
Brian Johnson
Kit Bevan
Shaqui Le Vesconte
Martin Willey
Tim Mallett & Kindred Productions
Catherine Bujold
Anthony Wynn
Bob Kotsopolous
Steve Warnek
Warren Friedrich
Christopher Paulsen
Renèe Feit
Jorge Carmo
Victor Marino, Jr.
Gordon Moriguchi
Todd Morton
Chris Thompson

And finally, to Roy Bjellquist, for organizing the cons that brought David and Robert together in person.

We would also thank Covid-19 … unbelievably the only thing we can thank it for is all of the lockdown time which provided us the opportunity to write this book.

CONTENTS

FOREWORD

by Christopher Penfold

Nearly half a century has now passed since the day when Gerry Anderson approached me about working with him on the development of what was, initially, a new series of *UFO*. That eventually mutated into *Space: 1999* and I am humbled by the fact that work I did then is still enthused over and inspirational to dedicated fans the world over. So my heartfelt thanks go out to all of you who have been so committed to keeping the faith.

Many of the people who were my colleagues at that time have sadly but inevitably passed away. And, although it is thankfully not the case, I sometimes have the feeling that I may be the last man standing. So, when David Hirsch and Robert Wood approached me to write the Foreword for their new book, I was not only flattered but also delighted by the prospect of a new publication that will breathe fresh life into what has become a cult classic. You can't, it seems, keep a good show down!

The passage of time does funny things to memory and re-visiting the show with the attention to detail that David and Robert have applied to their research for this book has caused me to resuscitate, revaluate and reconsider my memories in ways that have been deeply rewarding.

The title they have chosen for their book is taken from the episode 'Black Sun' which was written by David Weir and extensively re-written by me to make it compatible with the production resources that were available at the time. That was done under considerable pressure and, in my memory, I had made the episode my own. I felt confident that I had kept as close as possible to the spirit of David Weir's story, but it was not until I was able to re-read his original draft that I realized just how much of his inspirational work I had retained. It must be nearly fifty years since I had seen that draft, so it was a welcome surprise to discover that David and Robert had been able to unearth a copy which they made available for me to read.

'To everything that might have been' is the first part of the toast that Victor Bergman and John Koenig make to each other as they quaff Victor's 60 year-old brandy believing that, within hours, they will have disappeared into the maw of the black hole. Deployed here as the title of the book, the phrase carries with it a tinge of regret. David and Robert have discovered an extraordinary amount of documentation that relates to the early development of *Space: 1999* and to the changes of direction it took during the making of the two series.

It is certainly true that when I first called Johnny Byrne and asked him to join the embryonic script department, and when George Bellak arrived from New York to head up the department, we had confident aspirations and huge ambition. Yes, the series would offer a new and distinctive approach to space fiction; yes, it would achieve an American network sale; yes, it would be a huge success and yes, the show would run and run and run. As we know only too well, most of those ambitions were not achieved but, as I look back now, my memories of that adventure are not dominated by a sense of regret. We took risks, we boldly went, we made a handful of episodes that have become cult classics and yes, we committed some howlers and made a few horrors. But nearly fifty years of dedication by fans like you, the readers of this book, is good enough for me to think very positively of what we did collectively achieve.

I attended a convention recently in Bethlehem, Pennsylvania and, as I was checking into the hotel, a tall, lean and distinguished looking man was standing next to me. When he heard me give my name to the receptionist, he turned to me and said, 'Excuse me, I've wanted to meet you for years. I'm a rocket scientist and I work for NASA and none of that would have happened if I hadn't been captivated by your show when it first came out.' And later, at the same convention, a woman approached me and said she was a doctor. She, too, said that it was down to seeing Barbara Bain taking a leading role as a medical professional that gave her the will to pursue her ambition at a time when it was relatively rare for a woman to do so. It is so gratifying to know that when the pursuit of gender and ethnic equality and diversity are so high on the progressive agenda today, that they were taken for granted nearly fifty years ago on Moonbase Alpha.

Elsewhere in this excellent book you will find a memoir which I wrote at the authors' request about my friend, George Bellak. His time working on the show as head of the script department was relatively brief, but his influence lingered throughout Series One and to very good effect. But I'd like also to pay tribute here to Johnny Byrne whose contribution to the scripts of Series One reached far beyond the episodes for which he is credited as author. Johnny's chain-smoking enthusiasm and irrepressible good humor did so much to sustain us through pressure and stress and it is my great privilege to be able to celebrate here a professional and personal friendship that is one of my most highly valued memories of working on *Space: 1999*. And, like my friendship with George Bellak, it continued until the end of his life.

If we three were the core of the script department on the first series, I was incredibly fortunate also to be able to draw on the support, wisdom, experience and creative imagination of two unofficial colleagues – Martin Landau and Barbara Bain. Often, after they had finished a long day of shooting, I would go back to their house in Little Venice to go through the latest draft of the next episode. To this day Barbara continues to insist that I was just out of Cambridge University, but I had, in fact, already got two drama series under my belt as writer and script editor and I was all of 30 years old. However, they took me under their wing and my learning curve went into the steepest incline. Their knowledge and firsthand experience of that vital transition between script and screen was invaluable and I remain grateful to this day for all that I learned under their generous tuition.

The greatest debt owed by all of us who were involved in *Space: 1999* is, of course, to Gerry and Sylvia Anderson. But I hope it won't be thought invidious of me to mention three more members of the team that they had so judiciously put together. Keith Wilson and Brian Johnson each had their own respective genius contributions to make. They were both involved from the very beginning and were so seminally instrumental in defining the look of the show which has endured to this day.

And finally, I would like to remember Charles Crichton. For my money, as a director, Charles was in a league of his own. Like me, Charles had begun his film career as a film editor – in his case, at Michael Balcon's Ealing Studios. *Space: 1999* was not the most exalted show that Charles worked on during the course of his long and glittering career, but he brought to it the same exacting high standards that he would have brought to any of his distinguished feature films. He would spend hours with me during pre-production, going through and refining the script and then, during shooting, he would encourage – even insist – that I should attend the screening of rushes each day so that we could learn from what had been shot the day before and see where the script might be improved for what he was yet to shoot. As with the time I spent with Martin and Barbara, the learning curve was steep, and the experience was both invaluable and unforgettable.

So, far from being tinged with the regret that is hinted at in the chosen title of this excellent book, my own memories – which have been prodded into sharp relief by the research that David and Robert have done – are warm, affectionate and tinged with justifiable pride in what, collectively, we all achieved together. It will be sure to add to the enjoyment that you dedicated fans continue to derive from your devotion to *Space: 1999*.

Christopher Penfold – February 2021

INTRODUCTION

by Robert E Wood

David Hirsch and I had long been friends online, familiar with each other through our writings on the cult-classic science fiction TV series *Space: 1999* – David as author of the *Moonbase Alpha Technical Notebook* and longtime contributor to *Starlog* magazine, and I as author of *Destination: Moonbase Alpha – The Unofficial and Unauthorised Guide to Space: 1999*. It was only a matter of time before we met in person at a *Space: 1999* convention, which finally happened in September 2017.

The next time we met, in September 2019, David showed me his collection of extremely rare documents, story outlines, and scripts from the early pre-production period of the series. As we discussed the documents it dawned on both of us at the same time that what we were looking at could form the basis for an amazing book. We conferred with Christopher Penfold – who was a guest at the convention – and showed him some of the documents. His reaction was further encouragement, and our plans began to coalesce.

But David's collection of material wasn't everything we would need …

Sadly, actor Martin Landau had passed away in July 2017, and by this time in 2019 his estate was in the process of selling some of the items he had collected throughout his career. In the ensuing months I was lucky enough to be able to acquire from the Landau estate a wealth of additional uniquely rare *Space: 1999* documents, extensive correspondence, call sheets, cast lists, shooting schedules, and more.

As David and I subsequently reviewed all of our material as a whole and began to sketch an outline for this book we became increasingly aware of the amazing scope of the documents, and of the previously unimaginable perspective on the series that they provided. We found ourselves assembling countless missing links to the puzzle of *Space: 1999*'s development and production. Documents that had only existed for decades as vague remembrances, believed long-lost in the mists of time, were once again revealing themselves.

Some things seem pre-determined in life. People are drawn together for purposes, and I think that somehow David and I were drawn together at the right time, in the right place, to ensure that this treasure trove of information would not be lost and could be shared with our fellow Alphans, as *Space: 1999* fans call ourselves.

David and I are also extremely grateful to Christopher Penfold for his ongoing good-natured support and his significant contributions to this book. As one of the people most integral to the genesis of the series, his perspective and remembrances are invaluable.

Our title for this book, *To Everything That Might Have Been – The Lost Universe of* Space: 1999, links perhaps the most famous quote from one of the most popular episodes of the series ('To everything that might have been... To everything that was' from 'Black Sun') with what truly is a lost universe of material documenting what might have been if things had gone slightly differently during *Space: 1999's* early development, or in the transition between the first and second series, or indeed even after the series ended!

In that sense, the word 'lost' in our title points toward possible alternate realities of what might have been. Just as our Rogue Moon could wind up anywhere in the universe, so too could the direction of the TV series. What would Commander Koenig have been like had Larry Hagman, Doug McClure, Robert Culp, or even William Shatner been cast instead of Martin Landau? How different would it have been if the Italian actors they were planning on casting had indeed been hired to play Professor Danilo Sabatini or Chief Pilot Carlo Catani? What would life on the Moon have been like if the colony really was a powder keg of fear and dissatisfaction? If a heavily armed Moon City was at constant war with alien races, as depicted in early pre-production documents? Would the series have been more successful or an unmitigated failure? At each turn – and there are countless directions it could have gone – you are about to discover in these pages that *Space: 1999* had the potential of becoming a very different series entirely.

The word 'lost' also refers to the fact that much of the material in this book had literally been lost. Johnny Byrne had lost his copies of his Critical Commentary on Year One. Copies of many other documents included here have never surfaced anywhere else in the decades since the series ended. The fact that they continued to exist, packed away in boxes, and awaiting discovery, is remarkable. It is a lost history, now rediscovered.

Some of what you will read in this book recounts specific facts and details about *Space: 1999*, some fills in considerable historic gaps in our knowledge of its genesis and production, and some extrapolates from documents and correspondence, connecting the dots to reveal remarkable glimpses of what might have been.

So, here you have it: *To Everything That Might Have Been – The Lost Universe of* Space: 1999. It is an honor to be able to share this material with you, and a privilege to further document this amazing series, *Space: 1999*, and the odyssey of Moonbase Alpha, which – as foretold by the mysterious alien queen Arra in the episode 'Collision Course' – shall know no end.

UFO 2

by David Hirsch

Space: 1999 was the culmination of an almost 16-year journey for series creators and producers Gerry and Sylvia Anderson. This big budget, lavish A-List cast vehicle was the pinnacle event in a career that started with a modest low-budget, quarter-hour, children's puppet series.

In 1957, Gerry Anderson had formed an independent production company, A P Films, with his friend, cinematographer Arthur Provis. Struggling to secure work, they could not pass on the chance to produce a series of 52 episodes for *The Adventures of Twizzle*. Created and written by the prolific novelist Robert Leigh, the program was successful enough to secure A P Films another commission for the first 26 episodes of the follow-up series *Torchy, The Battery Boy (1959)*.

Desperate to improve the visual quality of the medium, Anderson struck out on his own to create, with composer Barry Gray, the ambitious western-themed series *Four Feather Falls (1960)*. Here, puppets now had moving mouths that were synced to the dialogue, performed on detailed 3-dimensional sets, and actually appeared to even ride horses. This would establish the goal for Anderson's manifesto; that each new series would make some quantum leap forward creatively and technically. He named this process 'Supermarionation'.

Anderson's desire to circumvent the inability of the marionettes to walk convincingly resulted, in partnership with art director Reg Hill, in the creation of a sci-fi vehicle for their next series, *Supercar (1961)*. Though pleased with the success of *Four Feather Falls*, Granada Television was unwilling to finance the expensive new series. Lew Grade, head of the rival ATV Network, was eying the value of international sales through his US-based distribution arm, ITC (Independent Television Corporation), and offered to bankroll the new show. *Supercar* went on to become a major hit in the United States, particularly in New York City.

While *Supercar* often experimented with mood lighting and clever camera angles (in particular the fan favorite episode 'Calling Charlie Queen'), the sale of their following series, *Fireball XL5 (1962)*, to the NBC-TV Network gave the A P Films team the ability to go even further, creating dark, mysterious outer space locations, weird alien populations and landscapes, all highlighted by Barry Gray's jazzy score and groundbreaking experimental electronic effects.

Further milestones were established with each successive series. *Stingray* (1964) was now in colour and had puppets with changeable expressive faces, while *Thunderbirds* (1965) ran as an action-packed full-hour drama and spawned two feature films. *Captain Scarlet and the Mysterons* (1967), set a new level of realism where the marionettes were now in perfect human proportion instead of characterizations and the sets were so detailed that they could have passed for full-scale locales. The following series, *Joe 90* (1968), favoured character-driven plots over fantastic vehicles and visual effects.

By the late 1960s, Lew Grade had felt that the puppet series had been played out. In England alone, all the series were rerun so often that there was little room in the network schedule for a new series. He was also unimpressed with Anderson's attempt to combine puppets and live-action exterior footage for *The Secret Service* (1969). After viewing the completed first episode, Grade was baffled by lead Stanley Unwin's double-talk routine. Convinced international sales were impossible, he ordered the series to shut down immediately after the thirteen episodes in production were completed. The Supermarionation era had come to an end.

The Andersons had always desired to move into live-action, though their first venture, an adaption of an Edgar Wallace story, *Crossroads to Crime* (1960), was agreed all around to be a less than satisfying product.

They had frequently developed various concepts for a live-action venture over the years, but it wasn't until Universal Studios agree to partner with them to film their script (co-written with Donald James and an uncredited Tony Williamson) for *Doppelgänger*. Released in the US on August 28, 1969 and retitled as *Journey to the Far Side of the Sun*, the film told the story of a twin, but mirror planet on the opposite side of the sun. Roy Thinnes, fresh off *The Invaders* (1967-68) TV series, starred in a film that proved a perfect vehicle to showcase the marriage of live-action with Derek Meddings convincing miniature effects.

Impressed with the final results and assured they could maintain that quality for a weekly TV series, Lew Grade was willing to finance the Anderson's first live-action series, *UFO*. Co-created with Reg Hill, the production began filming in 1969 at the MGM British Studios in Borehamwood, England. The most expensive TV series at its time, they also adapted the vehicles, props and costumes from *Doppelgänger* to give *UFO* a movie-of-the-week look. The scripts were also unlike anything the Andersons had written and produced before, presenting tales that were dark, often with unhappy endings, pushing the series' format to its limits.

The sudden closure of the MGM studios after the completion of the first block of 17 episodes forced a move to Pinewood Studios for the remaining nine episodes.

The Andersons, with Reg Hill, were then commissioned by Grade to produce the Robert Vaughn adventure *The Protectors* (1972). To be filmed on location and in England, this new series followed ITC's tried and true action format. It was to run only half an hour to appeal to the new US Prime-Time Access Rule, which gave 7:30 p.m. slots back to local stations.

Derek Meddings, whose effects team had taken over the company's entire puppet stage facility in Slough to shoot *UFO*, was not required for *The Protectors* and, with no outside work to keep the studio open, Century 21 Productions (formed from A P Films during *Thunderbirds*) was shut down. The Andersons and Hill formed a new corporate banner called Group Three.

Meddings moved into feature films, becoming the effects supervisor on the Bond films, starting with *The Man with the Golden Gun* (1974). He eventually opened his own effects studio, The Magic Camera Company.

UFO, which had begun airing in England in 1970, finally reached the United States in the fall of 1972. Though it had not achieved a full network sale, ITC had secured a lucrative sale to the CBS Network's 'Owned and Operated' stations (ie not independent stations that simply aired CBS Network programs). Placed at 7:00 pm on Saturday, it was the lead-in to the network's mega-hit line-up that began with *All in the Family*. Initially *UFO* was a ratings hit and Grade gave Anderson a budget to develop a second series.

The Head of ITC's New York office, Abe Mandell, mandated that the second series be revamped to take place totally in space. He felt the Earth-set stories were not as appealing as the space adventures and demanded that the new format prevent any terrestrial-set plots. Anderson envisioned moving the format further into the future from the first season's setting of the 1980s. This jump of only ten or so years into the future had allowed location shooting with little or no redress. Free from that limitation, the format was jumped to the year 1999. The tiny moonbase manned by SHADO (Supreme Headquarters Alien Defense Organization) would now become the vast Moon City, now manned by several hundred personnel. A fleet of fighter craft were based there to stave off the hordes of alien invaders.

With his department heads immersed on *The Protectors*, Anderson turned to Keith Wilson, who was Assistant Art Director under Bob Bell, to begin designing the lavish lunar complex. Christopher Penfold, whose work Anderson admired on *The Pathfinders* (1972), took over script editing duties from Tony Barwick.

After several months, it became evident that ratings for *UFO* were dropping. Convinced CBS was no longer interested in a second series, Grade pulled the plug on *UFO 2* (or *UFO: 1999*) in the early part of 1973.

Fabergè, who had been a major financial partner in *The Protectors*, opted out of committing to a third series and the Andersons spent much of the early part of that year scrambling to develop a new project. A self-financed attempt to return to puppetry, *The Investigator*, used marionettes as miniaturized people interacting with live actors and filmed on location in Malta. The result was a disappointment and wasn't even pitched to friend George Heinemann at NBC-TV. He did eventually buy Anderson's *The Day After Tomorrow – Into Infinity* for the network's *NBC Special Treat* (1975 - 86) educational series, but they did not pick this 'back-door pilot' up for series.

Convinced that there was still potential in all their pre-production efforts on *UFO 2*, the Andersons pitched the concept of an original half-hour space adventure wherein the inhabitants of a city of the Moon would be cast adrift into the vast unknown void. *Menace in Space* postulated that the humans themselves would be perceived as the hostile invaders. Eventually re-titled *Space: 1999*, Gerry and Sylvia then wrote a half-hour pilot script, 'Zero G'.

Grade and Mandell saw value in this revised format and, with dreams of that ever hoped for American TV network sale, the project eventually blossomed into the most expensive television series ever mounted at that time.

THIS (HALF-HOUR) EPISODE

by David Hirsch

In the early 1970s, the American TV landscape was changing, and regional stations had reacquired time slots back from the three major networks. There was suddenly a demand for 30-minute programs and ITC stepped up to fill the void with offerings such as *The Adventurer* (with Barry Morse and Catherine Schell) and the Gerry Anderson-produced *The Protectors* (featuring Tony Anholt).

Though the second series of *UFO* would most likely have retained the one-hour format, the revamped series was originally proposed as a fast-paced half-hour. To provide a detailed presentation of the evolution of a TV series, a degree of repetition in the material was necessary.

PRE-PRODUCTION DOCUMENTS

The following three documents chart the development of the series' initial concept, characters, and storylines. None of these documents are dated, but the order has been established by the authors based on the progression of the material contained within.

A few notes on these documents:

1. **'Early Series Proposal'.** This is the first known official ITC document outlining the series that would become *Space: 1999*. It is brief, untitled, and referred to here as 'Early Series Proposal'. While outlining a brief concept and point-form details, it contains no characters.

2. *MENACE IN SPACE*. This detailed document refers to 26 Half Hour episodes and retains numerous elements carried over from what would have been *UFO*'s second series. The Commander and Dr Janet Bowman are the only two characters mentioned.

3. *SPACE: 1999* **(Working Title) ADVANCE PROGRAM INFORMATION**. This document continues to reference 26 Half Hour

episodes. It now outlines three main characters including The Commander, The Lieutenant, and the Chief Medical Officer, who is now male. Once again, there are no names proposed. Included are eight brief storylines featuring a number of concepts that eventually became filmed episodes and some amazing title suggestions such as 'Stop the Moon – I Wanna Get Off!' It also contains the earliest known proposed title for the pilot episode, 'The Last of the Earth Men'. These storylines were possibly developed by original Story Editor Christopher Penfold and the Andersons. The proposal also now details a projected budget of at least $110,000 US per episode to show that ITC is promising a Network-quality product.

'EARLY SERIES PROPOSAL'

Action In Space

1999

At the dawn of the 21st Century, 300 men and women from Earth maintain an early warning system on the Moon. Aliens launch a devastating thermonuclear attack on the far side of the Moon[1] redistributing critical forcefields. The gravitational relationship of Earth and Moon is abruptly negated and the Moon is violently thrust out of orbit, marooning the 300 Earth men on a world adrift in outer space on an endless odyssey to the infinite regions of the farthest galaxies.

Sets And Hardware

Sets

All sets are futuristic. Exteriors and interiors are complex representations of space technology and include:

- Moon City
- Geodesic domes
- Domestic and industrial structures (dwelling, recycling plants, etc)
- Spaceport
- Control Sector

---

[1] This is the earliest mention of a thermonuclear event thrusting the Moon out of Earth's orbit. However, the plotline relating Aliens disrupting the gravitational forces was exclusively used in the 'Zero G' pilot script.

- Surface and subsurface installations
- Defence and communications systems

Hardware
- Lunarmobiles
- Hoverhoppers
- Moonbuggies
- Explorers
- Reconnaissance Rockets
- Interceptors
- Interplanetary Transport
- Computer Complex
- Medical Life Apparatus
- Voice Print Units

** AND MORE!

Note: Numerous pieces of pre-production design artwork by Keith Wilson were included in this document, as well as a Chris Foss painting of an early design for the spacecraft that would eventually become known as the Eagle.

Early MTU design landing at Moon City. By Chris Foss.

Moonbase Control by Keith Wilson.

The atomic waste deposit area by Keith Wilson.

Based on a scene that appears in George Bellak's 'The Void Ahead', two technicians are shown working above Moonbase Alpha as Koenig's M.T.U. comes in for a landing. They were also to appear later, hurled to the ground as Nuclear Waste Area Two erupts. By Keith Wilson

Originally, the location of the series was conceived as a vast complex known as Moon City. By Keith Wilson

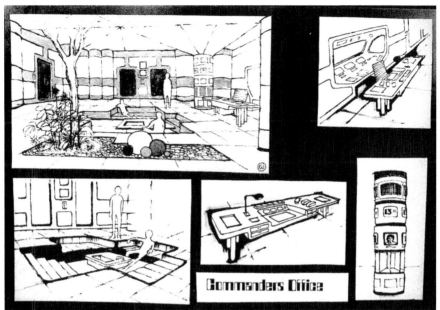

The Commander's Office originally had a much warmer design, one of several holdovers from the SHADO Moonbase 'Central Park' concept in UFO. *By Keith Wilson*

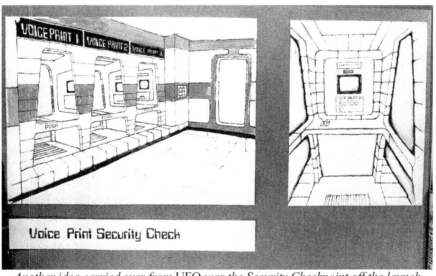

Another idea carried over from UFO *was the Security Checkpoint off the launch pads. While unused on the final set, a bubble-covered communications point can be seen off the Travel Tube entry/egress portals. By Keith Wilson.*

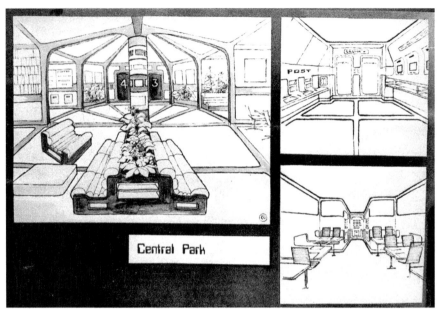

A centre for relaxation and group gatherings, 'Central Park' was originally created for UFO. Wilson carried the concept into Space: 1999 *as the original Writer's Guidelines called for a central area where people relaxed and ate. It wasn't until the Series Two episode 'Seance Spectre' that such a locale would be seen. By Keith Wilson.*

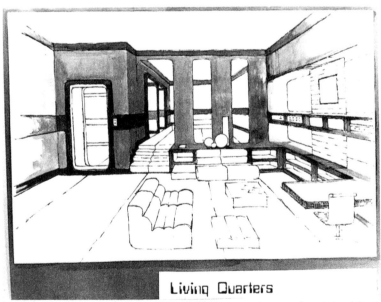

Bi-level design for typical crew quarters. This concept was only retained for Main Mission and Koenig's Office. By Keith Wilson.

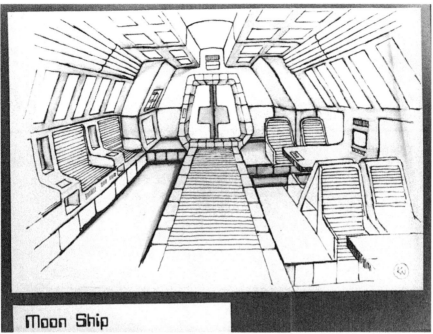

Moon Ship

Early design for the passenger module of the Moon Ship, or M.T.U., which later became the Eagle Transporter. Set design inspired the interior of the Travel Tube car. By Keith Wilson.

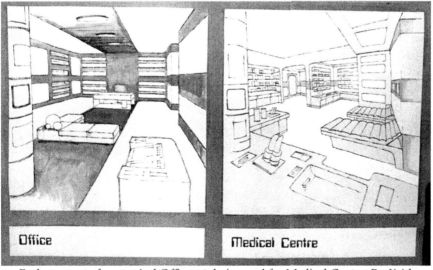

Office

Medical Centre

Early concepts for a typical Office set design and for Medical Center. By Keith Wilson.

Unused alien planet interior concept. By Keith Wilson.

Another unused alien planet interior concept that may have been adapted for use on Star Maidens, *a series Wilson designed between Series One and Two of* Space: 1999. *By Keith Wilson.*

Planet Zenno concept art adapted into the final matte painting for the episode 'Missing Link'. By Keith Wilson.

Alien planet or Moon surface concept art showing astronauts working outside an Eagle module serving as base camp. Note the early Moon Buggy design. By Keith Wilson courtesy Jorge Carmo.

Concept design for Helena's encounter with the Triton computer in 'Ring Around the Moon'. By Keith Wilson.

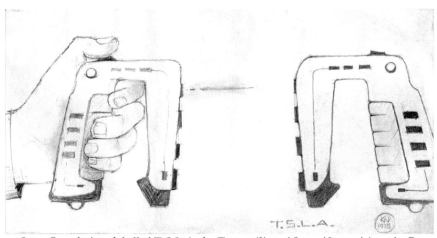

Stun Gun design, labelled T.S.L.A. for Tranquilizer / Stun / Laser / Atomic. By Keith Wilson.

Alien planet concept art reminiscent of the unused city glimpsed in the 'This Episode' sequence of 'Another Time, Another Place'. By Keith Wilson.

Concept art for Captain Zantor in 'Earthbound'. By Keith Wilson.

MENACE IN SPACE

The following document is reproduced from Marc Martin's website, www.ufoseries.com, and due to the lack of transition between the 'Sets and Hardware' section to the character Dr Janet Bowman, it is presumed to be missing an introductory 'Characters' heading and description for the Commander and potentially other characters. No other copy of this document is known to exist.

ADVANCE PROGRAM INFORMATION

MENACE IN SPACE
(working title)

26 NEW HALF-HOUR
SCIENCE-FICTION ADVENTURES
IN OUTER SPACE

Possible Titles

'The Intruders'
'Space Intruders'
'Journey Into Space'
'Space Journey'
'Outer Space'
'Space Probe'

WHY SCI-FI?

Never has the interest in science-fiction entertainment been higher. Books, movies and television programs about space adventure are experiencing marvelous popularity across a wide range of demographics.

This milieu, combined with feedback from the 136 stations which programmed our *UFO* series last season, has encouraged ITC to produce a brand-new series of science fiction stories.

WHY ITC?

Because we've been doing it successfully for a dozen years.

Our new science fiction series will be delivered to a ready-made science-fiction audience by the same team which helped get that audience ready. For the past 12 years, Gerry and Sylvia Anderson have specialized in producing science-fiction movies (UA, Universal) and television series (ITC) – working with a virtual repertory company of special effects technicians, designers, architects and engineers to achieve some of the most spectacular effects on the screen.

Together with Reg Hill, who collaborated with them on UFO, the Andersons have developed this new series of outer-space adventures. It will again be produced by ITC, with most of the same talents who have been working closely together for 12 years!

THE CONCEPT: FAR OUT ACTION

ITC's 'everybody-in-the-pool' theory is that the best way to combine story continuity and action is to keep everybody in an action environment – UFO was earthbound and required a full hour for development and narrative form. Our new series is conceived as a half-hour action format and to keep it moving, all the action is far out in space.

Set near the turn of the next century, in 1999, every exciting story depicts an adventure of the colony of earthmen who must wander through the universe on a small world which once was Earth's moon. All the 'business' is either on this world-ship, on other worlds and their ships – and in the space/time continuum which varies according to the moods of the art director!

In the limbo of outer space, limits are set only by the imaginations of the writers, art directors, set designers and other creative people involved in the production.

New hardware and special effects are being created for the new series. Everything about it will literally be new: stories, costumes, props, special effects, writers and cast.

THE FORMAT

Earth is destroyed[2] and the Moon, released from its orbit, wanders in space. On it are 300 men and women from all nations of Earth, originally based there to man an early-warning system and to repel invaders. Now they are Earth's sole survivors, on a quest for a new planet compatible with their needs. Ironically, they are considered the invaders, by inhabitants of other

---

[2] In this proposal, the Aliens are not present to cause the disaster. Simply, the Moon is set adrift when the Earth is destroyed. This was Gerry Anderson's answer to Abe Mandell's mandate that no action take place on Earth. This concept was dropped because Mandell felt this might upset viewers. It is interesting to note the duality of the title, is the 'Menace' what faces humans out there, or are they the threat?

planets.

Their conflict is with the life forms encountered on other worlds, with the elements of outer space – and with the problems of sustaining life on their new world as it wanders on its unexpected odyssey across the universe.

SETS AND HARDWARE

All sets, of course, are futuristic. Since WANDER was originally a base on Earth's moon, a system of geodesic and other domes has been constructed, both for the maintenance of atmosphere and for protection from the elements. Additional exteriors include domestic and industrial structures, armament and observation equipment. Interiors are highly sophisticated and complex representations of space technology.

HEADQUARTERS

The moon is 2,160 miles in diameter. Control of it as it speeds through space is maintained within a compound about twenty miles square and protected by an elaborate security ring of fences, photo electric fields and domes. Only top security personnel are permitted within these boundaries, and fewer still within the Commander's Control Sector. Inside the general compound there is a stratofield, with hangars for various lunar craft. There is also a circular metal disc about 30 yards in diameter. This disc is actually an armor-proof cover which opens in sections, like the petals of a metal flower, to give access to a cylindrical tube leading down to the heart of the H.Q. complex. The only vehicles to land in this cylinder are the fully computer-controlled vertical take-off HOVERHOPPERS, used for local transport of WANDER personnel. At its base, the cylindrical access tube become hexagonal and each of the armored walls protects access to one of the six corridors which lead out like an asterisk from the hexagonal heart.

As the HOVERHOPPER lands it lines up automatically in front of the corridor pre-selected by its passengers. A telescopic metal tube then moves out through the armored wall to the craft. In the door of the tube is a numerical keyboard on which the passengers pick out the appropriate code of the day. If they are code-correct, the door opens and admits them to the corridor they have selected. The master corridor of the six gives access to the Commander's office and the control room.

COMMANDER'S OFFICE

Access from the corridor is by further key-code and voice-print identification. The office/control room complex is wedge shaped, the apex of the wedge being the access door from the corridor. On the Commander's desk is a visual display unit on which he can monitor any of the information sources which feed constantly into the control room. He can also communicate direct by videophone with any area of WANDER.

For general information he relies on a multitude of computer sources throughout the complex; but he also has in his office a personal Commander's Computer called COMCOM.

COMMANDER'S COMPUTER (COM COM)

This has been programmed with all possible or imaginable permutations of factors that could affect the Commander's decision-making. In purely technical matters he can 'consult' this computer and get a logical answer which will often form the basis of a decision. It is a machine which he has lived with and which he has fed facts and information; it is a tool which he has himself brilliantly equipped with the data necessary to do his own job efficiently and quickly. With all of WANDER's problems the buck stops with the Commander and he uses the computer to help him decide. However, there are many WANDER problems whose solution cannot be based on the assessment of technical information. Whenever he puts in a problem with human or moral elements, the computer's reply is: 'Impossible to answer: your decision.' And now the Commander is entirely on his own.

EARLY-WARNING SYSTEMS

To give early warning of the approach of U.F.O.s in space WANDER has set up a manned base on the Moon to monitor all approaches. They are the back-up systems to S.I.D.

'FIRST BASE'

Nickname for the first section of Emergency Base to go into action. It is a complex consisting of control room, living quarters, leisure sphere and sick bay. It is manned by Control personnel and a team of pilots who fly the Interceptors. There are launch bays for these craft, and a landing area for lunar craft. The complex is protected by moon-to-space guided missiles and by the Interceptors.

INTERCEPTORS

To take advantage of early warnings of approaching U.F.O.s, WANDER supports a fleet of single-seater, high-speed craft designed to be able to intercept and destroy U.F.O.s in space before they enter WANDER's gravity field. They are equipped with space-to-space rocket missiles and are controlled by a pilot who is directed from Control.

MOONMOBILE

Designed for travel over the surface of the Moon, this 'buggy' is used to investigate U.F.O. crashes or meteorite strikes.

LUNARMOBILES

To combat U.F.O.s that have actually landed on the moon, WANDER has a fleet of tracked armored vehicles manned by a crew of two and firing ground-to-ground missiles.

MOONSHIP

This is the basic rocket vehicle which carries personnel and equipment on short reconnaissance flights.

HOVERHOPPERS

For short-haul personnel transport to and from the H.Q. there is a fleet of these fully automatic, computer-controlled, vertical take-off craft. They carry up to four passengers whom they fly into and out of the H.Q. Cylinder, responding to the destination requests which they key into its computer.

TRAVEL TUBE

For movement of personnel between H.Q. and the various vehicles on the stratofield there is a fully automated, underground travel tube.

At H.Q. a passenger gains access to a travel capsule by punching up the correct key-code. Inside the capsule he selects his destination by punching up another numerical code on the capsule key. The capsule is then whistled along the underground tube in a cushion of air.

DR JANET BOWMAN[3]

Senior member of the Space Therapy Division of WANDER, although under 30, Janet Bowman is responsible for physical fitness of the entire population of her world. She is a splendid example of her work, and as competent as she is good looking. Since the preservation of life is a top priority, Dr Bowman is a member of The Commander's Council, a cabinet-like group of

---

[3] A subliminal nod to *2001: A Space Odyssey*? This is the only character named.

top advisors with whom he is continually meeting.

ACTION... AND VIOLENCE

The problems of personal violence are avoided by placing the concept outside the understanding of the 300 WANDER residents... who understandably hold all life sacred. Realizing that what they have is all they get, hurting each other is unthinkable in their society – and not a bad idea for ours.

Action, on the other hand, is the major ingredient of the series – and it is not confined to space-ship interiors. Neither are the plots confined to a rigid format. The open-end structure of this outer space series is as limitless as the structure of space itself.

ADVANCE PROGRAM INFORMATION

SPACE: 1999
(working title)

26 BRAND NEW FIRST-RUN SCIENCE-FICTION HALF-HOURS

IN COLOR ON FILM

Possible Titles

The Intruders
Menace in Space
Space Intruders
Journey Into Space
Marooned in Space: 1999
Outer Space
Space Probe
Space Journey: 1999

WHY SCI-FI?

Never has the interest in science-fiction entertainment been higher. Books, movies and television programs about space adventure are experiencing tremendous popularity across a wide range of demographics.

THE CONCEPT: FAR OUT ACTION

ITC's 'everybody-in-the-pool' theory is that the best way to combine story continuity and action is to keep everybody in an action environment. UFO was earthbound and required a full hour for development and narrative form. Our new series is conceived as a half-hour action format and to keep it moving, all the action is far out in space.

Set at the turn of the next century, in 1999, every exciting story depicts an adventure of the colony of earthmen who must wander through the universe on a small world which was once Earth's Moon. All the 'business' is either on this world-ship, on other planets and their ships – and in a varying space/time continuum.

In the limbo of outer space, limits are set only by the imaginations of the writers, art directors, set designers and other creative people involved in the production.

New hardware and special effects are being created for the new series. Everything about it will literally be new: stories, costumes, props, special effects.

THE FORMAT

The Moon, blasted out of its Earth orbit, wanders in space. On it are 300 men and women from all the nations of Earth, originally based there to man an early-warning system and to repel invaders. Now they are marooned in space – on a quest for a new planet. Ironically, <u>they</u> are considered the invaders by inhabitants of other planets.

Their conflict is with the life forms encountered on other worlds, with the elements of outer space – and with the problems of sustaining life on their new world as it wanders on its unexpected odyssey across the universe.

Action on SPACE: 1999 will be set away from Moon City as well as in it. Both interior and exterior sets and props will be constructed for scenes on alien planets and ships.

We realize that a successful series must not lock its characters into the same familiar sets week after week and have allocated major budgets to this important aspect of production.

$110,000/$120,000

The budget for each half-hour episode is $110,000 to $120,000. Minimum. This is a guarantee.

It reflects the highest budget for a half-hour series ITC has committed in 15 years of production. Sets, props, costumes – and the most comprehensive special effects yet mounted for a TV series have been figured into this budget.

THE STORY

In 1999, Earth is threatened by attack from alien worlds. The common enemy unites all the nations of Earth, which sign a treaty suspending domestic hostility. An elite defense force is organized from all countries, and 300 men and women maintain an early-warning system on the Moon.

This system enables them to repulse an alien attack, but not before devastating thermonuclear explosions on the far side of the Moon redistribute critical force-fields. The gravitational relationship of Earth and Moon is abruptly negated and the Moon is violently thrust out of orbit. The 300 men and women on the Earth-outpost find themselves marooned in space!

The Commander of Moonbase becomes, in effect, the head of government of this new world. A council composed of officers, scientists and medical personnel decide that it will be their primary mission to find a way back into Earth's orbital range. Failing this, they must locate a compatible planet on which to settle. In the meantime, they are prepared to continue functioning in outer space the same way they have been functioning in an Earth orbit. Food, air and water recycling installations are powered with atomic and solar energy. All systems necessary for the maintenance of life as it was on Earth are operative – making the Moon totally self-supporting.

The marooned Earthmen begin their fateful journey through the incredible vastness of space. Soon they learn that they are regarded as intruders and considered a menace to the Universe. Suspicious aliens attack and they must match wits and weapons against fantastic life forms found throughout the galaxies on their unexpected odyssey.

Principal leads are THE COMMANDER, THE LIEUTENANT and THE CHIEF MEDICAL OFFICER. At least one of these leads will be an American actor of status in U.S. television markets.

THE COMMANDER

The awesome responsibility of commanding Earth's outpost in space was assigned to a leader chosen for his combination of outstanding leadership qualities, superior space knowledge and unequalled administrative ability. A former test pilot and celebrated astronaut, he won the command over candidates from all nations because their leaders acknowledged that he knew the job better than anyone in the entire world. He is a self-assured career man with the ability to inspire loyalty and fidelity among the elite core of Earthmen on the Moon.

THE LIEUTENANT

The Commander's right-hand man, he is virile and attractive. Essentially a man of action. The Lieutenant shies away from any permanent attachment to either a desk or a girl. His background is generally similar to that of The Commander, although he is younger and more disposed to action than administration.

CHIEF MEDICAL OFFICER

A close associate of The Commander, it is the doctor's responsibility to maintain the species of Man on an artificial Earth, marooned in the infinity of space, where the rules of medical science as he has learned them are constantly bent and broken.

SETS AND HARDWARE

All sets, of course, are futuristic. A system of geodesic and other domes has been constructed, both for the maintenance of atmosphere and for protection from the elements. Additional exteriors include domestic and industrial structures, armament and observation equipment. Interiors are highly sophisticated and complex representations of space technology.

HEADQUARTERS

The Moon is 2,160 miles in diameter. Control of it as it speeds through space is maintained within a compound about twenty miles square and protected by an elaborate security ring of fences, photoelectric fields and domes. Only top security personnel are permitted within these boundaries, and fewer still within the Commander's Control Sector. Inside the general compound there is a spaceport, with hangers for various lunar craft. There is also a circular metal disc about 30 yards in diameter. This disc is actually an armor-proof cover which opens in sections, like the petals of a flower, to give access to a cylindrical tube leading down to the heart of the H.Q. complex. The only vehicles to land in this cylinder are the fully computer-controlled vertical take-off HOVERHOPPERS, used for local transport. At its base, the cylindrical access tube becomes hexagonal and each of the armored walls protects access to one of the six corridors which lead out like an asterisk from the hexagonal heart.

As the HOVERHOPPER lands it lines up automatically in front of the corridor pre-selected by its passengers. A telescopic metal tube then moves out through the armored wall to the craft. In the door of the tube is a numerical keyboard on which the passengers pick out the appropriate code of the day. If they are code-correct, the door opens and admits them to the corridor they have selected. The master corridor of the six gives access to the Commander's office and the control room.

COMMANDER'S OFFICE

Access from the corridor is by further key-code and voice-print identification. The office/control room complex is wedge shaped, the apex of the wedge being the access door from the corridor. On the Commander's desk is a visual display unit on which he can monitor any of the information sources which feed constantly into the control room. He can also communicate direct by videophone with any area of Moon City, and with selected areas of the unsettled parts of the Moon.

For general information he relies on a multitude of computer sources throughout the complex; but he also has in his office a personal Commander's Computer called COMCOM.

COMMANDER'S COMPUTER (COM COM)

This computer complex has been programmed with all possible factors that could affect the Commander's decision-making. In purely technical matters he can 'consult' this computer and get a logical answer which will often form the basis of a decision. It is a machine which he has lived with and fed facts and information; it is a tool which he has himself brilliantly equipped with the data necessary to do his own job efficiently and quickly. With all of Moon City's problems, the buck stops with the Commander and he uses the computer to help him with critical decisions.

CENTRAL CONTROL

The Control Room is the broad end of the wedge and when the Commander has to be directly involved in its activities, the wall behind his desk parts, his chair swings round and he can now look down into the complex area from his high dais. It is the nerve-center of Moon City's early-warning systems, The Control Room maintains constant surveillance of the space around the Moon via a continuous flow of radar data. The Control Room is a monitoring and communications center as well as the means by which the Commander directs all his forces in action. It is equipped with a multitude of TV monitors, radar scopes, videophones, recorders and other radio and telephone devices. It is manned round the clock by highly trained personnel.

EARLY WARNING SYSTEMS

Manned bases have been built outside Moon City to monitor all approaches and give early warning of any unexpected or unauthorized activity in space near the Moon.

EMERGENCY BASE

The first section of the early warning defense system to go into action is Emergency Base, a complex consisting of control room, living-quarters, leisure sphere and sick-bay. It is manned by Control personnel and a team of pilots who fly the Interceptors. There are launch bays for these craft, and a landing area for lunarcraft. The complex is protected by moon-to-space guided missiles and by the Interceptors.

INTERCEPTORS

To take advantage of the early warnings of approaching alien spacecraft, Moon City supports a fleet of single-seater, high speed spaceships designed to intercept and destroy alien bodies in space before they enter the Moon's gravity field. They are equipped with space-to-space rocket missiles and are controlled by a pilot who is directed from Central Control.

MOONMOBILE

Designed for travel over the surface of the Moon, this 'buggy' is used to investigate any activity on the surface of the Moon, including meteorite strikes and other landings.

LUNARMOBILES

To combat alien ships that have actually landed on the Moon, there is a fleet of tracked armored vehicles, manned by a crew of two and firing ground-to-ground missiles.

MOONSHIP

This is the basic rocket vehicle which carries personnel and equipment on short reconnaissance flights and serves as a skylab for long hauls.

HOVERHOPPERS

For short-haul personnel transport to and from the H.Q. there is a fleet of these fully automatic computer-controlled, vertical take-off craft. They carry up to four passengers whom they fly into and out of the H.Q. Cylinder, responding to the destination requests which they key into its computer.

TRAVEL TUBE

For movement of personnel between the H.Q. and various points in Moon City, and for access to vehicles on the spaceport there are fully-automated, underground travel tubes. At H.Q. a passenger gains access to a travel capsule by punching up the correct key-code. Inside the capsule he selects his destination by punching up another numerical code on the capsule key. The capsule is then whistled along the underground tube in a cushion of air.

THE SCRIPTS

Science Fiction is a highly specialized genre. For this new series, scripts are being prepared by the leading writers in the field. Here are storylines for the first eight episodes.

Author notes have been added in italics.

THE LAST OF THE EARTH MEN

The moon soars free of the solar system with 300 men and women — on a desperate odyssey across time and space.

The first of a multitude of proposed titles for the series pilot, all of which share the core plot of the Moon breaking free of Earth orbit and hurtling throughout uncharted space.

WAR GAMES

Approaching an alien planet in a far galaxy, the earth men are treated as invaders and met with hostility.

Adapted by Christopher Penfold into the classic visual effects extravaganza, this pitch is the only one that retained its original title. This is also one of several episodes based on the format outline theme that the Alphans will be treated as potential hostile invaders.

THE MONO MENACE

Alien life, bred from a single cell, with a single purpose: destroy the men from earth.

This plot line appears to have been unused in any filmed episode and there is no information if it ever made it beyond this stage. More than likely, it was probably abandoned due to VFX limitations.

THE TROJANS

Aliens infiltrate Moon City. Their leader: a female.

This appears to be the seed idea for Dione's matriarchal society in Bob Kellett's 'The Last Enemy'. One could suppose that her alleged request for asylum was the infiltration concept. It has been rumored that Barbara Bain suggested this story.

ANOTHER EARTH

A compatible planet seems to be found — but all is not what it seems on the Utopian world.

The title 'Another Earth' invites comparisons to 'Another Time, Another Place' by Johnny Byrne, both in the similarity of title and the Alphans return to Earth. The storyline, however, could possibly have also been an inspiration for the mysterious planet in 'Guardian of Piri' or the peaceful alien society in 'War Games', both penned by Christopher Penfold.

REVOLUTION

The Commander's authority is challenged, as an unexpected space hazard threatens to destroy Moon City.

Similar in plot to the Year Two episode 'The Seance Spectre' by Donald James, wherein a group of Alphans plot a mutiny (the script's original title) while Koenig investigates a stellar phenomenon.

A MOON FOR ALL SEASONS

The moon begins to develop into another earth, but there is a serious snag.

Christopher Penfold fleshed out this plotline into 'The Last Sunset', wherein mysterious aliens give the Moon an atmosphere to prevent the Alphans from landing on their planet.

STOP THE MOON — I WANNA GET OFF!

Two Earthmen decide to go it alone on an alien planet, with unexpected results.

This evolved into the more seriously titled 'The Testament of Arkadia' by Johnny Byrne, in which the Moon is stopped dead in space, and Luke Ferro and Anna Davis become the new Adam and Eve of an ancient world.

ACTION... AND VIOLENCE

The problems of personal violence are avoided by placing the concept outside the understanding of the Moonbase personnel, who hold all life sacred. Hurting each other is unthinkable in their society.[4]

Action, on the other hand, is the major ingredient of the series – and it is not confined to space-ship interiors. Neither are the plots confined to a rigid format. The open-end structure of this outer space series is as limitless as the structure of space itself.

All network standards concerning continuity, violence, sex and other regulatory matters of public responsibility will be complied with to assure that SPACE: 1999 is produced in complete accordance with the NAB Code.

SPACE: 1999 is produced by Gerry and Sylvia Anderson. For 12 years, the Andersons have led the way in both television and motion picture production of science fiction film.

Among the Anderson's many credits are two full length feature films:

JOURNEY TO THE FAR SIDE OF THE SUN – Universal Pictures
THUNDERBIRDS ARE GO – United Artists Corporation

Television series for ITC include:

UFO
THE PROTECTORS
THUNDERBIRDS

---

[4] George Bellak, the American writer who took over developing the series when it pivoted to a one-hour format, wanted the interpersonal relationships of the Moonbase personnel to be more volatile. However, when he left before shooting began, the format – once again under the guidance of Christopher Penfold – returned to a more idyllic atmosphere.

STINGRAY
CAPTAIN SCARLET
FIREBALL XL-5
SUPERCAR

All feature outstanding special-effects and innovative production techniques, many of which have since become standard in the industry.

WHY ITC?

Because we've been doing it successfully for a dozen years.

Our new science-fiction series will be delivered to a ready-made science-fiction audience by the same team which helped get that audience ready. For the past 12 years, Gerry and Sylvia Anderson have specialized in producing science-fiction movies (UA, Universal) and television series (ITC) – working with a virtual 'repertory company' of special-effects technicians, designers, architects and engineers to achieve some of the most spectacular effects on the screen.

SPACE: 1999 is custom made for U.S. syndication. The new series is the first in fifteen years that ITC has made with the U.S. as its <u>prime</u> market. It was the Prime Time Access Rule that created this marketing decision. And in order to produce prime time quality, ITC has committed network budgets of $110,000 to $120,000 for each episode.

SPACE: 1999 is the only network budgeted, network quality half hour series made for U.S. prime time access periods available for fall start from Independent Television Corporation.

'ZERO G'

Half-Hour Format Pilot Script
by Gerry & Sylvia Anderson
Early 1973
Unfilmed

INTRODUCTION

It is not known how many scripts were written for the half-hour format, but one script for the first episode was found in the files of the New York office of ITC. 'Zero G' was written by series creators Gerry and Sylvia Anderson, who had provided all the pilot scripts for their TV series from *Fireball XL5* (1962) to *UFO* (1969). When the series was expanded to a one-hour format with a larger budget, the Andersons' script was abandoned.

This first draft was completed sometime in early 1973 and appears somewhat rough. Characters are ill-defined, emphasizing plot and format over the human element. The two-act format left little time for much character development, but this may have been written merely as an example to demonstrate the series' potential to Lew Grade and Abe Mandell, and not as a shooting script.

SYNOPSIS

In the year 1999, Earth has launched deep space probe C. 42 to unlock the mysteries of another planet. As the members of WANDER, the World Association of Nations Defending Earth Rights, await the data, they find themselves also under observation by a strange alien craft hovering high above their complex within Moon City.

Space Commander Steve Maddox is somehow abducted from his quarters by the leader of the planet Uranus. The creature accuses the human race of a clearly historic propensity to violence and their plan to spread this into deep space.

Awakening back at Moon City, Maddox reports his experience to Doctor Marc Miller. As the probe data is about to reach the Moon, the alien craft interferes with the transmission, proving Maddox did experience his encounter on the alien planet.

Shortly thereafter, a Modular Transportation Unit from Earth, Moon Ship Zero Three, mysteriously crashes. Even the astronaut who recovered the flight recorder is mysteriously affected by a strange force. There is no doubt that they are under attack by forces beyond their understanding!

Attempting to attack the alien craft with an armed MTU, the Space Commander finds himself again confronted by the leader, now satisfied his suspicions have proven correct.

The aliens reveal they have the ability to alter gravity. It was by this power that they caused the crash of the moon ship. Now, they reduce the Moon's gravitational pull with Earth by 70% and the ancient satellite is sent hurling into deep space.

STORY DIFFERENCES

This first draft script was written to showcase the new format evolved from the material developed for the cancelled second series of *UFO*. In particular Moon City was created for the previous series as ITC wanted the main location limited to outer space.

INSPIRATION

Several ideas contained within 'Zero G' wound up incorporated into later episodes.

Maddox's encounter with the Alien Leader through some mysterious form of teleportation was later adapted by Edward Di Lorenzo into 'Missing Link', where Koenig was transported to the planet Zenno, encountering the scientist Raan and his daughter Vana.

The hovering Alien spacecraft, with its pulsating green light finally appeared in story consultant Christopher Penfold's 'Alpha Child' as three vessels holding alien fugitives.

The reconnaissance space probe, C.42, is actually inspired by the *UFO* episode 'Close-Up', written by Tony Barwick. In that story a probe was launched by SHADO to study the Alien home planet, which was always hinted at being located within our solar system in the end titles. It may, or may not have been Uranus, or one of its 27 known moons.

The description of the Travel Tube car docking with the MTU hatch also appears inspired by a sequence in the pilot for *Stingray* (1963). A similar conveyance moved along a clear tube, which extended to link it with a Terror Fish submarine berthed at the underwater city of Titanica.

TECHNOLOGY

'Zero G' features the first appearance of the talking computer.

MTU -- Modular Transportation Unit -- 'A number of MTUs are already on their pads each with a different configuration,' demonstrating the versatility of the Modular Transportation Unit.

LAUNCH PAD BOARDING TUBE — 'A large tube extends from one of the buildings and connects up to the entrance of the MTU in the immediate foreground. Through the portholes in the slide of the tube we are able to see the cylindrical compartment that Maddox and Miller are traveling in, move through the tube and stop at the entrance of the MTU' (see *Stingray* pilot).

TRAVEL TUBE — 'A six-seater cylindrical compartment that transports personnel through a tube system to all parts of Moon City.'

COMMUNICATIONS COLUMN

VIDEO-SCAN — 'It is a large screen to one side of the control center.'

LASER BEAM GENERATOR - 'A pencil-like beam…'

TV CAMERAS SCANNING MOON SURFACE

RECONNAISSANCE PROBE C.42

ALIEN SHIP (WITH GREEN PULSATING LIGHT)

CHARACTERS

SPACE COMMANDER STEVE MADDOX — 'A Man in his prime — an ex-astronaut who led the first manned expedition to Mars. Highly trained — tough, dedicated. Space oriented — a man of the future — in the future.'

DOCTOR MARC MILLER — 'Doctor of Space Research, his vast knowledge of space science gives him a key position in Moon City.' 'The two men have vastly different responsibilities in the WANDER Organization, but a strong bond has developed between them during their tour of duty in Moon City.'

DOCTOR GORDON — Female medical officer.

LT CARON — Second in command.

CONTROLLER

GIRL OPERATOR

URANUS ALIEN LEADER — 'He is dressed in a skin-like material of geometric design that matches his environment.'

COMPUTER — Talking Computer

FIRST PILOT — MOON SHIP ZERO THREE

SECOND PILOT — MOON SHIP ZERO THREE

MOONBASE ALPHA SETS / LOCATIONS

MOON CITY — Modular

WANDER, the World Association of Nations Defending Earth Rights

SPACE COMMANDER'S OFFICE — 'It is of modular construction — spacious — futuristic.' 'Maddox rotates in his chair and depresses button on his fingertip control. The wall he now faces divides, and his office becomes an integral part of the control center beyond.'

CONTROL CENTER & OBSERVATION GANTRY

SPACE COMMANDER'S QUARTERS

TRAVEL TUBE & CORIDOR

MTU COMMAND MODULE

MTU SECTION - 'Array of large buildings with vertical take-off launch platforms.'

URANUS ALIEN PLANET EXTERIOR — 'Exotic foliage with a vivid flame-colored sky.'

URANUS ALIEN CONTROL ROOM

(DH)

THESE (ONE-HOUR) EPISODES

by David Hirsch

As the format continued to be developed, the series morphed back into a full hour. ITC had in mind A-List stars as their leads, and combined with elaborate sets and visual effects, only the longer format could command what they had hoped would be a lucrative sale to the American TV networks.

To make the show more appealing stateside, ITC and the Andersons began a search for American talent. Lists of Writers and Actors (see Chapter 8) were compiled in depth. Ideally, their goal was to find people willing to relocate to England for the length of the production, though some would attempt to work long distance. This would prove problematic in these pre-internet days, though it was not unheard of.

It was decided that American writer George Bellak (see Chapter 9) would now be responsible for developing the series' format. Christopher Penfold, who had held that position since *UFO 2*, would now assist him as Story Consultant.

Bellak's responsibilities would include fleshing out characters and format details, developing the first episode and commissioning stories from other American writers. He was not a science-fiction writer, so his focus was not on the fantastic, but gritty reality. His characters were decidedly human, his Moonbase a powder keg of emotions. While the first episode script hints at a metaphysical influence, Bellak and his initial crop of writers sought to write more character-driven stories.

The following four documents chart the revised development of the series concept, characters, and storylines. Only one of these documents is dated, the final version of the series Guidelines. The order of the other documents has been established by the authors based on the progression of the material contained within. Once again, in an effort to show how *Space: 1999* quickly evolved throughout 1973, many details are repeated unchanged, or with minor changes from one document to the next.

1. *SPACE: 1999*. This brief promotional document reflects the format change to 26 One Hour episodes. Characters now include The American Commander, The Space Captain, and the Chief Medical Officer, who is still male, all unnamed.

2. **GUIDELINES** & PILOT (first version). This undated version of the series Guidelines (or Writer's Guide) credits George Bellak as Story Consultant and includes an untitled story outline for the pilot episode. This was the most detailed fleshing out of the series format. The setting is now named Moonbase Alpha with its functions described in detail. Characters like Commander John Robert Koenig and Doctor Helena Russell are named and given detailed biographies. Other characters like the Professor and Chief Pilot have early names and nationalities.

3. **GUIDELINES** (final version). This final version of the series Guidelines is dated 3 September 1973 and is credited as having been written by George Bellak (Story Consultant) and Christopher Penfold (Associate Story Consultant). The Moonbase, props, and spacecraft are presented in exacting detail (though some concepts would still be dropped or altered). The character of the Professor is unnamed (probably awaiting casting), the Chief Pilot is now Italian, as is a female technician (most likely Sandra Sabatini).

4. *SPACE: 1999* **ADVANCE PROGRAM INFORMATION**. Intended to promote the now 24 one-hour episode series to American television stations, this document includes the casting of actors Martin Landau, Barbara Bain and Barry Morse, along with the stories for nineteen episodes. Although they are not listed in production order, the last five are, culminating with 'The Troubled Spirit', which was filmed in late November and early December 1974, giving an approximate timeline for the release of this document.

SPACE: 1999

TELEVISION SCIENCE FICTION FILM SERIES

- 26 ONE HOUR EPISODES

PRODUCTION COMPANY

GROUP THREE PRODUCTIONS LTD.,
EMI/MGM STUDIOS,
ENGLAND

PRODUCERS

GERRY & SYLVIA ANDERSON

RECENT PRODUCTIONS

'U.F.O.'
'THE PROTECTORS'

DISTRIBUTION COMPANY

I.T.C. NEW YORK/LONDON

PRESIDENT: MR. ABE MANDELL

STUDIOS

EMI/MGM ENGLAND

PRE-PRODUCTION

COMMENCED.

STUDIO FLOOR SHOOTING

COMMENCING 5TH NOVEMBER 1973 FOR APPROXIMATELY 50
WEEKS.

FOREWORD

The year 1990... with the use of highly sophisticated equipment, radio waves have been intercepted from outer space which confirms the theory that life exists outside our solar system. The major powers on Earth unite and create a manned permanent base on the Moon... its purpose, to maintain surveillance of deep space and become the first outpost of Earth's defense system. Further analysis of the signals reveals that inter-stellar travel is already taking place.

By 1999, the Moon Base is complete and operational. Vast stocks of nuclear fuel have been deposited at various points on the far side of the Moon. Unaccountably, one of the stockpiles is detonated. There is a chain reaction which causes a devastating thermo-nuclear explosion. The gravitational relationship of Earth and Moon is abruptly negated, and the Moon is violently thrust out of orbit.[5]

THE SERIES

The 300 men and women on the Earth outpost find themselves marooned in space and the Commander of Moonbase becomes, if effect, the head of government of this new world. A council composed of officers, scientists and medical personnel decides that it will be their primary mission to find a way back into Earth's orbital range. Failing this, they must locate a compatible planet on which to settle. In the meantime, they are prepared to continue functioning in outer space the same way they have been functioning in Earth orbit. Food, air and water recycling installations are powered with atomic and solar energy. All systems necessary for the maintenance of life as it was on Earth are operative - making the Moon totally self-supporting.

The marooned Earthmen begin their fateful journey through the incredible vastness of space. Soon they learn that they are regarded as intruders and considered a menace to the Universe. Suspicious aliens attack and they must match wits and weapons against fantastic life forms found throughout the galaxies on their unexpected odyssey.

MAIN CHARACTERS

Principal leads are THE COMMANDER, THE SPACE CAPTAIN and THE

---

[5] The 'gravitational relationship of Earth and Moon' being 'abruptly negated' continues to be a hold-over from the Anderson's 'Zero G' script.

CHIEF MEDICAL OFFICER.

THE AMERICAN COMMANDER

The awesome responsibility of commanding Earth's outpost in space was assigned to a leader chosen for his combination of outstanding leadership qualities, superior space knowledge and unequalled administrative ability. A former test pilot and celebrated astronaut, he won the command over candidates from all nations because their leaders acknowledged that he knew the job better than anyone in the entire world. He is a self-assured career man with the ability to inspire loyalty and fidelity among the elite core of Earthmen on the Moon.

THE SPACE CAPTAIN (i/c Deep Space Reconnaissance)

A man of great experience in space technology whose prime function is now advance reconnaissance of planets in the paths of the Moon's trajectory.

CHIEF MEDICAL OFFICER

A close associate of The Commander, it is the doctor's responsibility to maintain the species of Man on an artificial earth, marooned in the infinity of Space, where the rules of medical science as he had learned them are constantly bent and broken.

GUIDELINES & PILOT

SPACE: 1999 GUIDELINES
(First Version)

PRODUCERS: GERRY AND SYLVIA ANDERSON

STORY CONSULTANT: GEORGE BELLAK

Consider that it is the year 1999.

Some years back the major powers on earth, having determined that life exists outside our solar system, have united and created a manned permanent base on the moon, with the purpose of maintaining surveillance of deep space, and of becoming the first outpost of earth's defense system.

MOON BASE ALPHA the center of our series, is a complex of interconnected command centers, laboratories, and living areas; each building self-contained as to gravity and atmosphere production, and each building linked to the other by a series of 'travel tubes' which allow movement from one to another, above ground and within view of the desolate moonscape.

MOON BASE ALPHA is designed to be spectacularly self-sufficient. All of its wastes are re-cycled, its food and water chains are perhaps eighty percent chemically produced. The rest is supplied by regular space shuttle which goes to and from the Earth, bringing replacements, visitors, and personnel. ALPHA is organizationally in constant communication with Earth Control, is basically <u>under</u> its control, though the operations' chief is the Moon Base commander advised by a council composed of Section Chiefs.

The personal of MOON BASE ALPHA consists of approximately three hundred men and women, specialists in their field, who have signed on for an eighteen-month tour of duty. These people work in one of six sections. Each of these sections has its own building and a commander who takes part in the major decisions affecting the base. The sections are:

MAIN MISSION. The main mission, basically, is the scientific investigations of space and defense of Earth. The Central Control office of MAIN MISSION is the place from which probes are launched, rockets sent off, and communications with the earth maintained. All this is done with the aid of computers, visual equipment, audio equipment, and sophisticated telemetry. The commander of this section is also the commander of the entire moon base.

MEDICAL AND PSYCHOLOGICAL M. AND E. (Maintenance and experimentation). This section is charged with the maintenance of the physical and mental health of base personnel. The work also involves medical and psychological experimentation upon all factors affecting people in space. On occasion the head of this section will be called upon to make decisions involving choices of base personnel for specific missions.

TECHNICAL AND ENGINEERING. This section is composed of the lower echelon computer people, rocket people, air people, all the engineering troops who keep the complex machines working.

RECONNAISSANCE SECTION. This section consists of space people who make the deep probes into space. They are the spearheads and the chartists for many operations.

SECURITY. This is a composite small force of people trained as security guards for moon base installations. They also, being trained as space arms specialists, form a highly effective mobile force of space soldiers who, when actual warfare is imminent, are in the fore-front.

SERVICE UNIT. These are the people who have the basic working responsibility for the environment of the buildings, the food services and the like.

The living arrangements of the base personnel are somewhat spartan, though exceedingly functional, and resolve themselves into units which are occupied by either married couple, or single inhabitant. There are no children at ALPHA; the 18-month tours of duty obviate that.

The base personnel live a structured life. They work for a stated period of time and, if there are not alerts, are on their own for whatever recreation the base affords. These may include all kinds earth sent and cassette entertainments, such as 3-dimensional film transmissions, holographs, current music, television, etc. It is postulated that within the limits possible, the Earth Command has done all it could to keep moon base life as normal as possible.

As an instance of the above, the personnel take their meals in a very pleasant, though highly automated kind of restaurant (no restaurant personnel can ever be seen, all of the installations are almost one hundred percent labor-saving, thus eliminating manpower requirements). Since there is no sun, with its healthful rays, upon this base, the medical department has had constructed a gymnasium with very special exercise equipment, and a solarium, with an artificial sun giving off the needed spectrum so that base personnel, sunless though they are, have very healthy-looking tans.

The base personnel move through outer space, when they do, in a very advanced spaceship, which is a modular unit, capable of converting part of itself into a low-flying vehicle for local, over-the-surface-of-any-planet travel, while the mother ship orbits in space. The mother ship can have as a complement anything up to ten persons with equipment and stores for a comparatively lengthy exploration.

It should be noted that for story purposes, the main scene playing areas of ALPHA will be:

- Central Control (full of equipment);
- The private office of the base commander, which is adjacent to Central Control;
- The private office of the Head of the Medical Section;
- The various offices and labs of the Technical Sections as needed;
- The living quarters of the people involved in the stories.

As for moon exteriors, the moonspace, basically, is alike all over, and is reached through various airlock egresses by base personnel when suitably space-suited up so they can survive outside the building environment.

To speak of how futuristic we are going to be for a moment, it might be profitable to indicate that we are striving for a combination of futurism (extrapolation from current knowledge) and a connection with a recognizably human and current reality. By which we mean that when a base spaceman goes to sleep at night, it may be in a very modern shaped, plastic affair which, once into, he switches on his heat light but he sighs with either tiredness or contentment when he does so. There are even certain prior history hangovers possible, such as a drink of scotch every now and then by certain of the older personnel who don't like the taste of the new synthetic brew which is non-alcoholic, but which makes you feel a mellow glow. The key is the combination of startlingly new and comfortingly familiar.

Now, having described, to some extent, the way of the Moon Base Alpha lifestyle, we must immediately state that all of that is true, only for a limited time. Because, in the very first show of the series, the moon will suffer a massive atomic explosion in an unhappily man-made accident. As a result, a chunk of the moon will be ripped off and flung into space, causing the moon itself to go careening out of orbit and headlong into the void, with the moon base upon it. Communications with Earth will be broken and the moon base will be left upon its own to survive, to seek a friendly planet to colonize, and to defend itself against other space-lives, for now they are invading aliens.

We can postulate, by the way, that the very nature of the horrendous accident allows the moon base people to survive somewhat because the crater exposed by the moon chunk being ripped away becomes a source of raw material, necessary to be fashioned into essentials for moon base living.

Despite Alpha's predicament, once the base is stabilized as much as possible, and systems function, perhaps not perfectly but rather well, as much of the pre-explosion flavor as possible is maintained. People still have to eat, work, sleep, and exercise in order to keep going. And so the restaurant, the gym, the solarium, some of the cassettes, the holographs still work. And so a kind of life goes on, even with emergencies. As it always does.

The leading characters in *Space: 1999* are as follows:

JOHN ROBERT KOENIG

John Koenig is not only the American Commander of the moon base, but at forty he is an astrophysicist of very high repute. A man who started in science when he was only in his teens, John Koenig, product of an old midwestern farming family, went on to M.I.T. an early honors. He became a pilot and an astronaut. His practical and theoretical abilities being recognized, as well as an unquestionable leadership ability, he was responsible for the planning and control of many outstanding space missions. Though something of a maverick, because of his knowledge and abilities, Koenig was asked to help work on Alpha's designs. He did so and was thus, gradually drawn into the project. As we pick ALCOM KOENIG up (Spacese for Alpha Commander) he has accepted the post of new Base Commander and is making arrangements to take charge.

In most cases, this will be back story, but it should be kept in mind, for story purposes, that Commander Koenig is faced with crises before he has fully absorbed the ordinary routine of the Moon Base operations.

On the personal side, John Koenig is an interesting and somewhat complex man. He has two streaks in him, one, rather ruthless and efficient:

the 'mind as computer' aspect, and, on the other hand, a moody and introspective strain. Born in 1959, he is <u>not </u>the total space child. He has had, along with science, more humanities education than some others of his generation. As a matter of fact, he was married for five years to a woman who was a highly gifted artist.

From where John Koenig stood, the marriage was a gratifying one. Not so, for his wife. She had sublimated some of her own life to his, and at this point, decided to do so no longer. John was exceedingly unhappy over this decision but loved her enough to make the separation an amicable one.

All this was over six years ago, but John Koenig carries the scars with him and holds back at relating deeply to women. As to men, Koenig demands a lot, but he demands a lot of himself.

He isn't fantastically happy with the current 1999 state of humanity, but he has hope for the future, and feels that the human race can only evolve into any kind of ideal state if it goes on — and so he is dedicated to its survival.

Still, having said that, it should be understood that he is a man with one foot somewhere in the past and one foot somewhere in the future.

DR HELENA RUSSELL. Sp. Med. Ast-Psy.

Dr Helena Russell's cool good looks belie her abilities and her responsibilities. For Dr Russell is Chief of the Medical Section and has twenty-five highly skilled medical personnel under her direction and control.

Helena Russell, is a woman in her early thirties (born, say in 1965) whose father was a West Coast physician of great energy and drive. Influenced by her father, and driven by her own achievement mechanism, not to mention the strong feminist liberating movement of the times, Helena drove through Medical School meeting and marrying a fellow student.

The man she married, Telford Russell, moved into space medicine, a rapidly expanding specialty. Helena went along with him. Telford became a medical mission man — going out into space. Helena, now in her late twenties, worked at NASA and delved into space disorientation and psychology, becoming an expert in those areas. Then a mission disappeared into space — simply vanished — never to be heard from again. Telford was on that mission, and Helena, to all intents and purposes, was widowed.

Helena grieved and then went on working and living her full and liberated life. She rose in her profession. One year ago, she was offered the post of Chief of Medical Section on MOON BASE ALPHA and was accepted. Thus, as we pick Dr Russell up, she has been on ALPHA for twelve months working and living, and to some extent retiring emotionally in that space womb environment.

Helena Russell is a very responsible person, a fine professional, but she is a woman nonetheless. By which we mean that she has her own side, a very feminine side, apart from the somewhat uni-sexed ambience of the Moonbase.

Helena does holographic sculpture. She likes all kinds of music. She has a flair with her uniform. She has a certain style. She is, despite the times, an individual and no one forgets that.

In the ongoing series, she may have to test that individuality more than once.

PROFESSOR DANILO SABATINI. Ast-Phy.

This interesting and wise Italian astrophysicist in his late fifties, comes to Moonbase Alpha as a visitor to take his first look at some of the components a number of his students designed. He remains as an accidental addition to the small colony hurtling through space.

Sabatini, born in the early forties, is a brilliant teacher and theoretician. Rarely involved in worldly things, Sabatini, nonetheless, achieved a reputation as a tremendous mind in Field-Force theory. From his conjectures has come much of the space hardware in current use.

John Koenig was one of Sabatini's outstanding students years ago. Since then, a bond of affection has grown up between them.

Professor Sabatini looks upon his times with a somewhat rueful eye. He is more of a throwback — a nineteenth century scientist — philosopher — humanist — and he is a counterbalance to the twenty-first century we are about to enter.

J. W. GRAYSON P.C.1.

To an extent, Jim Grayson is Professor Sabatini's antithesis. This 26-year-old Britisher, is a Probe Captain, First-Class, a veteran of nine deep space adventures and both a technician and activist.

Probe Captain Grayson is the Chief of the elite Reconnaissance Section — those men who plan and execute the space probes, the exploration into space, either manned or unmanned. These are the men who are in the forefront of developments and danger. These are the men upon whom, very often, the entire Moonbase will depend.

Jim Grayson has an almost unshakable belief in technology. Born in 1963, he grew up with complicated visuals and mega-decibel audio, media mixed and matched. He has been in the program since he was twenty-two, right out of the Technicon.

Highly trained, highly motivated, Jim Grayson is a doer. He has the brashness of youth and the total belief in his mission that only someone his age could have.

With minor exceptions, the characters described above will be our running characters. They must be given two lives — one of themselves, and one as cells in a unit involved in a planet-shaking emergency — a life and death struggle for human survival.
If that can be made to happen, the combination of science-fantasy and reality will have been achieved and deep dimension, as well as gut excitement, will be generated.

UNTITLED OPENING EPISODE STORYLINE

This story will open with the Moonbase already in operation for some time under the command of someone other than John Koenig. Koenig has just been appointed the replacement Commander and is about to leave on the space shuttle for the base.

One of the side operations of the Moonbase has been the solution of a very vexing Earth problem, namely, how to dispose of the generations of worn out, but still highly radioactive nuclear fuel which have resulted from Earth installations.

For some time now an area on the dark side of the moon has been used as a dumping ground for all of this material, so as to leave Earth uncontaminated. In the last twenty years a new and highly sophisticated metal has been used for nuclear energy and the residue of this material has also been deposited on the Moon. This 'garbage' program is overseen by a technical group headed by a scientist-politician named Grivas. Grivas is an older, once important scientist who, now worried about his position, has left science behind and is much more subservient to the political winds that blow. Since this agency is internationally run, Grivas makes more concessions than he should to pressures and ideas.

Professor Sabatini has taken an interest in this nuclear dumping and, with only theoretical evidence to back him up, has told John Koenig that he is fearful of some kind of accident on the Moon due to the mingling of specific quantities of this new nuclear material. Koenig agrees with him, but Grivas, for political reasons does not. Thus, even before leaving Earth, Koenig is in conflict with Grivas over an issue he considers potentially dangerous.

John Koenig goes to take up his command. Sabatini goes along to check out nuclear waste piles in an attempt to confirm his theory.

Once at Moonbase and while Commander Koenig is getting acquainted with the installation, taking charge, etc., it becomes apparent that efforts to research the disposal dump and experiment upon it are being thwarted by Grivas' orders. Koenig fights against this as best he can. There are moves and counter moves, and suddenly it appears the instruments indicate the nuclear temperature and radiation, etc. of the slagpile is rising rapidly towards a crisis point.

Alert is called. Methods of dealing with the emergency and cooling the pile are invented instantly, and, cautiously, with great danger to all concerned, are put into operation. But to no avail. The pile goes up. There is an incredible nuclear explosion and chain reaction at the site of the disposal area. The Moon undergoes a violent shock. The tip of the moon, a large area perhaps one hundred miles square, wretches itself loose and becomes solar dust. The moon itself is pulled out of its orbit and goes careening off in an unknown trajectory.

The effect on Moonbase can be cataclysmic. Koenig and his people fight to keep the base's environmental stability going. They manage, in the end, to do this. Moonbase Alpha survives, partly crippled but operative. The question now is, however, with all communication with Earth broken, and all hope of ever getting back home dimmed, where will they go and how will they survive.

The only answer is to zoom through the heavens on this monumental Moon journey and to hope to find some place in the cosmos which they can colonize and make their own again. But even as this decision is taken, word comes in from the space probers that all indications are that immediate space dangers confront them. But with no way out they must now go on and face them.

GUIDELINES

3 SEPTEMBER 1973

SPACE:1999 GUIDELINES
(Final Version)

SPACE 1999
A GROUP THREE PRODUCTION

GUIDELINES FOR WRITERS, PRINCIPAL ARTISTS, PRODUCTION
DEPARTMENT, SPECIAL EFFECTS DEPARTMENT, ART DEPARTMENT

BY
GEORGE BELLAK (STORY CONSULTANT) and
CHRISTOPHER PENFOLD (ASSOCIATE STORY CONSULTANT)

EMI-MGM Elstree Studios, Borehamwood, Herts.[6]
3rd September 1973

(N.B. This document will be revised from time to time, either in the form of
amended pages of different color or by a replacement of the whole.)[7]

1. INTRODUCTION

Consider that it is the year 1999.

Some years back the major powers on earth, having determined that life
exists outside our solar system, have united and created a manned
permanent base on the moon, with the purpose of maintaining surveillance
of deep space, and of becoming the first outpost of Earth's defense system.

2. MOON BASE ALPHA

---

[6] *Space: 1999* was originally scheduled to film at EMI/MGM Elstree Studios in
Borehamwood. Set construction had begun, but when MGM pulled out of the studio in
September 1973, threatening the studio with closure, the production was moved to
Pinewood Studios in Buckinghamshire in what production designer Keith Wilson described
as a 'moonlight flit'. Oddly enough, a similar situation occurred during the production of
UFO when MGM also closed another studio (MGM British Studios) after the 17th episode
('Sub Smash'), forcing a shift to Pinewood Studios.
[7] No further revisions are known to exist.

(a) Layout / Moon Base Alpha

Moon Base Alpha, the center of our series, is a complex of interconnected command centers, laboratories, and living areas; each building self-contained as to gravity and atmosphere production, and each building linked to the other by a series of 'travel tubes' which allow movement from one to another, above ground and within view of the desolate moonscape.

(b) Organization / Moon Base Alpha

Moon Base Alpha is designed to be spectacularly self-sufficient. All of its wastes are re-cycled, its food and water chains are perhaps eighty percent chemically produced. The rest is supplied by regular space shuttle which goes to and from the Earth, bringing replacements, visitors and personnel. Alpha is organizationally in constant communication with Earth Control, is basically under its control, though the operations' chief is the moon base commander advised by a council composed of Section Chiefs.

(c) Personnel / Moon Base Alpha

The personnel of Moon Base Alpha consists of approximately three hundred men and women, specialists in their field, who have signed on for an eighteen-month tour of duty. These people work in one of six sections. Each of these sections has its own building and a commander who takes part in the major decisions affecting the base. Members of each section are visually distinguishable by the color coding of the left sleeve of their uniform. This color coding will be extended to the work location of the sections and to the living quarters of the personnel who comprises them.

The Commander will wear a sleeve color that is unique on Moon Base Alpha.

3. THE SECTIONS

(a) Main Mission (color code to be decided)

The Main Mission, basically, is the scientific investigation of space and defense of the earth. The Central Control office of Main Mission is the place from which probes are launched, rockets sent off, and communication with Earth maintained. All this is done with the aid of computers, visual equipment, audio equipment, and sophisticated telemetry. The Commander of this section is also the Commander of the entire moon base.

(b) Medical and Psychological M & E (color code to be decided)

(Maintenance and Experimentation) This section is charged with the maintenance of the physical and mental health of base personnel. The work also involves medical and psychological experimentation upon all factors affecting people in space. On occasion the head of this section will be called upon to make decisions involving choices of base personnel for specific missions.

(c) Technical and Engineering (color code to be decided)
This section is composed of the lower echelon computer people, rocket people, air people, all the engineers who keep the complex machines working.

(d) Reconnaissance Section (color code to be decided)
This section consists of space people who make the deep probes into space. They are the spearheads and the chartists for many operations.

(e) Security (color code to be decided)
This is a composite small force of people trained as security guards for moon base installations. They also, being trained as space arms specialists, form a highly effective mobile force of space soldiers who, when actual warfare is imminent, are in the fore-front. They will wear over their uniforms a distinguishing band over the shoulder and across the chest.

(f) Service Unit (color code GREY)
These are the people who have the basic working responsibility for the environment of the buildings, the food services and the like.

4. ALPHA ROUTINE
(a) Living
The living arrangements of the base personnel are somewhat spartan, though exceedingly functional, and resolve themselves into units which are occupied by either a married couple, or a single inhabitant. There are no children at Alpha; the 18-month tours of duty obviate that.

But in spite of the spartan modular similarity of the basic structure of the living quarters they will nevertheless strongly reflect the personalities of the people who occupy them. Eighteen months in a totally strange and unsympathetic environment is a long time and we can assume that, in the interests of keeping the personnel as contented as possible, provision would be made for them to pursue their normal Earth-bound leisure interests. Psychological advice would be available to them before being posted — advice as to what in the way of objects from their earthly lives they might like to take with them to make their stay on Alpha as palatable as possible. Each person would be restricted to predetermined limits of volume and weight, but within those limits, a weird collection of idiosyncrasies would be reflected in the incongruous Earth objects that they took to decorate their space environment. A collection of butterflies, perhaps, or an antique chair. Even actual leather-bound, printed books as an alternative to the microfilmed literature that is pumped, on request, into the video-screens in their rooms. This is the only way in which we hope to populate Moon Base Alpha with credible human beings with whom we can readily identify.

The base personnel live a structured life. They work for a stated period of time and, if there are not alerts, are on their own for whatever recreation the base affords. These may include all kinds of Earth-sent and cassette entertainments, such as 3-dimensional film transmissions, holographs, current music, television, etc. It is postulated that within the limits possible, the Earth Command has done all it could to keep moon base life as normal as possible.

(b) Feeding
As an instance of the above, the personnel, when on duty, take their meals in a very pleasant, though highly automated kind of restaurant (no restaurant personnel can ever be seen, all of the installations are almost one hundred percent labor-saving, thus eliminating manpower requirements).

When they are off duty they might choose to relax and eat in the privacy of their own quarters, in which case the meal of their selection would arrive automatically as one of the service facilities, adding a touch of recognizable domesticity to the flagrantly futuristic setting.

(c) Relaxing
Since there is no sun, with its healthful rays, upon this base, the medical department has had constructed a gymnasium with very specific exercise equipment, and a solarium, with and artificial sun giving off the needed spectrum so that base personnel, sunless though they are, have very healthy-looking tans.

5. TRANSPORT
(a) Travel Tube
Movement about Alpha itself is by travel tube. This is a basic travel capsule with seating for up to ten people. Every room or corridor has a door which will give access to the travel tube. When an individual wants to move from one part of Alpha to another he goes to the travel tube door and selects his intended destination on the appropriate scale of his IDX (see Section 6(a)). He then points the IDX at the key-plate beside the door and the tube capsule will appear, the door will open, the traveler will enter and the door will close automatically after him. His destination has been cued by the IDX and so he has to do nothing but get out when the tube stops and the doors open. As with passing through doorways, the movement is handled by CENTRAL COMPUTER (see Section 6(b)) so that if the individual requests the tube to

take him to an area for which he does not have clearance then it will refuse to take him.

For travel to the Moon's surface, the travel tube will take people to an airlock which will not let them out unless they have been: --
1.authorized
2.wearing appropriate space suit

The travel tube will also carry astronauts and passengers from Alpha to the MULTIPLE TRANSPORTATION UNITS which wait on launch pads ready for blast off. In this case the travel tube itself will telescopically extend to one or other of the two entrances to the vehicle, so that people will be able to walk from the travel tube compartment into the passenger capsule of the MTU without necessarily having to don a space suit, or at least a helmet.

(b) The M. T. U. (Multiple Transportation Unit)
The MTU is the only space vehicle that Alpha has left to it after episode one. Originally intended to provide a shuttle service between Alpha and the orbiting space station onto which docked the deep space penetration vehicles and the Earth ships, the MTU has had to be adapted to all space travel purposes after the catastrophe which blasts the Moon out of Earth orbit and away on its random trajectory through space.

Basically, it's a workhorse, a thoroughly utilitarian spacecraft. It consists of a basic frame section -- a container platform driven by three main nuclear motors. It can land like a helicopter, and once in flight the main motors will drive it horizontally, like an airplane. Attached to the main platform are four fuel pods which also support the undercarriage sections. On the outer edge of these pods are vernier motors for directional control.

The whole craft is manipulated from the Command Module, where there is seating capacity for two people, pilot and co-pilot. Under normal circumstances, they will have access to the Command Module through the main passenger cabin of the MTU, via an airlock. In the event of an emergency, the Command Module can be detached from the main frame of the MTU and used as a 'lifeboat'. In this case there would be room for more people to crowd in uncomfortably and for a short period of time. There are attached to the side of the Command Module also small vernier motors which will give it very limited propulsion power and a modicum of directional control.

In this form the Command Module could also be used by not more than two people for short-haul trips over the surface of the Moon itself.

On occasions such as this, when the Command Module is used in separation from the main MTU, the crew gain access by a subsidiary entrance in the side of the Module itself, to which the travel tube can be connected.

But under most normal circumstances the MTU will be used as a complete unit. That is, as a main frame with main vertical and horizontal engines, and with a Command Module attached. And to this main frame different containers can be fixed for different purposes. A conventional container would have seating for ten people plus cargo holds. But from time to time new containers will be devised for specific purposes, e.g., a fuel container, to give the MTU deep space range, or a self-contained laboratory and living quarters for a couple of scientists which can be put down on the surface of an alien planet and left for a while. Should it be necessary for Alpha to repel an alien attack, then the container could house a complete weapons system. There are a lot of these MTUs at Alpha — but they are all the Moon-men have.

6. COMMUNICATIONS

(a) IDX (Temporary name)

The 'IDX' is a multi-purpose communication device, held comfortably in the palm of the hand. At one end is a miniature two-inch TV monitor, and set into it also are microphone and speaker, so that it is first of all a portable videophone. Secondly, it carries an electronic identification code. This emits no audio or visual pulse, but when the 'IDX' is aimed at the 'key' plate beside each door it will electronically signal the door to open. Provided, of course, that the individual concerned is security cleared to pass through that particular door. This action, of aiming the 'IDX' at the key plate will be something that the staff so automatically and without thinking — like we turn the handle to open a conventional door. The moment they do think about it is the moment when it has dramatic significance — when the door does not open as expected, because for one reason or another the computer has rejected their automatic request for admission. When the computer does so reject an application, it will immediately be brought to the notice of the SECURITY SECTION who will want to question the reject. So, by means of the 'IDX', the movements of every member of the Alpha staff are logged in the CENTRAL COMPUTER.

(b) The Central Computer

All of the information, on whatever subject, that concerns the working operations of Alpha is stored in the CENTRAL COMPUTER.

Of course, much of this information is classified, and the only person on the base who has access to all the information is the Commander.

But everyone on the base has access to the computer to a greater or lesser degree. They get the information simply by asking for it through their 'IDX' and if they ask for information to which they are not entitled, then the computer will refuse to divulge. Its method of selection is straightforward. The same electronic key that gives people access to specific areas, also governs their access to the computer's information. So whenever a request is made the computer knows instantly, by means of the electronic key, who is making the request and the extent of the information to which that particular individual is entitled.

Depending on the type of information requested, the Computer divulges in different ways. If it's a short answer to a specific question, then the Computer will communicate verbally. If the information is of a visual nature, the Computer will ask the questioner to go to the nearest communication post and observe the television monitors there. Or, thirdly, if the information is complex and extensive, the Computer will offer it in the form of a read-out which will appear from slots placed under each door key plate, so that there is one in every room, and in each communication post. So wherever people are about Alpha they are always in immediate contact with all the data necessary to deal with unforeseen circumstances. But things will happen, of course, which are beyond the Computer's ken.

In this way the Computer does not think. It remains a purely mechanical device whose capability is no more than the sum of all the data that fallible humans put into it. It has, therefore all the fallibility of the humans who feed it. It will be possible for individuals to trick the Computer, but when humans find themselves in the trickiest situations the Computer will provide them with no more help than a straightforward statement of accumulated facts.

(c) Communications Post (Temporary name)
There will be a constant background of audio and visual information of a general nature relating to aspects of life on Alpha. Reports of space conditions, news of the base, progress reports on probes, duty schedules -- routine chatter about daily life. And this information is available to everyone through the Communications Posts which are found in every communal area. There will be one in Central Control, one in the Solarium, one at every corridor intersection. In the form of a free-standing column, the Communications Post has mounted in it a series of key lights whose signals everyone will know. There will be larger TV monitors than the miniature 'IDX' screens, so that visual data like graphs or astronomical diagrams can be projected from one place to another. It will also contain slots through which the computer can offer larger read-out information. The Communications Posts are always alive -- always flickering and talking and always in the background of shots. They are a constant presence, an inescapable fact of life on Alpha.

7. HEALTH
DR HELENA RUSSELL, Head of the Medical Section, is not a general practitioner and it is no part of her function to bandage sprained ankles or treat minor wounds. All that routine maintenance will be carried out by the minions of the medical section and we don't particularly want to see it.

HELENA RUSSELL and the MEDICAL LABORATORY are there because the ALPHA MISSION has mankind out on a limb of environmental uncertainty where the frontiers of physical and psychological normality are frequently crossed. HELENA RUSSELL is on Alpha to observe and analyze unknown mental and physical conditions brought about by the strange environment. After episode one, of course, the situation will be even more acute and on HELENA RUSSELL's ability to respond to, and cope with, the strains inflicted by a random and involuntary space journey will depend the survival of the Alpha humans.

Her laboratory will be equipped for experiments and operations of a very advanced nature. Human and mechanical spare-parts surgery; deep freeze preservation; psycho-therapeutic re-orientation and psychosurgery. Examination and analysis of the mental and physical nature of captured aliens will take place in this laboratory and under HELENA RUSSELL's aegis.

As far as the permanent inhabitants of Alpha are concerned their medical condition will be perpetually monitored as follows:

In the sleeve of everyone's uniform is built a concave lens which gives to the wearer a constant monitoring of his or her physical condition. The data is gathered by printed circuits and electrodes built into the uniform itself, and transmitted constantly, via the 'IDX', to Central Computer.

If a person's temperature or metabolic rate puts on a sudden surge, then wherever the individual may be, the Computer brings the matter directly to the attention of a medical operative. If an individual is suddenly faced with a fearsome or dangerous situation, then the ensuing adrenalin discharge will be recorded by the Computer and he may be questioned about it later. If a person is asked a straight-forward question which for some reason he is unable to answer truthfully, then the Computer will record the lie — unless of course, the individual has been clever enough to foil the Computer by taking something like a spot tranquilizer to conceal the lie. All this is routine, and unnoticed until something unusual happens.

8. WEAPONS

The circumstances of Alpha will give rise to strife within and without the base. But basically it is not in Alpha's interests to kill. Each member of the community is on the Moon because he has some highly desirable qualification. If he becomes psychologically disturbed to such an extent that he proves violent, it would be a waste of irreplaceable manpower to destroy him. In general the practice, will be to stun anyone engaged in an act of violence, and then either to re-align him psychologically, or to put him in cold store until time is available for that purpose.[8]

In the case of an alien intruder or captive who offers violence the need to preserve him alive is even greater, since he may provide invaluable information about the nature of a hitherto incomprehensible enemy.

So the weapon that Alpha personnel carry with them is small, but multi-purpose — a TSLA. The initials describe the emissions from each of the four antennae: Tranquilizer, Stun, Laser, Atomic. There are four selections of the grip for purpose and intensity. The first choice is a tranquilizer which will give an opportunity to prevent actual violence but will still enable the user to talk to his victims; secondly a neuronic stun will stop a man instantly and make him unconscious so that he will need medical attention to revive him; thirdly, a laser which will pierce known metals and matter and stop some alien spacecraft without actually destroying them; and lastly the chain ray which engenders an atomic reaction in any matter that it strikes and so causes a totally destructive explosion.

Scaled-up versions of these weapons are incorporated in the combined weapons system of the military MTU, additional to the guided weapons which carry the offensive further away from the defenders.

9. TIME SCHEME

Earth-time for the series is not too far ahead — 1999. Therefore on Alpha itself we are striving for a combination of futurism (extrapolation from current knowledge) and a connection with a recognizably human and current reality. By which we mean that when a base spaceman goes to sleep at night, it may be in a very modern shaped, plastic affair which, once into, he switches on his heat light, but he sighs with either tiredness or contentment when he does so. There are even certain prior history hangovers possible, such as a drink of scotch every now and then by certain of the older personnel who don't like the taste of the new synthetic brew, which is non-alcoholic, but which makes you feel a mellow glow. The key is the combination of startlingly new and comfortingly familiar.

But a different time scheme altogether will apply when Alpha, in the course of its random journey, either stumbles across, or is directly accosted by, other forms of life in the Universe. Alien technology need not be Earth-related in any way. Alien beings may take any shape or form (always providing they can be convincingly represented in visual terms) and in relation to Earth, alien development can be as far in advance or retarded as imaginable.

---

[8] In the series itself, Alpha did not have 'cold store' / cryogenic technology, but the Alphans were fascinated when they came across other beings who had mastered immortality.

10. THE STORY

Now, having described to some extent the way of the Moon Base Alpha lifestyle, we must immediately state that all of that is true, only for a limited time. Because, in the very first show of the series, the Moon will suffer a massive atomic explosion in an unhappily man-made accident. As a result, a chunk of the moon will be ripped off and flung into space, causing the Moon itself to go careening out of orbit and headlong into the void, with the moon base upon it. Communication with Earth will be broken and the moon base will be left upon its own to survive, to seek a friendly planet to colonize, and to defend itself against other space-lives, for now they are invading aliens.

We can postulate, by the way, that the very nature of the horrendous accident allows the moon base people to survive somewhat because the crater exposed by the Moon chunk being ripped off becomes a source of raw material, necessary to be fashioned into essentials for moon base living.

Despite Alpha's predicament, once the base is stabilized as much as possible, and systems function, perhaps not perfectly but rather well, <u>as much of the pre-explosion flavor as possible is maintained</u>. People still have to eat, work, sleep, and exercise in order to keep going. And so the restaurant, the gym, the solarium, some of the cassettes, the holographs still work. And so a kind of life goes on, even with emergencies. As it always does.

11. THE LEADING CHARACTERS

The leading characters in *SPACE: 1999* are as follows:-

(a) JOHN ROBERT KOENIG

John Koenig is not only the American Commander of the moon base, but at forty he is an astrophysicist of very high repute. A man who starting in science when he was only in his teens, John Koenig, product of an old midwestern farming family, went on to M.I.T. and early honors. He became a pilot and an astronaut. His practical and theoretical abilities being recognized, as well as an unquestionable leadership ability, he was responsible for the planning and control of many outstanding space missions. Though something of a maverick, because of his knowledge and abilities Koenig was asked to help work on Alpha's designs. He did so and was thus gradually drawn into the project. As we pick ALCOM KOENIG up (Spacese for Alpha Commander) he has accepted the post of new Base Commander and is making arrangements to take charge.

In most cases, this will be back story, but it should be kept in mind, for story purposes, that Commander Koenig is faced with crises before he has fully absorbed the ordinary routine of the Moon Base operations.

On the personal side, John Koenig is an interesting and somewhat complex man. He has two streaks in him, one, rather ruthless and efficient, the 'mind as computer' aspect, and, on the other hand, a moody and introspective strain. Born in 1959, he is not the total space child. He has had, along with science, more humanities education than some others of his generation. As a matter of fact, he was married for five years to a woman who was a highly gifted artist.

From where John Koenig stood, the marriage was a gratifying one. Not so, for his wife. She had submitted some of her own life to his, and at this point, decided to do so no longer. John was exceedingly unhappy over this decision but loved her enough to make the separation an amicable one.

All this was over six years ago, but John Koenig carries the scars with him and holds back at relating deeply to women. As to men, Koenig demands a lot, but he demands a lot of himself.

He isn't fantastically happy with the current 1999 state of humanity, but he has hope for the future, and feels that the human race can only evolve into any kind of ideal state if it goes on — and so he is dedicated to its survival.

Still having said that, it should be understood that he is a man with one foot somewhat in the past and one foot somewhere in the future.

(b) DR HELENA RUSSELL Sp. Med. Ast-Psy.

Dr Helena Russell's cool good looks belie her abilities and her responsibilities. For Dr Russell is Chief of the Medical Section and has twenty-five highly skilled medical personnel under her direction and control.

Helena Russell, is a woman in her early thirties (born, say in 1965) whose father was a West Coast physician of great energy and drive. Influenced by her father, and driven by her own achievement mechanism, not to mention the strong feminist liberating movement of the times, Helena drove through Medical School meeting and marrying a fellow student.

The man she married, Telford Russell, moved into Space Medicine, a rapidly expanding specialty. Helena went along with him. Telford became a medical mission man - going out into space. Helena, now in her late twenties, worked at NASA and delved into space disorientation and psychology, becoming an expert in those areas. Then a mission disappeared into space — simply vanished — never to be heard from again. Telford was on that mission, and Helena, to all intents and purposes, was widowed.

Helena grieved and then went on working and living her full and liberated life. She rose in her profession. One year ago, she was offered the post of Chief of Medical Section on Moon Base Alpha and was accepted. Thus, as we pick Dr Russell up, she has been on Alpha for twelve months working and living, and to some extent retiring emotionally in that space womb environment.

Helena Russell is a very responsible person, a fine professional, but she is a woman nonetheless. By which we mean that she has her own side, a very feminine side, apart from the somewhat uni-sexed ambience of the Moon Base.

Helena does holographic sculpture. She likes all kinds of music. She has a flair with her uniforms. She has a certain style. She is, despite the times, an individual and no-one forgets that.

In the ongoing series, she may have to test that individuality more than once.

(c) <u>PROFESSOR</u> - (name to be decided)

This interesting and wise English astrophysicist in his late fifties, comes to Moon Base Alpha as a visitor to take his first look at some of the components a number of his students designed. He remains as an accidental addition to the small colony hurtling through space.

The Professor, born in the early forties, is a brilliant teacher and theoretician. Rarely involved in worldly things, the Professor nonetheless achieved a reputation as a tremendous mind in Field-Force theory. From his conjectures has come much of the space hardware in current use.

John Koenig was one of the Professor's outstanding students years ago. Since then, a bond of affection has grown up between them.

The Professor looks upon his times with a somewhat rueful eye. He is more of a throwback -- a nineteenth century scientist -- philosopher humanist -- and he is an intellectual counterbalance to the twenty-first century we are about to enter, although physically he is much more a part of it than he appears. For he has a mechanical heart, which responds much more slowly to nervous stimuli than does a normal human heart. This makes him unsusceptible to panic or to emotional stress of any other kind. Unless someone who understands his condition is ruthless enough or desperate enough to interfere with his mechanical heart and so upset his finely tuned metabolism.

Two further characters have yet to be cast:

1. An Italian man of 28 who will be in charge of space reconnaissance.

2. A 23-year-old Italian girl who will be an expert in sensor devices.

With minor exceptions, the characters described above will be our running characters. They must be given two lives -- one of themselves, and one as cells in a unit involved in a planet-shaking emergency -- a life and death struggle for human survival.

If that can be made to happen, the combination of science-fantasy and reality will have been achieved and deep dimension, as well as gut excitement, will be generated.

12. STANDING SETS

The main scene playing areas for Alpha will be: —

- 1. Central Control (full of equipment)

- 2. ALPHA Commander' Office (adjacent to Central Control and becoming at times an integral part of it.)

- 3. Commander's Living Quarters (slightly more expansive than standard)

- 4. A standard modular living quarter (capable of adaption to any individual)

- 5. Corridor (with doors off to work sections or living quarters dressed as required, or travel tubes)

- 6. Interior travel tube compartment.

- 7. Interior Command Module of Multiple Transportation Unit (MTU)

- 8. Interior Passenger compartment MTU.

These are the standing sets. The number of additional sets available for each episode can be discussed at storyline stage.

ADVANCE PROGRAM INFORMATION

FACTS ABOUT SPACE: 1999

SPACE: 1999

THE MOST SPECTACULAR AND EXPENSIVE SPACE SCIENCE FICTION
SERIES EVER PRODUCED FOR TELEVISION

24 BRAND NEW NETWORK BUDGETED, NETWORK QUALITY
FIRST-RUN SCIENCE FICTION HOURS
IN COLOR, ON FILM

Starring

MARTIN LANDAU
BARBARA BAIN
BARRY MORSE

THE PREMISE

Near the end of this century space travel has become commonplace and necessary. During a series of routine trips between Earth and Moon, radio signals are heard, establishing without a doubt, the existence of life forms in space. This extraordinary discovery unites, for the first time in the history of mankind, all the peoples of Earth in a common effort to defend itself against the potential threat of these unknown life forms.

Moonbase Alpha, an early-warning defense system installation, is established on the surface of the Moon. It is manned by 311 men and women representing all the nations of the world.

At this juncture in history, atomic power has, coincidentally, become the principal means of man's energy needs. The storage of atomic waste matter poses severe environmental problems on Earth and so a decision is made to store atomic waste matter on the far side of the Moon.[9]

THE STORY

September 1999.

As SPACE: 1999 begins, the folly of man's decision to store atomic waste matter on the far side of the Moon results in a catastrophe unequalled in the history of mankind. A series of spectacular thermonuclear explosions occur that tear away portions of the Moon and completely alter its gravitational relationship with Earth. The Moon is blasted out of Earth's orbit!

With Moonbase Alpha intact, the Moon careens inexorably away from Earth. It can never return, and becomes the only world for the 311 helpless, hopeless inhabitants, whose goal now is to find a compatible planet on which to settle.

Self-sustaining, the base is able to maintain survival conditions. Food, air and water recycling installations are powered with atomic and solar energy. All systems necessary for the life functions of the people, and the computer-governed operations of the complex machinery, are operative – making the runaway Moon totally self-supporting.

Thus a fateful journey of 311 men and women through the incredible vastness of space begins. Their adventures… their quest for survival… their search for a compatible planet… and defense against the fantastic life forms found throughout the galaxies and with the awesome forces of the universe itself, becomes the springboard for our weekly episodes.

THE SIX AND A HALF MILLION DOLLAR SERIES

The budget for each hour episode of SPACE: 1999 is $275,000.
It is the highest budget for an hour series ITC has committed in 20 years of production.

Stars, guest stars, writers, directors, sets, props, and costumes are the very best. And the most comprehensive special effects yet mounted for a television series – special effects so extraordinary and so spectacular –

---

[9] The reference to 'the dark side' of the Moon has finally been corrected here to 'the far side', however – as anyone familiar with the pilot episode 'Breakaway' knows – in the opening moments of the show it is identified on-screen as 'the dark side of the Moon'. If one is generous, it could be claimed that the screen caption is correct as that side of the Moon was indeed in darkness at that point in the story.

demanded and dictated the filming of this series on 35mm film. Not on 16mm film. Not on videotape.

CUSTOM MADE FOR THE U.S. TELEVISION MARKET

SPACE: 1999 is the first series ITC has specifically custom-tailored for American audiences.

Both above and below the line personnel feature American talent whose stature and skills are absolutely tops in the industry.

To assure our success, we drew upon extensive research and our own experience, took the best elements of every successful science-fiction TV series, and incorporated them into SPACE: 1999.

Because of ITC's special situation and distinguished position in the industry, special waivers were secured from British trade organizations and unions, increasing the number of American actors, writers, directors and other talent used to make television programs in England.

- We have three excellent and established stars in the leads: Martin Landau, Barbara Bain and Barry Morse.
- We commissioned scripts from leading science-fiction writers and seasoned American television pros including George Bellak to put the imprint and style of American TV on SPACE: 1999.
- We hired the very best directors in the industry, including Lee H. Katzin, to set the pace and patterns of American TV.
- Under the guidance of producers Gerry and Sylvia Anderson, we created the most outstanding special effects ever seen on television, and seldom seen in motion pictures.
- We have more sets than any other television series has ever had – both interior and exterior – including new planets or locations on every episode.
- Because of ITC's special situation, this series has the look that would have cost ten million dollars if filmed in Hollywood.
- Meticulous care was taken with every word of dialogue and every bit of business.

In every respect, SPACE: 1999 is a first-class, first-rate, spectacular series. It has all the elements for a successful science-fiction series PLUS everything audiences require in contemporary entertainment. It is precisely this PLUS value, which ITC's special situation in the world market is able to deliver, that makes the difference between a moderately successful series and a super-series like SPACE: 1999.

THE LANDAUS: MARTIN LANDAU/BARBARA BAIN

SPACE: 1999 is the first TV series in which Martin Landau and Barbara Bain have worked together since their marathon run in MISSION: IMPOSSIBLE. Both life members of the famed Actors Studio, where Martin also teaches, they have continued their separate television and motion picture careers, and are re-united professionally for the first time in a TV series. Barbara Bain holds the distinction of being the only actress in the history of TV to have won an Emmy -- three years in a row -- as Best Actress for her role in MISSION: IMPOSSIBLE.

In SPACE: 1999 Martin Landau stars as Commander Koenig, leader of Moonbase Alpha... chosen for his combination of outstanding leadership qualities, superior space knowledge and unequalled administrative ability. He won the command over candidates from all nations because their leaders acknowledged that he could do the job better than anyone else in the world.

Barbara Bain stars as Dr Helena Russell, chief medical officer on the new world of Moonbase Alpha. Her responsibilities include the maintenance of life on Alpha including the psychological and emotional stability of its inhabitants. Her sphere of influence extends to Commander Koenig, with whom she has an understandably close relationship.

BARRY MORSE

Best known to American audiences for his role as Lt. Gerard on THE FUGITIVE, Morse has appeared on many other series including DR KILDARE, WAGON TRAIN and THE SAINT. He is soon to be seen co-starring with Brian Keith, John Mills and Lilli Palmer in a new prime-time adventure series, THE ZOO GANG, on NBC-TV. One of the most distinguished international actors, he has been seen in many motion pictures and on both the British and Broadway stages, as well as on television, where he has won the Best TV Actor Award five times. Schooled at the Royal Academy of Dramatic Art, he has been Adjunct Professor in the Drama Department of Yale University.

In SPACE: 1999, Morse stars as Professor Victor Bergman, a scientist whose remarkable work is most responsible for the establishment of Moonbase Alpha. At one time Commander Koenig's mentor and teacher, the professor has remained a close friend and together with him and Dr Russell they form the triumvirate which makes the critical decisions on which the fate of the space travelers depends.

PRODUCERS

Gerry and Sylvia Anderson, long associated with ITC, produced SPACE: 1999. For the past 12 years they have produced science-fiction feature films for Universal and United Artists and outer-space television series for ITC. Their credits include the motion pictures JOURNEY TO THE FAR SIDE OF THE SUN (Universal) and THUNDERBIRDS ARE GO (UA). For television, they produced series for ITC including UFO, THE PROTECTORS, THUNDERBIRDS, STINGRAY, CAPTAIN SCARLET, FIREBALL XL-5 and SUPERCAR. Working with a virtual 'repertory company' of special effects technicians, designers, architects and engineers, they have achieved some of the most spectacular effects on the screen, many of which have since become standard.

DIRECTORS

Only the very best directors in the industry have been hired to direct this series. Among them are Lee H. Katzin, one of the most prolific and highly regarded craftsmen in the industry, and Charles Crichton, internationally hailed as a master of suspense and action.

Katzin has directed THE SALZBURG CONNECTION, LE MANS, WHATEVER HAPPENED TO AUNT ALICE?, ANGRY ODYSSEY and other feature films. For television he has directed made-for-TV movies for all three networks, and his work includes ORDEAL, ALONG CAME A SPIDER, HONDO, THE STRANGER, VOYAGE OF THE YES, THE AMERICAN EAGLE and VISIONS. In demand for network series, Katzin has directed episodes of MCMILLAN AND WIFE, MOD SQUAD, THE FELONY SQUAD, IT TAKES A THIEF, MANNIX, RAT PATROL, WILD WILD WEST, RAWHIDE, BRANDED, STONEY BURKE and many more including MISSION: IMPOSSIBLE – the long-running series in which Martin Landau and Barbara Bain originally starred.

Altogether a record number of American directors was allowed to participate in the scripting of this series, as was an American story supervisor.

STORY EDITOR

To assure that SPACE: 1999 would be an American series for American audiences, George Bellak was relocated in England where he developed a set of guidelines, organized the writers' pool and supervised the initial stories and concepts. One of the most experienced writer/editors in show business, Bellak has won the WGA Award and been nominated for an Emmy. Among his television credits are those for THE DEFENDERS, CANNON, THE NURSES, EAST SIDE-WEST SIDE and many more going back to the classic stories on PLAYHOUSE 90, STUDIO ONE, CBS PLAYHOUSE and others. He was a contract writer at Columbia Pictures and 20th Century-Fox and has also authored plays produced on Broadway and in London.

SETS

For SPACE: 1999 we have built more sets – both interior and exterior – than any other television series has ever had. In addition to the standing sets for the continuing locations, there are new planets or locations on every episode, and a new set of sets for them. This costs extra, but it makes the difference.

SPECIAL EFFECTS

For SPACE: 1999, we have created the most outstanding special effects ever seen on television, and seldom seen in feature films except for those produced by the same team that made SPACE: 1999 – Gerry and Sylvia Anderson. For openers, we blow up the Moon!

FASHION

RUDI GERNREICH, who created the topless bathing suit and whose latest contribution to style is this season's so-called bottomless bathing suit, designed the costumes for SPACE: 1999.

THE STORIES

BREAKAWAY

The biggest explosion in the history of man destroys the dark side of the Moon hurling it violently out of Earth's orbit.[10] On a manmade Moonbase, the 311 survivors of the nuclear blast begin an unexpected journey across the universe, searching for a compatible planet on which to settle. Conflicts and fear dominate these early hours of space travel and subject the survivors to the tensions and anguish of a thrilling struggle for survival.
FORCE OF LIFE

---

[10] Once again, there is no 'dark side' of the Moon, but there is a far side which always faces away from Earth.

Terror strikes Alpha as one of the Moonbase's technicians is possessed by a frightening outer-space force which transforms him into an energy-consuming monster. He goes on a rampage, destroying everything he touches by absorbing its heat, freezing everything he touches. Finally he heads for the giant generators of the Moonbase itself. Unable to stop him, and in peril from his deadly touch, Commander Koenig orders laser beams turned on him. Charred by enormous blasts from the guns, the monster's blackened, burned out body is regenerated by the energy! Pulsating with light, he advances relentlessly on the very energy source of Alpha itself, threatening the entire expedition with destruction.

BLACK SUN

The runaway Moon is on a deadly collision course with an asteroid which suddenly burns out and becomes a terrifying 'black sun' – a whirlpool-like phenomenon of deep space which devours everything around it, including light.[11] With only three days to avoid destruction, the Moonbase personnel construct anti-gravity towers and build an immense forcefield. A survival party is dispatched from the Moon in a space 'lifeboat' and those remaining are sucked inexorably into the fearsome black sun as time, space, and even matter are cancelled.

MATTER OF LIFE AND DEATH

Helena's husband returns from the dead to warn Moonbase personnel away from a seemingly compatible planet. Composed of anti-matter, his touch hurls Helena across the room and all who come in contact with him suffer similarly violent reactions. Disregarding his warnings, Commander Koenig and a landing party embark in a spaceship for the forbidding alien planet, where they find the anti-matter reaction multiplied. Disaster strikes in enormous waves, as first the spaceship is destroyed, then the Moon itself seems to explode. In horror, Helena and Commander Koenig watch as enormous shock waves hit the planet, wiping out everything in the aftermath of a holocaust that must mean the end of everything for the space travelers.

EARTHBOUND

An alien spaceship crash lands on the runaway Moon and the bodies of six

---

[11] The asteroid does not burn out and become a black sun. It is on a collision course with the Moon until being diverted by the forces of the black sun and being torn apart by gravitational stresses. After the asteroid blows up, the Alphans spot the black sun (although it takes them a while to positively identify the space phenomenon) and realize that the Moon itself is being drawn into it.

figures are discovered in a state of suspended animation. They are refugees en route to Earth from a dying planet. Frozen down for 3 1/2 centuries, they are looking for a compatible planet on which to live. When one of the aliens is accidentally destroyed, Koenig agrees to let the Alpha computer select one of his crew as a replacement. But Commissioner Symonds is so determined to return to Earth that he forces the decision by breaking into the power station and threatening to destroy the entire Moonbase unless Koenig agrees to let him go.

RING AROUND THE MOON

A space probe on its way to destroy Earth encounters the runaway Moon and plans to eliminate it as well, considering Earth and its satellites a menace to their home planet. They are completely unaware that their planet Triton itself has disintegrated millions of light years ago, and this mission is useless. Among the fantastic powers demonstrated by the hostile aliens is that of decomposing atoms, enabling them to transport Dr Russell from Alpha to their spaceship, where she becomes a living link between the alien computer and her own. When the aliens have completed assembling all of Alpha's data, they will destroy it and its personnel. Koenig desperately searches for a way to break the power of the strange creatures and save the lives of Moonbase Alpha personnel. He decides on a daring attack and forces his way into the alien craft.

ANOTHER TIME, ANOTHER PLACE

A huge, churning mass appears in space and rushes at incredible velocity toward the runaway Moon. The mammoth, spiraling cone of spitting colored gasses is only one of the awesome hazards in an adventure which finds the Moon on a collision course with... itself. Caught in a 'time-trap', the Moon and everyone on it is duplicated as a result of the spectacular 'collision' and past and future become one for Commander Koenig and the others, who meet themselves out of time, in the phenomenon of Space, beyond 1999.[12]

MISSING LINK

Five million light years away from Earth, Koenig is kidnapped and brought to a beautiful planet of light and luxurious surroundings. While Dr Russell's

---

[12] A rather vague and strange ('in the phenomenon of Space, beyond 1999') synopsis that nevertheless does reveal the basic premise of the episode. The 'mammoth, spiralling cone of splitting coloured gasses' was depicted somewhat more simply on-screen as a particle storm.

medical computer and all the other futuristic equipment supports Koenig's physical body, his life force is being examined on the alien planet, where a beautiful woman tells him that her father is an anthropologist using him as a sort of 'missing link' to their own past – millions of years ago. They plan on keeping Koenig there permanently, while back on Moonbase Alpha, his crew fights desperately to bring him back alive.

GUARDIAN OF PIRI

In an exciting discovery, the Alphans come upon the most marvelous planet of all: a paradise where machines run the necessities of life and the people enjoy luxury, peace and contentment. Only a beautiful woman, the Guardian of Piri, controls the machines and regulates the planet. All others are 'free' to do nothing at all. When members of Moonbase Alpha are lured to Piri, they become convinced that this is the life for them and that here they will find their new home. In truth, the planet is dead. Where there is no aim in life, there is no life. The promise of absolute permanent euphoria is really a cancellation of human functions – and Koenig soon recognizes his crew lolling about in a trancelike state. His heroic efforts to resist the planet's insidious influence begins to fail, but a dramatic encounter with the Guardian of Piri brings the adventure to a startling climax.

VOYAGER'S RETURN

Moonbase Alpha is threatened with destruction from an unmanned spacecraft sent from Earth 15 years earlier. In its erratic rampage, the malfunctioning ship has caused millions of deaths on other planets and is now approaching the Moon. Also bearing down on them is an outer space force bent on vengeance for those responsible for the interstellar carnage. Only one man can deactivate the ship. This is a scientist now working on Moonbase, who races against time to prevent further disaster in space, including the possible destruction of Alpha and everyone on it.

ALPHA CHILD

During a stupendous battle in outer space between rival spaceships, the first baby is born on the Moon.[13] A baby with a difference, it grows to the age of five years in only hours, then rapidly becomes a 'man' in his middle thirties. The body is to be used by aliens who have life but not form and face

---

[13] The Alpha child is born in the opening teaser of the episode, but there is no 'stupendous battle in outer space between rival spaceships' happening at the time. The alien spacecrafts don't arrive at Alpha until much later.

extinction on their own planet. Their fleet of spaceships has zeroed in on Moonbase Alpha and the Alpha child is apparently only the first they plan to use.

DEATH'S OTHER DOMINION

On a frozen planet of ice and sub-zero temperatures, Koenig and the Alphans discover an extraordinary people preparing to launch the greatest adventure in the history of the universe: a probe deep into space, spanning the entire solar system, and crossing from one galaxy to the next. How can they even consider embarking on so long a journey? Time is not a factor, for on this incredible planet they have discovered how to live forever! Most fantastic of all, Koenig realizes they are not aliens, but members of an Earth expedition believed lost on a proton storm 13 years earlier. In that time, they have travelled 800 years, and now they know they can never die. They urge the Alphans to join them, and they are tempted, until a dissident group leads them to discover the horrifying consequences of the experiment.

THE LAST SUNSET

The Moon is shaken by an unbelievable electrical storm, pressurized vapor endangers the Alphans... while in space, an Eagle is tossed mercilessly in turbulence surrounding the hostile planet. A reconnaissance team crash-lands on an alien planet, as a series of spectacular events threatens to bring Alpha's space journey to an abrupt and violent end. The blistering, scarlet sun of the planet Ariel, which has dwarfed the Moon throughout the adventure, now sets over Alpha in what may be its last day.[14]

COLLISION COURSE

After a tension-filled adventure in space, during which Alan Carter is almost killed, mines are planted which destroy an oncoming asteroid in an enormous explosion that fills the screen. The Alphans immediately discover an even greater menace: they are being drawn rapidly onto a collision course with an awesome planet many times their size. Again space mines are planted, but in the time left before detonation, Koenig goes to the planet in a spaceship. There he meets the ruler, a woman older than Earth itself, who tells him their meeting has been awaited in the body of time for millions of years. It will change life as they know it for both worlds. Koenig returns to

---

[14] Interestingly, this synopsis bears little resemblance to the final aired episode as the Reconnaissance Eagle never crash-landed on Ariel, but rather the Moon surface now enshrouded by an Earth-like atmosphere thanks to the aliens.

Alpha and cancels orders for detonating the mines. This means certain collision with the enormous planet dead ahead. Believing Koenig to be suffering from radiation hallucinations, Prof. Bergman and Helena Russell lead the crew in relieving him of his command. But with the help of Carter, to whom the ancient ruler has appeared several times in an extraordinary method of communication, Koenig is able to resume command by force. As the battle for control of their very lives takes place in Main Mission, the count-down runs out, the mines are not detonated, and the two masses of matter collide in a spectacular effect – with a surprising result!

THE FULL CIRCLE

Exploring a strange planet, Alpha personnel find themselves at war with a 40,000 year old enemy. Even more incredible, the enemy is... themselves! Caught in a time warp, their futuristic lives are superimposed over their ancient lives. Before realizing this awesome paradox, however, Sandra wounds the Cave Chief who, lies dying in the arms of his Cave Wife: they are the Cro-Magnon images of Koenig and Helena Russell! Professor Bergman, meanwhile, has run tests on another 'caveman' and discovered that the Stone Age creature is the pilot of a crashed Eagle ship. Has he time to stop Carter, now leading an expedition to kill his supposed enemies – who are in his own time the other members of his crew?

END OF ETERNITY

The runaway Moon encounters an asteroid that has been travelling a thousand years in space. Landing on it, Commander Koenig blasts his way into the sealed interior where a humanoid alien is found. Although the alien was injured by the blast he is completely recovered by the time Koenig's spaceship returns to the Moon. The alien is a scientist who has achieved man's dream of immortality: he cannot die! Banished by his people for creating a life which now has no meaning and is intolerable, he has been imprisoned, for all eternity in the asteroid. Now he hungers for destruction. Completely psychopathic, he runs amuck, destroying everything within his reach. No one is immune to his immense strength and powers of regeneration. And there is no way of catching or killing a man who cannot die! Finally, Koenig arrives at a desperate plan to trap him in an airlock and release him into space... forever.

WAR GAMES

A massive attack on Moonbase Alpha destroys the complex, wrenching its personnel out into space. Enormous towers crash to the ground as an unreal power from a strange planet creates a mind-boggling method of preventing inter-planetary war. Commander Koenig's confrontation with the aliens, on their own beautiful planet, is a dramatic contrast to the fury of the action on Alpha where the runaway Moon is threatened with total destruction.

THE LAST ENEMY

The runaway Moon's voyage through space plunges it into the center of an interplanetary war which threatens to destroy it. Two planets, out of each other's firing range because of the sun's position, seize upon the Moon as an excellent gun platform.[15] When one of the alien forces, led by a woman, 'confiscate' the Moon, the enemy commander – also a woman – counters with nuclear retaliatory measures that threaten to blow the Moon to smithereens.

THE TROUBLED SPIRIT

Conducting scientific experiments with Alpha's artificially nourished plant life, a vital link in the food chain on which Moonbase Alpha relies for survival, Alpha's Hydroponic Director is confronted by the hideously disfigured spirit of... himself! Meanwhile, efforts to establish communication between human and plant life take an ominous turn. Horror strikes and death comes suddenly to both plants and humans as Alpha's most serious crisis comes to a thrilling climax.[16]

SPACE: 1999

- The most spectacular and expensive space science-fiction series ever produced for television.
- 24 brand new Network Budgeted, Network Quality, First-run Hours, In color on 35mm film
- Starring Martin Landau, Barbara Bain, Barry Morse
- Six and a half million dollar budget

---

[15] The concept of two inhabited planets orbiting their sun on opposite sides was also featured in Gerry and Sylvia Anderson's 1969 film *Doppelgänger* (aka: *Journey to the Far Side of the Sun*).

[16] A confusing and vague synopsis. The 'efforts to establish communication between human and plant life' are the 'scientific experiments' that open the episode, not a separate storyline. The last sentence is particularly vague, but incorrectly states that 'death comes suddenly' to plants as well as humans. In the final episode the vengeful spirit only kills people, but as this synopsis is the last one included in this document it's probable that 'The Troubled Spirit' was still in the process of being written and this synopsis may have been generated from Johnny Byrne's initial concept for the episode rather than the finished script.

- Custom made for the U.S. television market
- Outstanding sets and special effects
- Action-adventure stories
- American writers
- American directors
- Produced by today's most prolific science-fiction filmmakers

NAME EVOLUTION

Throughout 1973, *Space: 1999* was an ever-changing work in progress. Many people contributed ideas over the course of development from creators Gerry and Sylvia Anderson, original Story Consultant Christopher Penfold, George Bellak, and perhaps even Abe Mandell. This handy chart shows how each character, prop, and locale was referred to over the course of the series' creation.

EARLY NAMES

SOURCE

FINAL NAME: Commander John Koenig

The Commander	Advance Program Information
The American Commander	Early Outline
Space Commander Maddox	'Zero G'
John Robert Koenig	Guidelines (1st Draft)
John Koenig	'The Void Ahead' (1st Draft)

FINAL NAME: Doctor Helena Russell

Dr Janet Bowman	Early Series Proposal
Chief Medical Officer (male)	Advance Program Information
Doctor Gordon	'Zero G'
Doctor Helena Russell	Guidelines (1st Draft)
Doctor Helena Russell	'The Void Ahead' (1st Draft)

FINAL NAME: Professor Victor Bergman

Doctor Marc Miller	'Zero G'
Professor Danilo Sabatini	Guidelines (1st Draft)
The Professor	Guidelines (2nd Draft)
Professor Penmarric	'Siren Planet'
Professor Bergman	'The Void Ahead' (1st Draft)

FINAL NAME: Captain Alan Carter

The Space Captain	Early Outline
Lt. Caron	'Zero G'
J.W. Grayson	Guidelines (1st Draft)
Grayson	'Siren Planet'
Probe Captain Catani	'The Void Ahead' (1st Draft)
Carlo Catani	'Breakaway' (Blue Pages)

FINAL NAME: **Controller Paul Morrow**
The Controller	'Zero G'
Vorkonen	'The Void Ahead' (1st Draft)
Main Mission Controller Bob Morrow	'The Void Ahead' (Temp. Final Draft)
Main Mission Controller Paul Morrow	'Turning Point'

FINAL NAME: **Data Analyst Sandra Benes**
Sandra Sabatini	'The Void Ahead' (1st Draft)
Sandra Benes	'Breakaway' (Broadcast Version)

FINAL NAME: **Computer Chief David Kano**
Computer Chief Ouma	'The Void Ahead' (1st Draft)

FINAL NAME: **Doctor Robert Mathias**
Doctor Fujita	The Void Ahead (1st Draft)

FINAL NAME: **Commissioner Simmonds**
Grivas	Untitled Opening Episode Storyline
Commissioner Symonds	'The Void Ahead' (1st Draft)
Commissioner Simmonds	'Turning Point'

FINAL NAME: **Commander Gorski**
Commander Grodno	'The Void Ahead' (2nd Draft)
Commander Gorski	'Turning Point'

FINAL NAME: **Eagle Pilot Collins**
Simpson	'Turning Point'
Carter	'Breakaway' (Blue Pages)
Collins	'Breakaway' (Broadcast Version)

FINAL NAME: **Eagle Transporter**
Moonship	Advance Program Information
Prober	'Siren Planet'
Probe Ship	'A Breath of Death'
M.T.U.	'Zero G'

FINAL NAME: **Moonbase Alpha**
Moon City	'Zero G'
Moon Base Alpha	Guidelines (2nd Draft)
Alpha Base	'The Void Ahead' (1st Draft)
Moonbase Alpha	'The Void Ahead' (2nd Draft)

FINAL NAME: **Main Mission**

Central Control / The Control Room	Advance Program Information
Control Center	'Zero G'
Main Mission	'The Void Ahead' (Temp. Final Draft)

FINAL NAME: **Commlock**

IDX	Guidelines (2nd Draft)
Commlock	'The Void Ahead' (Temp. Final Draft)

FINAL NAME: **Stun Gun**

Laser Beam Generator	'Zero G'
TSLA	Guidelines (2nd Draft)
Stun Gun	'The Void Ahead' (Temp. Final Draft)
Stun Weapon	'Breakaway' (Blue Pages)

FINAL NAME: **Communications Post**

Comm-Post	'Black Sun' (1st Draft)

FINAL NAME: **Moonbuggy**

Moonmobile	Advance Program Information

'THE VOID AHEAD' 'TURNING POINT' 'BREAKAWAY'

One-Hour Format Pilot Scripts
'The Void Ahead' First Draft Copy - Undated
'The Void Ahead' Unmarked Second Draft - Undated
'The Void Ahead' Temporary Final - Undated
all by George Bellak
'Turning Point' Final Shooting Script - 5 November 1973
'Breakaway' Amended Blue Pages Final Shooting Script - 22 November 1973
by George Bellak & Christopher Penfold (uncredited)

INTRODUCTION

The reinstatement of the one-hour, four-act format, and the arrival of George Bellak into the writing staff rescued Space: 1999 from the potential of being a mediochre series. The half-hour TV episode can be problematic for the action/adventure format. In only two acts, a well-plotted story has to be presented as 'Introducing a Problem' (Act One) and 'The Resolution' (Act Two). In between, a dramatic cliffhanger must be shoehorned in to bring the audience back from the commercial break.

Often, character drama must be limited or sacrificed to the plot. The original half-hour pilot script, 'Zero G', needed to cram in an awful lot of information, establishing how the Moon departed from Earth and what kind of universe the Moonbase inhabitants would face. Beyond the main characters of the Commander and the Professor, there was no time to put a spotlight on the rest of the supporting cast. They were merely background players with little or no personality.

Doubling the length allowed Bellak to cram in not only an ensemble of characters with personalities and back-stories but sell a very detailed and real location that was more science fact than fiction. He wrote at least three (that we know of) drafts, refining and tightening the action. Changes between each draft were based on casting, set design, and feedback from various quarters. Budget would also dictate how many characters, sets, and visual effects could be presented. Overall, it is evident that he was setting the bar high, expecting each episode to have a movie-of-the-week quality.

After Bellak left the production (see both the 'George Bellak' section written by Christopher Penfold and 'The George Bellak Situation' entry within the 'Correspondence' section of this book), Christopher Penfold created a shooting script from the material ('Turning Point') and all the amended script pages ('Breakaway') as the opening episode went before the cameras.

SYNOPSIS

Doctor Helena Russell is investigating possible radiation leakage at Nuclear Waste Disposal Area 2 on the dark side of the Moon. To her horror, another technician succumbs and dies.

John Koenig returns to take command of the Moon Base and expedite the launch of a critical deep space probe. The pilots appear to be suffering from the same mysterious illness that has befallen the workers. Initially dismissing Dr Russell's 'radiation' theory because of lack of evidence, Koenig is mystified by a mysterious erasure of a portion of a flight data recorder.

Despite no sign of radiation leakage, an older Waste Depot erupts, and Koenig's observation spacecraft is knocked out of the sky by unusual forces. Studying meters from the site, Professor Bergman theorizes that hitherto unknown 'magnetic radiation' is the culprit.

Koenig sets in motion a race to strip apart the vastly larger Area Two, but time runs out. The force of the explosion hurls the Moon out of Earth's orbit into outer space.

WRITER GEORGE BELLAK

'The Void Ahead' was written by American George Bellak who was originally hired to be the series' story editor alongside Englishman Christopher Penfold. Born April 9, 1919, his TV career began in 1951 writing the episode 'Cafe Ami' for the *Lux Video Theatre*. In 1958, he wrote a script for a proposed Republic Pictures TV series pilot vehicle for the popular pulp and radio character The Shadow. This and another episode were instead edited together and released theatrically as *The Invisible Avenger*. It was also re-released four years later as *Bourbon St Shadows*.

Bellak continued to contribute to various television series, including *The Untouchables* ('The Tommy Karpeles Story' 1960), the Boris Karloff hosted *Thriller* ('Choose a Victim' 1961), *The Alfred Hitchcock Hour* ('The Dividing Wall' 1963), *The Mod Squad* ('Confrontation!' 1969) and *Cannon* ('The Island Caper', 'Cain's Mark', 'Bitter Legion' 1972).

In addition to scriptwriting, Bellak was also an accomplished novelist with *Come Jericho* in 1981 and *The Third Friday* in 1988. He passed away on October 22, 2002.

REFERENCE MATERIAL

Bellak wrote a wholly original script for the series' revised one-hour format, adapting nothing from Gerry and Sylvia Anderson's earlier half-hour pilot 'Zero G'. After delivering at least three undated drafts, Christopher Penfold took over and refined Bellak's 'The Void Ahead' to incorporate finalized art direction and casting with his uncredited adaption first titled 'Turning Point' (dated 5 November 1973) and then further refined as 'Breakaway' (22 November 1973).

ANALYSIS

Bellak's undated first draft script was obviously written early in pre-production before it had been determined each episode would follow the format of pre-titles teaser, four acts and an epilogue. The story begins, as all versions do, at Nuclear Waste Area 2 on the dark side of the moon. Eventually shown on-screen in a futuristic style, Bellak first described the setting in a darker, more horrific, nuclear nightmare form. The Waste Pits are harshly lit by glaring floodlights and surrounded by a wire fence, dotted with warning placards. For the second draft, Area 2 now had laser barriers, but still warning signs. By the 'Temporary Final' draft, he described the area closer to its final form, no doubt having seen Keith Wilson's set design (which did include the warning signage).

Initially, Waste Technician Steiner was killed when his suit is punctured on the wire fence, but the second draft has him now bounce off the laser barrier and crack his visor on a rock.

Professor Bergman (whose name is finalized in the first draft), was not originally at the Waste Area with Dr Russell, rather busy writing about events in his notebook in his quarters. Bellak establishes him early on as the narrator (utilized in other early drafts) and, as acknowledged by Christopher Penfold, the series conscience and voice of reason. Perhaps Bellak intended Bergman to narrate the series overall, much as Helena did in Series Two.

Dr Russell's companion at the Waste Area was the Depot Chief Gundlach, a character who lasted right up into shooting (played by Michael Sheard), but cut out when 'Breakaway' was edited down to its final cut. For the third, 'Temporary Final' draft, Bergman joins her and Gundlach and remains into both 'Turning Point' and 'Breakaway'.

Bellak's last draft offers the break-down of what would become the first series' main title format, describing a 'FAST CUTTING MONTAGE forming an exciting trailer' of the coming episode. Surprisingly, he describes in detail a visual image of Barry Morse, which did not appear until several episodes later. Both Morse, Martin Landau and Barbara Bain are named in the final draft, so casting had to have been finalized on the lead actors by this time.

Penfold refined these details further; the main title would appear with 'each letter a different colour representative of the various Alpha Sections' over a long shot of the Moonbase and 'an Eagle overflying two spacemen in foreground.' Originally, the montage of the Moon being blasted out of Earth orbit was supposed to be replaced in the opening episode. The subliminal caption during the preview montage, 'This Episode', was meant to read 'Tonight's Episode'.

The 'Virus Infection' story finally appears in the 'Temporary Final', up until then the Meta Probe astronauts were only described as suffering from a 'mild stomach illness'. Penfold tightened the dialogue between the initial reunion of Koenig and Bergman to give the 'Virus Infection' a more ominous mystery.

Bellak's scripts describe many details of Alpha, such as the complicated docking of Koenig's 'Probe Ship' with a ladder, possibly based on early set designs that were later altered or abandoned. Locations and props feature early names that were used perhaps as placeholders until final terms were established (ie, Probeship becomes MTU and then, finally, Eagle).

Many of the early character names, Vorkonen, Murneau, Dr Fujita *et al*, reflect Bellak's desire to establish the Moonbase as a result of International co-operation. Female characters are presented on equal footing to their male counterparts (Rudi Gernreich's unisex uniforms would avoid *Star Trek*'s contradiction of sexualizing females by putting them in miniskirts). Supporting character nationalities were obviously changed as actors were cast (director Lee H Katzin was very involved in this) and it has also been reported that several Italian actors had to drop out due to problems working in English.

Subsequent drafts also play up a round-the-clock background TV newscast, foreshadowing the likes of CNN. Katzin wanted a flurry of imagery on the base monitors during 'Breakaway' to convey the mass of activity on the Moon (the lack of this in later episodes actually worked to establish their isolation in deep space).

The French engineer Murneau was obviously intended as a major character. Gone by 'Turning Point', in early drafts he comes across as the base's answer to *Star Trek*'s Mr Scott. Much of that character's function was eventually delegated to others, particularly Bergman, as the series' format whittled down the core players to primarily the staff of Main Mission.

Bellak, very early on, made a dramatic choice to give Koenig and Russell an adversarial relationship, something the recent Big Finish audio drama returned to. Had the series been produced with a set running order, this approach to their relationship could have developed in a dramatic fashion across several episodes, but the nature of television at the time necessitated the conflict be resolved by the end of this episode (it should be noted that in some regions, 'Dragon's Domain' followed 'Breakaway' which again had them at odds). By his last draft, Bellak had revised the two leading characters closer to their final aired personas, still wary of each other's motives, but mutually respectful.

Russell's conflict with the former Commander also remained in all versions until that character was all but eliminated from the final broadcast version, save for a brief appearance during Koenig's arrival. Called Grodno in the early drafts, this character played a major part in the second draft onward, only departing before Commissioner Simmonds' arrival. Bellak added a major scene between Koenig and Grodno where the former Commander tries to discredit Dr Russell. Christopher Penfold's re-writes also retained the now re-named Gorski's private conversation with Koenig before his departure.

The disappearance on a space mission of Helena's husband (called Telford in both this episode and Art Wallace's 'Siren Planet' first draft) was established in the first episode, as well as Bergman's mechanical heart.

Unused in the final aired series was the story of Koenig's youth, growing up on a farm and his conflict with his father. These concepts also made it into 'Siren Planet'.

Bellak hinted at a mysterious connection with the signals from Meta in his first draft, fleshing out a greater need to discover what the signal may be saying in the subsequent drafts. In his 'Temporary Final' and the 'Turning Point' / 'Breakaway' revisions, Morrow talks about how Computer has attempted to decode it, but to no avail.

The first draft has the Meta Probe being constructed on the base, instead of in orbit above. This was obviously cut out due to the unnecessary cost of creating the Probe's interior. We also lose the panicking probe technician, Allison. Bellak went to great lengths to pack his script with a lot of character conflict, focusing less on the science-fiction elements and more on the human drama. The people who worked on the Moon were emotional, with fears of the unknown. Perhaps, had Bellak not left the series, Moonbase Alpha would have become a more volatile place with frequent psychological and inter-personal conflicts. Early drafts by other writers seem to support this intended direction. The series two episode 'The Seance Spectre' belatedly touched on this with a group of disgruntled Alphans (that script was originally entitled 'The Mutiny' by author Donald James).

As set and visual effect designs were refined, Bellak incorporated these changes into his second draft, such as the appearance of the spacecraft hanger and an establishing shot of the base with two technicians working outside as Koenig's ship arrived. Keith Wilson's sketch of this sequence was used to announce the series going into production in the industry trade paper *Variety*, and planned for the main title card. The sequence was never shot, most likely due to the difficulty in compositing live-action figures convincingly into the miniature landscape.

Bellak also focused on establishing in detail just how the Nuclear Waste Areas could have exploded. He set up a disaster caused by the mixing of two different waste materials that produced a violent surge of magnetic energy. Unlike the Moon's appearance in the final aired episode, Bellak continued with his 'nuclear nightmare' scenario by describing the post-explosion Moon appearing with a tremendous piece ripped away. The series seemed to ignore the horrific potential of this imagery, even in the 'The Seance Spectre', where the Waste Dump is pretty clean (established as a third storage facility in the *Moonbase Alpha Technical Operations Manual*, Anderson Entertainment 2021).

Through all the drafts, Symonds (changed to Simmonds in 'Turning Point') remained alive at the episode's end, unlike E C Tubb's novelization where his neck was broken during the disaster. Though his future on the series was never addressed in other proposed scripts, the character replaced another in Anthony Terpiloff's 'Earthbound'.

As the Moon is hurled out of Earth orbit and set adrift in space, Bellak had Bergman drop a hint to a mysterious power that may be looking out for them, the genesis of the 'Mysterious Unknown Force' hinted at further in David Weir's 'Black Sun', Christopher Penfold's 'War Games' and Johnny Byrne's 'The Testament of Arkadia'. As the Professor stares at 'an image of the swirling heavens', he remarks, 'Ah — perhaps God has spoken to us.'

In the 'Temporary Final', the Alphans now look towards Meta as their salvation. This was excised from 'Turning Point' but restored in the revised pages of 'Breakaway'.

RUNNING TIME

It has been well documented in Gerry Anderson's biography and various interviews that there existed a longer version of the first episode. Christopher Penfold's 'Turning Point' and 'Breakaway' revisions are both 'shooting scripts', each sequence roughly timed out and in the same four-act one-hour episode format as all of George Bellak's drafts.

A rough edit that lasted much longer may have been due to director Lee H Katzin's meticulous coverage, longer visual effect sequences, and alternate live-action sequences created in additional re-writes or during shooting (ie, Koenig's small talk about Helena's replica microscope prize is absent from even the 'Breakaway' blue page revisions).

EXCERPT FROM 'TURNING POINT'
5 November 1973
pages 47 - 50

81 EXT. MOON BASE ALPHA. SFX.(0.04)81

An Eagle approaches.

82 EXT. LAUNCH PAD. SFX.(0.07)82

An Eagle settles down to land and the travel tube telescopes out towards it.

83 INT.TRAVEL TUBE(0.24)83

Koenig gets to his feet as the tube slows to a stop. He moves towards the door.

The door opens. Koenig waits. At the end of the airlock from the Eagle passenger module appears Commissioner Simmonds.

KOENIG
Commissioner.

Simmonds looks up, cold-eyed, extends his hand. Koenig shakes it.

SIMMONDS
Commander…

Koenig turns back into the travel tube. He directs his commlock at the selector panel. The door closes as soon as Simmonds is in the tube.

As the tube accelerates, Koenig indicates a seat for Simmonds. They both sit down.

SIMMONDS
My office tried to query you
on your emergency request for
my presence … You didn't seem
to be available.

KOENIG
(coldly)
I am now.

CUT TO:

84 INT.KOENIG'S OFFICE(0.55)84

ON BERGMAN

> BERGMAN
> When this project started
> we used Uranium 392 as fuel.
> In the last seven years we
> started mixing it with Cesium.
> Uranium was expensive, Cesium
> was cheap. It would seem that
> Uranium and Cesium are reacting
> adversely to each other,
> producing magnetic fields of
> incredible strength. That's
> our problem.

> SIMMONDS
> (great skepticism)
> Magnetism — causing brain damage?

> HELENA
> Atomic radiation causing cancer?

> KOENIG
> Magnetism is energy — all energy radiates.

> SIMMONDS
> (to Helena, dismissive)
> I'll be happy to look at a
> comprehensive report on the
> subject.

> KOENIG
> Commissioner, I don't think you
> understand the urgency of the
> situation. We've got one hell of
> a problem up here, and it's got to
> be thrashed out. Dr Russell and

Professor Bergman identified the
problem and analysed its causes.
Together we've got to solve it,
here and now.

Koenig presses a button on his desk. The screen lights up.

ON THE SCREEN

85 EXT.NUCLEAR DISPOSAL AREA 2.SFX.(0.05)85

A remote camera pans the desolate and deserted area. It holds on the crashed Eagle.

86 INT.KOENIG'S OFFICE(1.00)86

ON SIMMONDS

He watches the screen, shifting uncomfortably.

WIDE

BERGMAN
(refers to the screen)
Commissioner, the heat has started
to rise on the interior of Area
Two as well and it is murderous.
It contains one hundred and
forty times the waste of Area One.
(takes a breath)
With those quantities the
possibility of a chain reaction
cannot be ruled out.

SIMMONDS
(now he's nervous)
What are the chances it will burn
itself out -- like Area One?

KOENIG
You don't seem to be getting this,
Simmonds. We're sitting on top
of it and there is no chance.

ON SIMMONDS

Tries to control his fear.

SIMMONDS
What can be done?

BERGMAN
We can try to break the pile apart …
Rip up the fuel rods, destroy the
mass.
(he turns to Koenig)
If we can spread the mass over
a wide enough area, we might …

SIMMONDS
Then let's do it.

KOENIG
Yes, let's do it.

BERGMAN
But we have limited time.

CAMERA PANS about the tense faces and finally over to the screen of the Communications Post. A kind of tremor shakes the ground.

ON KOENIG

He reacts, knowing now what it means.

TIMING DIFFERENCES:

<u>Script timing</u> 2:30

<u>Final Screen Time</u> 1:47

The timings in Christopher Penfold's 'Turning Point' break down as follows:

SCRIPT TIMINGS:
Teaser - 244 seconds - 4:07 minutes

Main Title - 60 seconds - 1:00 minute
Act One - 710 seconds - 11:83 minutes
Act Two - 542 seconds - 9:03 minutes
Act Three - 465 seconds - 7:75 minutes
Act Four - 573 seconds - 9:55 minutes
Epilogue - 112 seconds - 1:52 minutes
End Title* - 30 seconds - 0.5 minutes

TOTAL RUN - 2,736 seconds - 45.6 minutes

* assumed running time based on final ET.

Based on the scripts, it appears there were no plans initially to present the first episode any length longer than the normal one-hour format. Perhaps if *Space: 1999* had been sold to a US TV network as hoped, or if Sylvia Anderson's idea of a Cannes Film Festival premiere (as discussed in the **Correspondence** section of book) had materialized, there would certainly have been enough extra footage to pad 'Breakaway' out. In the end, according to Gerry Anderson, Katzin's initial edit did not meet the standards the Andersons or ITC demanded, and a re-edit and re-shoots were ordered.

INSPIRATION

Beyond the Moon leaving Earth orbit, Bellak's scripts used none of the plot of Gerry and Sylvia Anderson's 'Zero G'. The Commander and the Professor are still the main characters, but the Doctor, relegated to a minor position in the Anderson's script, is now part of the core group.

TECHNOLOGY

Much of the technology described in Bellak's draft reflects a combination of futuristic thinking, such as portable communication devices and holographic imagery. For example, the first draft script has the Technical Section recreating an MTU crash through a 3-D hologram. Medical Center scans are all described as stereo images. However, just as *Star Trek* often remarked, recording devices still retain information on magnetic tape.

MTU –– Modular Transportation Unit –– 'A number of MTUs are already on their pads each with a different configuration, demonstrating their versatility. The craft was rechristened as an Eagle in 'Turning Point'.

LAUNCH PAD BOARDING TUBE –– 'A large tube extends from one of the buildings and connects up to the entrance of the MTU in the immediate foreground. Through the portholes in the slide of the tube we are able to see the cylindrical compartment that Maddox and Miller are traveling in, move through the tube and stop at the entrance of the MTU' (*see the Terror Fish boarding tube in the* Stingray *pilot*)

TRAVEL TUBE — Early drafts still establish the vistas of the Moon visible outside the car as it travels. This was no doubt eliminated due to cost.

COMMLOCK — This name is established in the first draft.

COMMUNICATIONS COLUMN — General information and communications device found around the base.

MOON-BUGGY - small two-person land transport outside the base.

SYNTHOCRETE - Artificial concrete-like material used to cap the Nuclear Waste Pits.

CHARACTERS

JOHN KOENIG — New Commander of the base.

PROFESSOR BERGMAN — Visiting scientist who developed the artificial gravity system. Former college teacher of Koenig.

DOCTOR HELENA RUSSELL — Chief Medical Officer.

GUNDLACH — NDU 2. Depot Chief

PROBE SECTION PILOT SERGIO CATANI - Chief pilot, later renamed Carlo Catani in 'Turning Point' (See SIMPSON below).

STEINER & NORDSTROM — NDU 2. technicians.

VORKONEN - Adjutant to Koenig. His name is changed to Morrow in the 'Temporary Final' draft and Paul Morrow in 'Turning Point'.

SANDRA SABATINI - Sensor Technician

COMMISSIONER SYMONDS - Head of the Earth Lunar Finance Commission. His name was re-spelled as Simmonds in 'Turning Point'.

COMMANDER GRODNO - Former commander of the base, re-named as

Gorski in 'Turning Point'.

OUMA - Computer chief.

DR FUJITA - Dr Russell's Japanese colleague in Medical Center.

SIMPSON - Koenig and Bergman's Eagle pilot to Area 2 who goes berserk and tries to smash an observation window in 'Turning Point'. Renamed Carter in 'Breakaway'. Nick Tate was cast in this role before director Lee H Katzin recast him to replace the Italian actor originally set to play Catani.

PROBE TECH FOUR ALLISON - Appeared in the first draft as a hysterical worker aboard the Meta Probe, later re-written as a technician at Area 2 when Koenig and Bergman are doing their own check of the Waste Pits.

SENSOR TECH THREE MANITIS - Died three weeks earlier working at ND.

FRANK and BORIS - Stricken Meta Probe Astronauts. Frank got the last name Warren and Boris became Eric Sparkman in 'Turning Point'.

COMPUTER (VO) — Talking Computer

NOTE: Character names (including spelling) changed over the course of the drafts. See 'Name Evolution' section.

MOONBASE ALPHA SETS / LOCATIONS

MOON BASE ALPHA — Modular construction interior.

CONTROL CENTER & OBSERVATION GANTRY ('The Void Ahead')
MAIN MISSION ('Turning Point')

KOENIG'S OFFICE

COMMANDER'S QUARTERS

MEDICAL CENTER

TECHNICAL SECTION

TRAVEL TUBE & WALK TUBE

LAUNCHING PAD

MTU COMMAND MODULE ('The Void Ahead')
EAGLE COMMAND MODULE ('Turning Point')

MTU SECTION ('The Void Ahead')
EAGLE PASSENGER MODULE ('Turning Point')

NDU 2. - Nuclear Disposal Unit 2, an eerie floodlit area surrounded by a physical fence, marked with warning signs.

DEPOSITORY BUILDING — NDU 2. monitoring area.

PROBE SHIP WITH ELEVATOR GANTRY - appearing in 'The Void Ahead' first draft only.

PROBE SHIP INTERIOR - appearing in 'The Void Ahead' first draft only.

TU FIVE — Training ship. ('The Void Ahead')

SPECIAL NOTATIONS

'The Void Ahead' Temporary Final features a detailed breakdown of the main title sequence which follows the same pre-title sequence as the final aired episode:

MAIN TITLES — MUSIC

(A)   *Close-Up Koenig — thoughtful — as he prepares for touchdown*

Caption over —

STARRING
MARTIN LANDAU

(B) *Close-Up Helena - shocked*

Caption over —

AND
BARBARA BAIN

TO EVERYTHING THAT MIGHT HAVE BEEN

(C) Exterior Alpha — High shot from the rim of the crater in which Moonbase Alpha has been built. In the foreground two technicians are laying cables on the rim of the crater. They stop what they are doing for a moment, look up to the MTU just barely visible, up above …

Caption over —

SPACE: 1999

(D) Close-Up 'Scope marked 'Radiation Levels' — Reflected in we see the face of Professor Bergman studying it intently.

Caption over —

ALSO STARRING
BARRY MORSE

*(E) FAST CUTTING MONTAGE forming an exciting trailer of the episode we are about to see, although it does not reveal the story pattern.
The concluding shot is Koenig's MTU touching down at Moonbase Alpha.*

'Turning Point' Final Shooting script dated 5 November 1973 features a further developed breakdown of the main title sequence:

STANDARD SERIES OPENING
SECTION ONE — MUSIC SYMPHONIC

*(A) Close-up Koenig against white background, left of screen.
Caption over right of screen, black lettering…*
MARTIN LANDAU

(B) Close-Up Helena against black background, right of screen
Caption over left of screen, white lettering…
BARBARA BAIN

(C) High shot of Alpha — Two technicians in the foreground laying cables on the rim of the crater. They stop to watch an *Eagle* approach
Caption over, each letter a different color representative of the various Alpha Sections…
SPACE: 1999

SECTION TWO - MUSIC MODERN

Fast-cutting montage using split screen technique to show the Moon being blasted out of Earth-orbit*

- *(Note: Section Two will be replaced by an alternative sequence for the pilot episode.)*

SECTION THREE - MUSIC SYMPHONIC

(A)   Close-Up oscilloscope *with colored trace and* reflected in it… close-up of
Bergman
Caption over red lettering…
BARRY MORSE

(B) Wide Angle — Master Computer
(C) Wide Angle — Int. Technical Section
Twenty Eagles lined up.

SECTION FOUR - MUSIC MODERN — SYMPHONIC CLIMAX

Fast-cutting montage forming a trailer of the episode about to be screened.
Caption interspersed in subliminal cuts…

TONIGHT'S EPISODE

'Turning Point' Final Shooting script dated 5 November 1973 features a
proposed breakdown of the end title sequence:

MUSIC OVERTAKES DIALOGUE

FREEZE ON HELENA AS SHE TURNS — PRODUCER CAPTION

FREEZE ON KOENIG AS HE TURNS — EXECUTIVE PRODUCER

THE EXPRESSIONS OF BOTH TELL US A BOND HAS BEEN FORMED
ACTIVITY IN MAIN MISSION HAS A FEELING OF HOPE

END CREDITS

In addition, the Amended Blue Pages from the 22 November 1973 shooting script for 'Breakaway' features the following:

Note:

The establishment of Moonbase Alpha is divided into 6 sections, and each section is visually identifiable by a separate color. Moonbase Alpha personnel will wear uniforms with one sleeve in the color of the section to which they belong. The sections, with their colors, are as follows:

Main Mission	*Flame*
Medical	*White*
Technical	*Rust*
Reconnaissance	*Orange*
Security	*Purple*
Services	*Yellow*

Temporary visitors to Alpha will wear uniforms whose sleeve will not be colored at all.

The Moonbase Alpha Commander will wear a uniform with both sleeves colored black.

CAST

Commander John Koenig	*Command*	*Black*
Dr Helena Russell	*Medical*	*White*
Professor Victor Bergman	*Visitor*	*No color*
Paul Morrow	*Main Mission*	*Flame*
Carlo Catani	*Reconnaissance*	*Orange*
Sandra Sabatini	*Service*	*Yellow*
Nordstrom	*Service (Spacesuit only)*	*Yellow*
Steiner (N.S.)	*Service (Spacesuit only)*	*Yellow*
Gundlach	*Service*	*Yellow*
First Newscaster_____		
Stewardess	*Service*	*Yellow*
Simmonds	*Visitor*	*No color*
Gorski	*Command*	*Black*
Frank Warren (N.S.)	*Reconnaissance*	*Orange*

Eric Sparkman (N.S.)	Reconnaissance	Orange
Dr Fujita	Medical	White
Operator	Service	Yellow
Carter	Reconnaissance	Orange
First Security Man	Security	Purple
Rescue Ship Pilot_____Voice only		
Jackson	Service	Yellow
Ellis (N.S.)	Service	Yellow
Ouma	Technical	Rust
Eagle Pilot (N.S.)	Reconnaissance	Orange
Eagle Co-Pilot (N.S.)	Reconnaissance	Orange
First Technician (N.S.)	Service (Spacesuit only)	Yellow
Second Technician (N.S.)	Service (Spacesuit only)	Yellow
Second Security Man	Security	Purple
Third Security Man	Security	Purple
Third Technician	Technical	Rust
Forth Technician	Service	Yellow
Fifth Technician (N.S.)	Service (Spacesuit only)	Yellow
Six Operatives	Main Mission	Flame
Three Alpha Staff	Assorted	Assorted
Second Newscaster_____		

SETS

EXT. NUCLEAR DISPOSAL AREA 2.
INT. DISPOSAL AREA 2 – DEPOT
INT. EAGLE PASSENGER MODULE
INT. TRAVEL TUBE
INT. CORRIDOR
INT. MAIN MISSION
INT. KOENIG'S OFFICE
INT. HELENA'S OFFICE
INT. INTENSIVE CARE UNIT
INT. TECHNICAL SECTION
INT. EAGLE COMMAND MODULE
INT. CORRIDOR (DISPOSAL AREA 2 – DEPOT)
INT. KOENIG'S QUARTERS
INT. DIAGNOSTIC UNIT
INT. FIRST NEWSCAST SET (EARTH)
INT. SECOND NEWSCAST SET (EARTH)
INT. SIMMONDS' OFFICE (EARTH)

(DH)

STORY OUTLINES

Presented here are a collection of scripts and storylines recovered from the ITC archives, with a few exceptions: the five-page treatment for 'Planet of the Eye' was provided by Shaqui Le Vesconte, who had acquired it from the author's estate and graciously shared it for inclusion in this book; 'Alpha People' was discovered in Martin Landau's collection; and the script for 'A Breath of Death' was acquired through fan sources.

These outlines detail the development of the series during 1973. The first section details the early proposals for four episodes that made it to air, while the section that follows features three proposals that were passed on.

PRODUCED EPISODES

'SIREN PLANET'

One-Hour Format Script
by Art Wallace
November 1973
Filmed as 'Matter of Life and Death', screenplay by Art Wallace and Johnny Byrne

SYNOPSIS

Prober One returns to Alpha after exploring a planet code-named Homeland II that appears to be ideal for settlement, but its crew is unconscious and there is an extra passenger: Helena's husband Telford Russell, who was presumed dead five years prior when the Astro Seven Exploratory Mission vanished near Jupiter.

Telford's medical assessment leads to further mysteries as all instruments show that he is dead. He subsequently disappears from his bed in Sickbay and – capable of changing his appearance – enters the Records Library and views personnel files.

Koenig and Penmarric set up a scanner behind a wall of the Staff Room as Helena leads Telford to the room for a pre-arranged interrogation by Koenig and Grayson while Penmarric conducts scans. Penmarric then shows Koenig the scans while Telford convinces Helena – through deceptively disguising himself as Koenig – to go down to the planet with him in Prober

Two. Koenig discovers the deception and tries to stop the launch, to no avail, but launches in pursuit with Grayson and Lt Stone in Prober One. They land on the rocky barren planet near Prober Two and set out separately in search of Helena and Telford.

Meanwhile on Alpha, Penmarric questions the two Prober pilots, who have regained consciousness. Each believed a family member was on the Prober with them. Penmarric believes they are dealing with an intelligence on the planet that can give substance and reality to human thought, but that none of the manifestations are real.

Telford leads Helena to a cave as hallucinations plague Grayson and Koenig, who uses an infra-red scanner to try to determine what is real and what isn't. The alien intelligence manifests as Koenig's father and explains that it has lured key members of Alpha's command staff to the planet in order to kill them, thus ensuring the rest of the Alphans won't decide to colonize the planet. With the aid of the scanner, Koenig sees through the hallucinations and rescues Helena.

WRITER ART WALLACE

'Siren Planet' was written by American Art Wallace, who had previously worked on other science fiction television series including *Tom Corbett, Space Cadet* (1950), *The Invaders* ('Labyrinth', 1967), and – likely most significantly in the context of *Space: 1999* – two episodes of *Star Trek* ('Obsession', 1967, and 'Assignment: Earth', 1968). Following his work on *Space: 1999*, Wallace's genre scripts included two episodes of the 1974 *Planet of the Apes* TV series ('Escape from Tomorrow' and 'The Gladiators'), and two supernatural thriller TV films: *The World of Darkness* (1977) and *The World Beyond* (1978). Wallace remains best known for his work on the gothic soap opera *Dark Shadows*, for which he created many notable characters. He wrote the original series Bible as well as the scripts for 65 episodes. 'Siren Planet' was his only contribution to *Space: 1999*, and he received co-writer credit on the final episode, 'Matter of Life and Death', alongside Johnny Byrne.

REFERENCE MATERIAL

A second 'Revised' version of the script exists and reflects the ongoing development of the series.

Two pieces of internal production correspondence also exist related to 'Siren Planet'. The first is a 15 November 1973 letter from Gerry Anderson to Abe Mandell. The second is a 16 November 1973 letter from Arnold Friedman (who was then the Creative Director of ITC New York) to Abe Mandell. Both letters are reproduced and discussed here.

STORY DIFFERENCES

Structurally, the First Draft doesn't contain a Teaser, but the Revised script introduces the Teaser and establishes that the end of it is the point at which Helena sees the face of the passenger on board the Eagle, who she recognizes, and whom the audience will soon discover is her husband, Telford Russell.

By the 'Revised' version a degree of early mystery has been excised from the script. In the opening pages of the First Draft there was the implication that something is strange about the planetary data (Penmarric says, 'I'd say they landed on a planet ideal for settlement. Breathable atmosphere, water vegetation… almost Earth-type with one strange omission… No animal life.') Penmarric, when asked by Koenig if there was any reason for the loss of communication with Prober One, speculates, 'Hostile organisms? Disease? No… but our knowledge of possibilities is limited by our experience, John. Bear that in mind.' This theme of the Alphans' limited knowledge as they encounter the unknown dangers of deep space would continue to reverberate throughout Year One.

On page five of the First Draft, Helena reflects on her husband's disappearance five years previously, which provides the planet (*Solaris*-like) the opportunity to seize on her memory of him in order to manifest the being the Alphans see as Telford Russell. This reference is not included in the Revised script.

As Act One draws to a close in the First Draft, Sandra Sabatini has a confusing encounter at the Alpha Records Library with Jim Grayson, who turns out to actually be Telford Russell, who is able to disguise his appearance. In the Revised draft, Sandra's substantial role throughout the story has been cut and replaced in this particular scene by a different encounter at Alpha's Computer Control. Here is an excerpt from the Revised script:

*****

INT. CORRIDOR NEAR COMPUTER CONTROL

There is not much activity in this corridor. A few Technicians passing by. Russell appears, dressed as a Technician. He moves down the corridor with the appearance of one who belongs there. No one pays any attention. He approaches a door, on which is the legend:

COMPUTER CONTROL
AUTHORIZED PERSONNEL ONLY

He tries to open the door, but it is locked. He glances at a small panel on the door jamb near the lock.

INSERT – PANEL

It is a small rectangular panel into which are set a cluster of numbered buttons… obviously a locking device.

RUSSELL

He tries punching some of the buttons at random. Useless. He cannot get in. Now he hears someone about to emerge from the library. Quickly he steps to one side, waits. The door opens, and a Technician emerges, carrying some tapes. The Technician moves on down the corridor after closing the door.

CLOSE SHOT – RUSSELL

Eyes following the Technician, concentrating.

CLOSE SHOT – TECHNICIAN

We are tight on the back of his head as he walks away.

TIGHT SHOT – RUSSELL'S EYES

As they concentrate on the back of the Technician's head.

ANOTHER ANGLE

Russell steps away from the wall, crosses directly to the door and, without any hesitation, pushes a sequence of buttons on the lock panel. We hear a click as the door is unlocked. He opens the door quickly.

INT. COMPUTER CONTROL

As Russell enters, closing the door behind him. The walls are lined with the master control panels of the computers that run all of Alpha's vital necessity.

The panels are labeled: COMMUNICATIONS, POWER, WASTE, DISPOSAL, TRANSPORTATION, ETC. He glances around quickly, searching for one particular set of controls. He sees what he wants.

POV – OXYGEN SUPPLY PANEL

The legend on this particular computer control panel reads 'OXYGEN SUPPLY'.

RUSSELL

He approaches the Oxygen Supply Computer Control Panel, studies it. The controls, themselves, are protected by a transparent panel. He tries to pull the panel aside, but cannot. He then glances at a buttoned locking device similar to the device on the door to the room. He looks at it in frustration, then makes a decision, starts hitting the buttons at random. Almost as soon as he hits the third button, an ALARM BELL sounds. (It will continue to ring throughout). Startled, Russell glances around. No way to shut off the alarm. He moves quickly to the door, tries to open it, but cannot. The door is locked.

INT. CORRIDOR NEAR COMPUTER CONTROL – ANGLE ON DOOR

The red light indicator over the door is flashing as the alarm continues to sound. WE ANGLE DOWN towards the corridor and see TWO SECURITY GUARDS, guns drawn, rushing towards the door. One of the guards swiftly pushes the correct sequence of buttons on the locking device. Then they push the door open and enter. As soon as the door had opened, the alarm had stopped.

INT. COMPUTER CONTROL – ANGLE ON DOOR

Russell is in the foreground, his back to the door, quite tense as the two Guards enter with drawn guns.

SERGEANT
All right, mister. What are you doing in here?

No response from Russell.

CLOSER – ON GUARDS

SERGEANT
Come on, mister. Turn around.

CLOSE ON RUSSELL

We are on the back of his head. Now he turns, and we see that it is Grayson!

> RUSSELL/GRAYSON
> Sorry to have caused you this trouble, Sergeant.

ANOTHER ANGLE

As the Guards stare at him in surprise.

> SERGEANT
> Captain! I didn't know it was you!

> RUSSELL/GRAYSON
> I slipped on the floor. Must have hit the controls
> with my elbow. I'm sorry.

> SERGEANT
> (still puzzled)
> That's all right, sir…

> RUSSELL/GRAYSON
> (with a smile)
> Anyway, I'm glad to see you're on your toes.

He exits. The Guards glance at each other, still puzzled.

INT. CORRIDOR NEAR COMPUTER CONTROL

As Russell/Grayson emerges from the room, pushing his way through the group that had gathered outside.

> RUSSELL/GRAYSON
> It's all over. Problem solved. All over. No more
> problem.

He makes his way through the crowd, walks briskly down the corridor, turns a corner.

INT. SECOND CORRIDOR

As Russell/Grayson turns the corner and finds he is in an unoccupied corridor. He leans against the wall with a sense of relief. And as we HOLD on him, his features begin to shimmer… and he gradually changes until we are no longer looking at Grayson. Once again, it is Russell. HOLD for a beat.

FADE OUT

<u>END OF ACT ONE</u>

*****

Throughout, numerous foreshadowing references in the First Draft to Alphans' fears (Grayson's fear of spiders, Helena's fear of a creature from her nightmares) were removed from the Revised version, although their fears end up manifesting on the planet anyway).

Then, in Act Two, as Telford Russell tries to convince Helena to go with him to the planet, the Revised script omits Telford's descriptions of his experiments and substitutes additional details of what he promises Helena she will find on the planet. Here is an excerpt from the Revised script:

*****

RUSSELL
Forget the regulations! Darling, it'll be worth it. You
won't be sorry. I promise.

HELENA
But why?

RUSSELL
Because there's something on that planet…
something so incredible, I couldn't even begin to
explain it.

HELENA
I think you ought to try.

RUSSELL
It's a… a force… I don't pretend to understand it,
Helena… a force that can fill your mind… that can
open up areas of knowledge you never even knew
existed. It's an unbelievable experience, and now
that I've found you again, I want you to share it
with me.

HELENA
Share what? I'm sorry, but I'm still confused.

RUSSELL
Knowledge, Helena. Pure knowledge…
understanding… peace… serenity… everything
man's been longing for since Adam took that first
big bite out of the apple.

HELENA
If it's that wonderful, why not tell Commander
Koenig or Professor Penmarric? I'm sure they'd be
more than…

RUSSELL
(interrupting earnestly)
Darling, I intend to tell them. I intend to tell
everyone. But not yet. Will you come with me?

*****

At that point the script cuts back to where it was in the First Draft, with Helena declining to go 'without official permission' and Russell promising to speak to Koenig and 'get that permission.'

As Act Three progresses, several scenes take a decidedly darker turn, starting with Lt Allan Stone's encounter with his Mother, who in the First Draft was quite pleasant as she invited him to follow her to his untimely death. By the Revised version, her appearance took on a more ominous tone:

*****

MOTHER'S VOICE
(a cry of desperation)
Allan? Allan?

He turns and stares.

ANOTHER ANGLE

A woman in her mid-fifties, thin and emaciated, her face wracked with pain, is clutching her stomach and holding out an entreating arm towards Stone. She is standing on the path where 'Koenig' had stood.

KOENIG'S VOICE
Lieutenant? Come in Lieutenant.

MOTHER
It hurts me so much, Allan. Please help me. Please.

STONE
(to communicator; barely able to talk)
You… you're not going to believe this, sir, but my
mother's here. At least, I think she is.

MOTHER
(writhing in pain)
Allan? Please? I can't stand it!

KOENIG'S VOICE
Listen to me, Stone. Listen carefully. Stay right
where you are. Don't try to move!

*****

At that point the Revised script continues as in the First Draft: Mother slips and almost falls into the ravine. She grabs a rock to keep from falling. Allan tries to save her but falls over the edge into the ravine. Her image disappears and he dies.

The following scene also contains more explicitly graphic horror imagery than in the First Draft, as Prof Penmarric questions the now-conscious pilots of the first Prober mission to the planet:

*****

INT. SICKBAY – CLOSE ON PARKS

On his bed, trying to talk coherently to Penmarric. Fujita standing nearby. In the other bed, Crimmins is sitting up.

PARKS
I know it doesn't make sense, but when we were
coming into the planet, everything looked so green
and beautiful. But when we landed, it was nothing
but rock. It was like… I don't know… a different
place.

CRIMMINS
We thought we'd lost our minds.

PENMARRIC
Did you see any visions? Any people you didn't
expect to see?

PARKS
How did you know about that?

PENMARRIC
Tell me about it.

PARKS
It was on the Prober, coming back... before we
blacked out. My father... you know, he was killed
in a plane crash. But he was there, in the Prober. All
bloody and torn up, like from the crash. But he was
alive... and he was talking to me.

CRIMMINS
And my sister. She was drowned about fifteen years
ago. But there she was, Professor... the water
dripping down... yelling for me to help her. I was
so scared, I wanted to scream.

PENMARRIC
And you're certain you took no one on board.

PARKS
So help me, I don't know what I'm certain of
anymore.

*****

Then, as Act Three concludes in the Revised script, and Telford lures Helena into the
cave, their scene has also taken on a more sinister tone:

*****

EXT. CAVE ENTRANCE – DAY

The entrance to a cave is at the base of a cliff. Russell and Helena approach,
Helena glancing around in concern, pause just outside the entrance.

RUSSELL
We go in here.

HELENA
I... don't think I want to.

RUSSELL
You're joking.

HELENA
(shakes her head)
Frightened... I think.

RUSSELL
Of what?!

HELENA
I don't know. There's... something about this place,
something about... you. I don't know, Telford, but I
think I want to go back to the ship.

She turns to leave.

RUSSELL
(almost a shout)
You can't go back!!

She turns, stares at him, startled by his tone. He moves up close to her, his
face distorted with fury.

RUSSELL
What did you mean... something about me? Would
you rather I were dead?! Is that what you want?! Is
that the image you've had in your mind all these
years... your husband's body rotting away, his flesh
eaten by maggots, his...

HELENA
What are you trying to do to me?!

RUSSELL
(pointing towards the cave)
In there, Helena! That's what we came for, and

that's where you're going!

She stares at him fearfully, then turns to run. She doesn't go far before he grabs her, swings her around roughly, and pushes her towards the cave.

RUSSELL
Start walking, Helena.

She looks at him fearfully, realizes she has no choice, turns and hesitantly enters the cave.

FADE OUT.

END OF ACT THREE

*****

In Act Four, as Koenig and Grayson reach the cave entrance, Grayson's giant spider hallucination that appeared in the First Draft has been Revised to be a 'huge snake… several feet in diameter,' but the scene plays out exactly as it did before.

Koenig's encounter with his Dad is similar in both versions of the script, with the addition of a darker element in a few added lines of dialogue, after Koenig says, 'You're not real', and scans his father:

*****

DAD
Now don't try to get rid of me, like you once did.

KOENIG
That's not true! I never…

DAD
Puttin' your own father in a nursing home! You
don't call that getting' rid of him?

KOENIG
I had no choice: You were sick! There was no one to
take care of you!

DAD
Then why's it been bothering you all these years?

> KOENIG
> Because I…

He breaks off as he suddenly realizes what he's doing… arguing with a figment of his own mind.

*****

The rest of Act Four plays out the same in both versions of the script. Then, in the Epilogue, there are a couple of changes. Sandra's dialogue has been given to Nurse Rizzo, and the final scene between Helena and Koenig has a couple more lines as Helena questions whether what they've experienced is really over:

*****

INT. HOSPITAL CORRIDOR

As they close the door.

> HELENA
> He's right, you know. How do we <u>ever</u> know
> what's real?

> KOENIG
> Helena, it's over.

> HELENA
> Is it?

> KOENIG
> Yes? There's only one reality… finding ourselves a
> home. And we'll do it, Helena. <u>We have to do it</u>.

And he walks off. She stands there, watching him go.

FADE OUT

<u>THE END.</u>

*****

There are numerous other minor differences between the two versions of the script.

ANALYSIS

Wallace's script bears considerable similarity to *Solaris*, the highly regarded, philosophical, and haunting Russian 1961 science fiction novel by Stanislaw Lem, which had been produced as a two-part Russian TV play in 1968, and then notably as a feature film that premiered at the 1972 Cannes Film Festival but did not premiere in the USA until 1976. While Wallace could have been aware of the TV and film versions, it is most likely that his inspiration came from reading Stanislaw Lem's novel.

Notable parallels include the ability of the planet to cull images of loved ones from the minds of the human characters and manifest simulacra of them (including the dead spouse of a lead character – in *Solaris*, Psychologist Kris Kelvin's wife Hari, and in 'Siren Planet', Dr Helena Russell's husband Telford; and the father of a lead character – again Kris Kelvin's father in *Solaris*, but this time Commander John Koenig's father in 'Siren Planet'); and the discussion of whether or not these beings are real or are hallucinations.

'Siren Planet' aspired to be a meditation on the nature of reality, humanity and existence, like *Solaris*, but clearly the script landed too close to its inspiration. Even the title, 'Siren Planet', alludes to the hypnotic call of the planet felt by the characters in *Solaris*, and by the inhabitants of Moonbase Alpha, who hope it will be their new home. And, as in *Solaris*, where the planet and its sentient ocean permit characters to envision its surface as they wish it, the 'Siren Planet' – even to its final on-screen incarnation – permits the Alphans to 'see what you want to see.' Does the planet actually look like the paradise the Alphans encounter, or the destroyed nightmare it devolves into, or in its reality does it look like something else entirely?

It is unclear whether the similarities to *Solaris* were apparent at the time to others involved in the script development process[17] as no reference is made to this being a concern in the Arnold Friedman letter. Either way, some of these similarities were removed from the script by the time of production, although the central concept of an alien planet manifesting the dead spouse of a lead character remained, along with the planet's ability to allow human characters to see dead loved ones and envision a world around them that is different than reality. And, like Kelvin's wife Hari in *Solaris*, who doesn't know who or what she is, Lee Russell is similarly confused, not knowing how he got to the alien planet or how long he had been there.

---

[17] 'At this point I had neither read the novel nor seen Andrei Tarkovsky's film. But it's not at all beyond the bounds of possibility that Johnny Byrne had seen it. Johnny was much more widely read in the genre of science fiction than I was and, indeed, he had a number of science fiction writers as his friends. If Art Wallace had found *Solaris* an inspiration in the first place, then Johnny would certainly have been enthusiastic about developing its themes as he took over the writing of the script.' – Christopher Penfold

TECHNOLOGY

Prober One and Prober Two appear in both versions of the script and are Moonbase Alpha's only two reconnaissance ships. It was obviously soon decided that two ships would be insufficient for the ongoing series.

Communication devices are audio only. The Commlock first appeared, with that name, in 'The Void Ahead' (Temporary Final Draft).

CHARACTERS

In the Revised script a couple of references to Prof Penmarric have been changed to Bergman, while the majority have not been updated yet.

In the First Draft both Nurse Rizzo and Dr Fujita appear, but by the Revised script Nurse Rizzo was largely removed (although she still appears) and her dialogue given to Fujita. Dr Fujita would later become Dr Bob Mathias.

Helena's husband is called Telford Russell in both early versions and would later be re-named Lee Russell.

Captain Jim Grayson would later become Catani, and then finally Alan Carter.

Sandra Sabatini would later become Sandra Benes. Sandra's large role in the First Draft is completely eliminated in the Revised version, and her final scene with Grayson has been changed to Nurse Rizzo.

The character Bartlett appears in both versions of 'Siren Planet' and functions primarily as a Communications officer. Bartlett first appears in the opening sequence, handling the communication efforts to contact Prober One, and then appears again briefly ('Central Control. Bartlett here.') in a superfluous section on page 43/44 where Koenig notifies Alpha that they have landed and are about to begin their search. By the time Johnny Byrne re-wrote the script as 'Matter of Life and Death' the Bartlett character evolved into Controller Paul Morrow. It is almost certainly a coincidence that a character called Bartlett (a nuclear physicist) would later appear in Year Two's two-part episode 'The Bringers of Wonder'.

MOONBASE ALPHA SETS / LOCATIONS

Central Control is the name used throughout 'Siren Planet' for what would become Main Mission.

Likewise, the Sickbay and Hospital referenced in both versions of 'Siren Planet' would become Alpha's Medical Center.

The First Draft includes significant references to records tapes being used on Alpha, and scenes set in the Alpha Record Library. By the Revised script, the Alpha Record Library locations were changed to Computer Control. A

Records Library did finally appear in the final filmed episode, Johnny Byrne's 'The Testament of Arkadia'.

The planet is referred to as 'Homeland II' in both the First Draft and Revised versions and would subsequently be re-named 'Terra Nova' (literally 'New Earth' as Helena points out in 'Matter of Life and Death') by Johnny Byrne.

There are numerous references to the Astro Seven mission as well as conflicting references to it as the Argo Seven mission throughout both the First Draft and Revised scripts. The most likely explanation is that Wallace originally called the mission the Argo Seven, then changed it to the Astro Seven but failed to update all the references in the script.

PRODUCTION CORRESPONDENCE

Gerry Anderson wrote a letter to Abe Mandell on November 15, 1973 primarily discussing scripts, including 'Siren Planet', in which he said, 'The Art Wallace story "Siren Planet" has now been dealt with by Chris Penfold, the British script editor, by telephone and Art Wallace is doing a considerable re-write on it basically to iron out certain inconsistencies in the story and to make Helena Russell react more believably in what can only be described as a mind-bending situation. This revision should have been dispatched to us via your office by the time you receive this letter. We will of course put the final touches to it when it gets back and feel very confident that it will make an excellent episode. We are placing this picture No 2 on the production schedule since the resources of our technical departments will have been strained to breaking point on the first episode. We agree with you however that it is not a suitable episode for you to submit to the Network as a No 2.'

Anderson put a positive spin on the 'Siren Planet' script, assuring Mandell, 'We will of course put the final touches to it when it gets back and feel very confident that it will make an excellent episode,' while also making a veiled acknowledgement that the script hadn't achieved their highest standards: 'We are placing this picture No 2 on the production schedule… We agree with you however that it is not a suitable episode for you to submit to the Network as a No 2.' That last line also confirms that Mandell and ITC New York had already provided earlier feedback on the script.

As Anderson says, the revisions had already been completed by Art Wallace, and 'should have been dispatched to us via your office by the time you receive this letter.' Indeed they were, as our second piece of internal production correspondence on the topic is dated the day after Anderson's letter, November 16, 1973, written by Arnold Friedman, Creative Director of ITC New York, to Abe Mandell, discussing the Revised version of 'Siren Planet'. He wrote:

I have the same basic reservations about this version as the one I read November 1. It is contrived, familiar and unresolved.

Most astonishing to me is that the basic point of the story – how we manifest our own fears and desires – has been played down, along with the spider. I suspect that Sylvia has prevailed here.

The rest is a silly hodgepodge of clichés and the whole comes off like a *Buck Rogers* adventure. There are still no sets on the alien planet; using barren landscape and caves is for El Cheapo Productions, not ITC.

There are many holes in the script, from my POV – and here are just some that really bother me:

1.   The dramatic shock experienced by Helena, in the teaser, is not shared by the viewers because they don't know who the man is (husband) and don't know he was lost in space five years ago.

In act one Helena tells us she hasn't seen the man in five years – and that he is her husband. Then we learn he was lost in space, but the impact is slight. We have been <u>prepared</u> and are not shocked by the news, as we would be if hit harder, earlier.

I suggest we do it all in the teaser. A man lost in space for five years is dramatic. A husband returning from the dead is dramatic, and also classic.

(END OF TEASER: HELENA REACTING OVER BODY OF STRANGE MAN.)

HELENA: This man was lost on a Jupiter probe five years ago.

KOENIG: That's impossible, Helena. Who do you <u>think</u> he is?

HELENA: John, I <u>know</u> who he is. He's my husband!

ZOOM CU OF HELENA… AND FADE.

2.   In Act 1, 'Telford' unlocks a door by manually punching a combination of buttons. I seem to recall from Gerry's 'Guidelines' that this sort of thing will be done by an

automatic device 'loaded' only with combinations for which that crewperson is cleared. Wallace's script does not conform with this guideline, and if the other scripts do, we have a serious inconsistency.

3.   About half the TV homes in this country have black & white sets, including mine. There are less color receivers in Great Britain. Wallace's use of color as a storytelling device is not a good idea and will leave b&w viewers baffled.

4.   I never understood why the prober would have a mechanism that locked it from the OUTside. (p.59). It makes no sense. When you drive home tonight, imagine that Smitty locked your car from the outside. How does that feel?

5.   P. 61. Helena On The Slab of Rock Amidst the Flames reminds me of all the *Hercules* movies Joe Levine brought over from Italy, and all the Virgins sacrificed in them, on the rocks. The scene was mandatory in those spaghetti tit-and-toga flicks, but just because we are co-producing this series with RAI doesn't mean we must use Italian stock-footage!

6.   P. 67. When Koenig stops Helena physically with the stun-gun, her mind is still aware, and the horror must fill it. What awful torture for her. I'd rather see her saved another way.

Even though Wallace has now sort of told us who the aliens are, it is still not clear, and I don't know if this is Wallace's idea of the afterlife, or what. Is that where you and I will go when we die?
Abe, I really don't want to write this memo. I'm just picking away. The script is not a good one, and that's all.'

Friedman and Mandell were obviously engaged in an ongoing discussion and critique of the early script drafts (presumably of various other scripts, not just 'Siren Planet', although this is the only letter between the two known to exist at the time of this book's writing). Mandell would then convey the criticisms from ITC New York to Gerry Anderson and the production team. As Friedman stated, he had read the First Draft on November 1, 1973, and wrote this critique of the Revised version on November 16, 1973. Friedman's criticisms are largely apt, but several deserve specific mention:

As he points out, the foreshadowing of the Alphans' fears (including the giant spider) was eliminated from the Revised version, thus detracting from the central concept that we manifest our own fears. Friedman's suspicion that 'Sylvia has prevailed here,' implies that he wasn't fond of her approach to story.

Friedman's suggestion for the end of the Teaser would indeed have been a much stronger hook than that in either draft of 'Siren Planet', and indeed it would have arguably been stronger than the hook that ended up appearing on-screen in 'Matter of Life and Death'.

Ultimately, Friedman's final line is most significant, 'The script is not a good one, and that's all.'

Subsequently, the script received a major re-write by Johnny Byrne, who recalled, 'They didn't have a second script. And so I found scripts that had been written before the series became a real series… I had to write a script that was geared to the actual production, [and I] based [it] on Art Wallace's [pre-existing] script, but there wasn't really very much in it… We had great trouble with 'Matter of Life and Death'. I can't quite remember what Art Wallace's script was like. I was under great pressure. Two weeks to get this thing ready and I was pitched in, as they say, into the deep end. So we came up with a story that concerned anti-matter.' (REW)

'BLACK SUN'

FIRST DRAFT - NOVEMBER 1973
by David Weir

SYNOPSIS

An asteroid threatening Moonbase Alpha suddenly alters course and explodes, the victim of some terrifying, invisible force. As Professor Bergman attempts to make sense of the odd data collected, Doctor Russell notices the man is under severe stress. Bergman's hypothesis points him in the direction of something he doesn't want to admit is out there.

MTU pilot Mike Meyer has been sent out to gather more information, but Bergman is too late to prevent him from meeting the same fate as the asteroid. Finally, the Professor reveals that he believes that in three days, the Moon will make contact with a phenomenon of such great gravitational pull, that nothing, not even light can escape. He calls it a 'Black Sun'.

With no way to alter the course of the rogue Moon, Bergman devises an elaborate plan to create a force field dome over Alpha that he hopes will protect in from the incredible forces within. In case the plan fails, Koenig launches a survival ship with five men and five women, including a reluctant Doctor Russell.

As the MTU escapes, the Moon enters the Black Sun. Koenig and Bergman experience forces beyond imagination. Time and reality bend, they even share their innermost thoughts, until they encounter a cosmic intelligence with a pleasant feminine voice, who guides them to safety.

WRITER DAVID WEIR

British writer David Weir's (1934-2011) credits include *Secret Agent* (aka *Danger Man*), *The Plane Makers*, *The Onedin Line* and *Crown Court*. He also created the English dubbing scripts for the Japanese TV series *Monkey* (*Saiyûki*) and *The Water Margin* (*Suikoden*), for which he also wrote a tie-in novel. His six-part 'Killers of the Dark' serial for the classic series of *Doctor Who* went unmade due to being deemed too costly to produce.

REFERENCE MATERIAL

The first draft was dated November 1973.

ANALYSIS

It had been established in early scripts that Professor Bergman was responsible for Moonbase Alpha's anti-gravity system. His apparent lack of knowledge of astrophysics and the inability to identify the 'Black Sun' early on seems unlikely as the September 1973 Writer's Guide clearly establishes that he is both an astrophysicist and an expert in force-fields. Weir either was uninformed of this fact or ignored it for dramatic effect. Certainly, Bergman's vast scientific knowledge was evident in later episodes.

Early character names still exist in the first draft. While the Professor's name was finalized, Italian nationalities still remain for Sandra Sabatini and Catani (due to ITCs plans to include Italian actors based on the co-financing deal with the RAI TV network).

Instead of simply Commander, Koenig is still referred to as Alcom (Alpha Commander), one of many 'Spacese' acronyms that were devised, then abandoned in the Writer's Guide.

The ill-fated pilot who investigates the Black Sun is named Mike Meyer here.

The Eagle Transporter still remains as the MTU. While the name Main Mission appears in the September Writer's Guide, Weir's draft refers to it as Alpha Control. IDX is another temporary name for what would eventually become known as the commlock.

Koenig has a monitor station in his office that Sandra can sit at, though this may be an earlier conceived then abandoned set concept. Weir also added a base restaurant, where Helena finds a sulking Bergman. This set would not appear in series one, but a variation of a communal space materialized in the second season episodes 'Séance Spectre' and 'The Lambda Factor'.

While the script and the final episode follow the same progression, much of Weir's visual effects described therein seem to have been beyond what could have been accomplished within the time and budget constraints of a 1973 TV series (as happened with his *Doctor Who* script). The relationship between Helena and Bergman is a little adversarial, unlike how Barbara Bain and Barry Morse would later play it. Bergman is also very metaphysical, possibly believing in a cosmic intelligence, which he initially dismisses in the final aired episode ('I'm a scientist, I don't know anything about God').

Weir's reference to a cosmic intelligence may have set off the running storyline that Alpha's journey was being guided for some greater good, though George Bellak's 'The Void Ahead' drafts hint at such a concept (again from Bergman). Koenig's plea to the aliens in Christopher Penfold's 'War Games' also backs up the notion of a potential guiding 'Hand of

God'[18].

One odd continuity error Weir makes in his first draft is with Sandra, whose name appears on the lifeboat list. However, after being present in the ship on page 57, she then shows up in Control Center when Alpha passes into and through the Black Sun.

Possibly due to an error by whoever typed up the script, Ouma's name suddenly changes to Oumi after page 26.

INSPIRATION

The first draft script utilizes the term *Black Sun,* despite the fact that it appears to have never been applied to this stellar object.

The concept of something so dense and powerful that nothing, not even light could escape its gravitational pull, had its origins in theories proposed by Albert Einstein in his 1915 presentation now known as The Einstein Field Equations. Though he never gave the phenomenon a name, this anomaly manifested itself as Einstein attempted to think about the effects of gravity relative to his Special Theory of Relativity.

Over the proceeding years, various physicists attempted to find solutions to many of Einstein's equations. One man, Karl Schwarzschild, found that there was a possibility for a star to become both small and heavy enough to exert a gravitational force strong enough to drawn anything in. He also postulated that there was a certain distance, 'The Schwarzschild Solution' (now known as 'The Event Horizon'), wherein objects were inexorably captured.

Thought his solutions to Einstein's equations were used, many physicists, in particular Arthur Eddington, could not accept the existence of collapsed stars. He instead proposed that stars could not collapse in *The Internal Constitution of the Stars,* published in 1926, and that these sources of radiation were due to the fusion of hydrogen into helium.

So well respected in his field by his peers, Eddington's theories were initially accepted by the astrophysics community, overshadowing not only Schwarzschild's, but those of Subramanyan Chandrasekhar. A student at the

---

[18] 'I certainly do not have, nor had, any belief in a conventional God. Inasmuch as we humans are ever masters of our own destiny, my belief (which accorded with Martin Landau's perception of his role as a leader) is that we make our own luck and that some humans are endowed with more cosmic intelligence than others. However, I was well aware that religion, in one guise or another, holds sway with much of the human population and I was very taken with David Weir's notion that our characters, in the throes of their very near-death experience and at what looked as though was about to be the end of their natural lives, would experience a moment of meeting with their maker – however irrational that might seem to both of them. And I was also taken with the notion that, in our persistently male dominated world, their perception of their maker should be a woman.' – Christopher Penfold

University of Madras in South India, he had read a paper by a protégé of Eddington, Ralph Fowler. Chandrasekhar realized that a white dwarf star could collapse into itself.

Both Eddington and Fowler dismissed his theories as insignificant, doing so publicly at a monthly meeting of the Royal Astronomical Society. Though initially devastated, Chandrasekhar eventually won the Nobel Prize in Physics for 1983 for writing an acclaimed book on stellar physics.

Over the following years, other scientists continued to study the energy source of various stars. Soviet physicist Lev Landau incorrectly proposed that stars had internal cores made up entirely of neutrons. Robert Oppenheimer, with several student collaborators at the University of California in Berkeley vigorously disputed Landau's conclusions. With Hartland Snyder, Oppenheimer proposed the collapse of a star into a denser mass (still not yet called a Black Hole).

In 1965, at the General Relativity and Cosmology conference in London, two Soviet physicists, Isaac Khalatnikov and Evgeny Lifshitz, presented a paper theorizing that the irregularities and asymmetries of a star would prevent it from collapsing into a singularity of a Black Hole. When a young British physicist, Roger Penrose had already proved his theorem that singularities would always occur, the two men found an error in their analysis that eventually proved that singularities always occur for a star sufficiently large. Penrose's Singularity Theorem, which postulated Black Holes could form when stars 1.4 times the mass of our sun collapsed, was accepted.

Though there was still no evidence that 'completely collapsed gravitational objects' actually existed in physical reality, in 1971, John Wheeler found it was easier to use the term 'Black Body' during his lectures. Soon, many other physicists adopted the name, which eventually morphed into the more commonly used 'Black Hole'.

There appears no evidence that 'Black Sun' was ever applied in any scientific paper. Weir may have read it mis-used somewhere or thought it more dramatically mysterious and threatening.

TECHNOLOGY

'Black Sun' is one of the few scripts that makes use of 'The Lens', a watch-like bio-monitor worn here by Bergman. It was also prominent in Johnny Byrne's 'Force of Life' when Zoref's victims died and, Donald James' story for series two, 'Journey to Where'. This piece of tech was possibly inspired by the heart monitors seen in the Gerry & Sylvia Anderson feature film *Doppelgänger* (aka *Journey to the Far Side of the Sun*).

MTU — Modular Transportation Unit — 'A number of MTUs are already on their pads each with a different configuration, demonstrating the versatility of the Modular Transportation Unit.

LAUNCH PAD BOARDING TUBE — 'A large tube extends from one of the buildings and connects up to the entrance of the MTU in the immediate foreground. Through the portholes in the side of the tube we are able to see the cylindrical compartment that Maddox and Miller are traveling in, move through the tube and stop at the entrance of the MTU' (*see* Stingray *pilot*)

TRAVEL TUBE — 'A six-seater cylindrical compartment that transports personnel through a tube system to all parts of Moon City'

COMM-POST - A communications column found all around Moonbase Alpha

IDX - Early name for the commlock.

LIGHT PENCIL TOOL - Bergman uses this device to work on his force-field generator spheres.

CHARACTERS

COMMANDER JOHN KOENIG

DOCTOR HELENA RUSSELL

PROFESSOR VICTOR BERGMAN

SANDRA SABATINI

PILOT MIKE MEYER

OUMA

CATANI

MOONBASE ALPHA SETS / LOCATIONS

MOONBASE ALPHA

COMMANDER'S OFFICE

CENTRAL CONTROL

CONFERENCE ROOM -- Not part of Koenig's office.

TRAVEL TUBE & CORRIDOR

MTU COMMAND MODULE

MEDICAL CENTER

ENGINEERING SECTION

RESTAURANT - The September 1973 Writer's Guide proposes staff eat in their quarters. Weir created a communal place which would have been a great location for social gatherings. A similar set appeared in the second series episodes 'The Seance Spectre' and 'The Lambda Factor'.

SPECIAL NOTATIONS

The last page of David Weir's November 1973 First Draft of 'The Black Sun' included:

NOTES:

I'm afraid I've spent a small fortune on SFX.

But what's the point of hiring a genius designer, and under-using him?

I won't presume to tell him how -- but a couple of notes:

God knows how you achieve a black sun effect. However, it might be worth trying to photograph a shiny, black-painted long tube exactly end-on against a black background, for the basic shape. Mainly, you see it as an absence of light, of stars where it blots them out, and by the ghosting effects at its peripheries.

The forcefield screens. Strictly, the invented technology calls for this arrangement of circular antigrav fields --

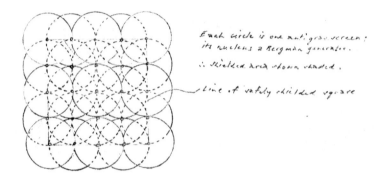

Which would look very pretty in different colors, but might be too complex. Then, and it's allowed for in the script, you could assume the antigrav fields transform into forcescreens merely by touching edges; and do not require to overlap, to double, over the whole shielded area,

With apologies to H G Wells.

Luck.

DW

NOTE: Weir's hand-written notations read:

Each circle is one antigrav screen;
its nucleus a Bergman generator.

∴ *shielded area shown shaded.*

Line of safely shielded square.

(DH)

'FLY TRAP'

Story Outline
Working Title: 'FLY TRAP'
by Donald Jonson
Second Version (1973)

SYNOPSIS

A strange asteroid approaches the Moon. Sensors detect it is composed of an unknown material and possibly hollow. Unknown to them, the interior contains an Alien Computer which begins to absorb all Moonbase Alpha's transmissions.

Caught in orbit around the asteroid, a Probe Ship is launched, only to be also trapped in a ring of light. The Commander fires a warning shot with a laser, then a nuclear missile, only for both to be deflected off into space.

An object is launched at the Moon. It's not an armed device, but some sort of unmanned vehicle. A team, including reconnaissance member Donovan, are sent out to investigate. Donovan is pulled into the craft, which returns to the asteroid.

The man is eventually returned, now under the thrall of some alien computer from the planet Uralt. They demand all the data in Alpha's computers, threatening to destroy the base.

Helena realizes Donovan is somehow connected to the asteroid, and the link is killing him. The Alien Computer admits it is aware of this fact and, once the human dies, another will replace him.

Checking his star charts, the Professor realizes Uralt's sun has gone nova and uses this information to convince the Alien Computer its mission is over.

SPACE 1999
STORY OUTLINE
WORKING TITLE: FLY TRAP

by Donald Jonson

Second Version

ACT ONE

1. The moon seen from afar.

2. Various sensors on the surface of another celestial body react to the approaching moon.

3. A computer unit. Not of terrestrial design. The lights on the control panels do not winking blink; they shimmer and oscillate. The image of the moon appears on a screen. The image becomes more sharply focused. A long, long zoom in – and then Moonbase Alpha appears on the screen.

4. Moonbase Alpha.

5. Command module. Commander & Professor. We learn that the moon is voyaging through deep space. Certain of the moon's supplies of essential raw materials will just about last out until the moon gets within range of Planet Delta B 3, which (spectroscopic analysis has revealed) possesses abundant quantities of the material in question.

6. Alien computer unit. As the commander and professor talk, sympathetic light vibrations are registered on a panel. The alien computer is recording dialogue. Other banks in the computer become activated. The computer is analyzing and
learning human speech (i.e., English).

7. Command module. An asteroid has been sighted. We see it on the commander's screen. He orders a routine survey.

8. Alien computer unit. It continues to assimilate dialogue. More banks become active. The unit is now very busy ingesting information.

9. Report to the Commander: the asteroid consists of an unknown material. Its weight is small – it seems to be hollow.

10. The professor's curiosity is aroused. He asks for and obtains a closer picture of the asteroid. Very odd! The asteroid is too small to support life, too big to be an artifact. And yet… it's not just a lump of rock, either…

11. Another sensor on the asteroid's surface is activated.

12. Alien computer unit. The moon's image on the screen. Points of light

move across the screen and converge until they form a continuous unbroken line round the image of the moon.

13. Command module. A very slight shudder through the building causes a couple of light objects (pencils, a plastic cup, e.g.) to fall to the ground. What's happening? The professor scrutinizes the picture of the asteroid.

14. Alien computer unit. The moon's image on the screen, as in item 12. Other images of the moon on other screens, in various degrees of close up. The computer completely activated now. Reacting to and registering dialogue not only from command module but also from every other module on Moonbase.

15. Command module.
    Commander: 'It seems to be in orbit.'
    Prof: 'Seems to be.'
    Commander: 'Isn't it?'
    Prof: 'No. We are.'
    Commander incredulous — then realizes it's true. The moon is orbiting the asteroid.

16. Command module. Commander broadcasts to all personnel. Quick shots of various parts of Moonbase as he says his piece. Some of these shots are seen on the screens of the alien computer. Commander: 'We are in orbit. Evidently there is life on the asteroid. Also very advanced technology, which is able to create powerful artificial gravitational field. As yet no cause for alarm. However, all personnel on emergency standby. Will attempt to communicate with asteroid.'

17. Commander orders communication procedure. (Writer's query: presumably a standard routine has been or will be devised whereby Moonbase attempts communication with alien cultures?)

18. The alien computer digests the Moonbase messages but makes no reply.

19. Command module. Commander consults professor and Helena. They agree a probe should be launched to try to establish contact.

20. Probe launched to asteroid.

21. Probe plotted on screen of alien computer. On another screen, points of light converge and form an unbroken ring.

22. Probe approaches asteroid.

23. Alien computer screen: probe approaches ring of light.

24. Inside probe: pilot finds he has gone into orbit round asteroid, cannot approach closer.

25. Alien computer screen: probe going round the ring of light.

26. Commander recalls probe.

27. Command module. Commander: 'All right. Let's wait for them to make a move.'

28. Command module. Several hours later. We can't go on waiting. Commander consults Helena and Prof. All three are reluctant to take hostile action against the asteroid, which until now has itself shown no hostile intent. On the other hand, they cannot afford to remain stuck in orbit.

29. Continuous attempts have been made to get in contact with the asteroid. No response at all.

30. The Commander decides to fire a burst from a laser at the asteroid — not in order to destroy it, simply as a warning that Moonbase cannot continue to accept this situation.

31. The laser beam is deflected from the asteroid by the invisible barrier (i.e., visible only on the alien computer screen).

32. The Commander now orders a nuclear missile to be launched at the asteroid. The missile is deflected. It explodes harmlessly in space.

33. A missile is launched from the asteroid at the moon.

34. The missile launch is detected on Moonbase. Emergency stations.

35. Moonbase launches an anti-missile-missile. It explodes prematurely. Laser beams are deflected from the approaching missile.

36. Missile lands near Moonbase. It is evidently not a missile after all, but some kind of space vehicle.

37. Commander attempts to communicate with vehicle. No response. No

sign of life.

38. Commander instructs Donovan (Reconnaissance) to investigate vehicle, with escort of security men.

(Editor's Note: Line 39 missing)

40. Donovan and escort approach vehicle. Donovan reports to Commander: the vehicle seems to have no doors or windows.

41. The alien computer records the dialogue.

42. An opening appears on the vehicle's hull. No door moves. No panel slides. The opening simply appears, without the apparent aid of any mechanism. A strange light shines from inside the vehicle. It is the same color as the rings of light on the alien screens. The light travels towards Donovan, seeming to flow along the ground like a ribbon. Donovan orders the security men to fall back. The light reaches Donovan. It seems to lock him in its grip. It is a tentacle of light. The tentacle pulls Donovan towards the vehicle.

43. The security men open fire on the vehicle. Their fire is harmlessly deflected.

44. Donovan is dragged to the vehicle.

45. The Commander orders the security men to stop firing. He calls Donovan. No reply.

46. Donovan is pulled into vehicle. The opening disappears.

47. The Commander continues to call Donovan. Still no reply.

48. The vehicle takes off.

ACT TWO

49. The Commander is calling Donovan. No reply.

50. Donovan in the space vehicle. We hear the Commander. Donovan seems to be in a trance.

51. The Commander instructs a subordinate to continue calling Donovan. He

must confer with Professor and Helena.

52. Vehicle lands on asteroid.

53. Command module. Council of war. Evidently the aliens want something from us. But what? And why do they refuse to communicate?

54. Vehicle proceeds to a kind of shaft.

55. Council of War: I have the feeling that Donovan has been collected as a sample, and now he's going to be examined. That's what we do with lower forms of life, isn't it?

56. Vehicle goes down lift shaft. Interior of the asteroid is of geodetic construction, something like a honeycomb.

57. Council of War: What can we do? Nothing. Wait and hope. Like laboratory animals.

58. Donovan, still in a trance, inside the vehicle. The vehicle opens. It is standing in the alien computer room.

59. The light-tentacles maneuver Donovan on to a horizontal slab. Other light-tentacles spring from the slab and pinion him to it. A transparent or translucent globe or helmet descends over Donovan's head. Lights flash on the computer panel and are answered by lights flashing within the globe.

60. Various shots of different parts of Moonbase. Silent personnel. Waiting for news. The Commander's voice over: Still no news.

61. Donovan's treatment continues. On the screens we see X-rays of his skull and a map of his nervous system.

62. Council of War. Donovan has been gone for 10 hours. Perhaps the aliens are trying to communicate with him? But why do both Donovan and the aliens remain out of contact with Moonbase?

63. Donovan once again in the vehicle. It ascends in the lift to the asteroid's surface.

64. Observers on the moon report blast off of vehicle to the Commander. Commander relays the message to all personnel.

65. Vehicle lands near Moonbase.

66. Commander watches from command module as vehicle opens up. Donovan steps out. 'Are you all right, Donovan?'
'I bring you greetings,' answers Donovan, 'from the inhabitants of Uralt.' The voice is recognizably Donovan's, but it is distorted, like a ventriloquist's voice issuing from a dummy. And he stares, like a man in a trance.

67. On the alien screens pictures of Moonbase appear, as seen through Donovan's eyes. We realize that Donovan has become a transmitter for the computer.

68. Moonbase. 'Uralt?'
'It is the name of a planet in another galaxy. I have been chosen as their representative.'
'I'm glad you're back, Donovan.'
'I have come to give you your instructions. You will obey them. Any failure to do so will be punished.'
'How?'

69. A port opens in the space vehicle. A beam of light is projected from it. The light strikes a boulder and vaporizes it. The port in the space vehicle closes.

70. Donovan: 'It is wiser not to disobey the inhabitants of Uralt.'

ACT THREE

71. Donovan's eyes.

72. Commander, Helena, Professor: as seen by Donovan.

73. Picture 72 on the screen of the alien computer unit.

74. Command module. Commander, Helena, Professor ply Donovan with questions. What happened on the asteroid? What do the aliens want from us? Where is Uralt? Donovan ignores all these questions. Occasionally he winces and touches his head. 'Are you ill?' He does not answer.

75. Alien computer unit. On the screen: the X-ray of Donovan's skull. A pinpoint of light appears on it. This is an activating mechanism.

76. Command module. Donovan recites: 'No form of life exists on the

asteroid. It is a robot. Its sole purpose is to gather information. It does this from any life forms that chance to come within its range. The information is transmitted to Uralt. Many such asteroids exist in many galaxies. They are all robots. They transmit information to Uralt.'

'What sort of information does Uralt require?'

'Everything. First, the data on computer tapes. Second, the contents of all the minds of all the personnel.'

'That could take months!'

'Time is of no importance to Uralt,' says Donovan.

But time is of the essence to Moonbase...

77. Moonbase computer room. Donovan, moving like a zombie, begins to reset the computer controls. The Computer Chief is alarmed: 'What the hell is Donovan doing? He's going to foul up the system! He doesn't know anything about the computers!'

'Maybe he doesn't know what he's doing,' says the professor, 'but whatever is controlling him knows perfectly well.'

Donovan completes the adjustments: 'We are now connected with the asteroid.'

'How? Where is the link?'

'I am the link,' says Donovan.

78. Moonbase computer room. The Professor says: 'I wish to ask the asteroid a question.'

Donovan replies: 'The asteroid does not give information to alien life forms.'

The professor says: 'It must answer this question. I wish to know where Uralt is located. I wish to communicate with Uralt direct.'

79. Alien computer room. The computer scans the Professor on a screen. A mechanism activated.

80. Moonbase computer room. Donovan says: 'Your question is accepted.'

He punches a key. Moonbase computer punches out a stream of figures. The professor studies the answer. Uralt is located in a galaxy approximately 500 million light years from here!

81. There is no possibility whatsoever of communicating directly with Uralt.

82. Donovan orders the Computer Chief to start feeding the tapes into the machine for transmission to the asteroid. The Commander tells the Computer Chief to obey Donovan. Which tapes? All of them. That will take days! Get on with it. The Computer Chief gets on with it.

'Now you can get some rest,' the Commander tells Donovan. 'You need it. That's an order.'

Donovan refuses. He has to stay with computer. Helena tries to reason with him. He threatens to become violent. She tranquilizes him with a TSLA.

83. Sickbay. Doctor completes checkup of Donovan. Nothing wrong with him physically. Assistant brings in X-Ray films. The head X-ray reveals that a (very small) foreign body has been implanted in Donovan's brain. The doctor is amazed. There is absolutely no sign of surgery to the head. Donovan is
taken off to his quarters to rest.

84. Command module. The Commander calls up the professor on the intercom. 'What shall we tell the personnel?'

'Tell them the truth. There is nothing we can do but wait and hope. We are totally at the mercy of the asteroid.'

The professor is examining star charts. 'What good will it do?'

'No good at all; it's a way of passing the time; I'm curious to see what Uralt looks like. That distant planet, which does not even know of our existence, but which has sentenced Moonbase to death.'

85. Command module. The Commander broadcasts a short grim message to all personnel.

86. Moonbase computer room. One tape has been transmitted. Thousands more wait to be processed. The Computer Chief switches off a panel as he unloads the transmitted tape and prepares another.

87. Alien computer room. One panel goes dead as transmission from the moon momentarily ceases. Then a bright pulsing light appears on the panel — an alarm signal. The X-Ray photo of Donovan's skull appears on a screen. The bright pulsing light flashes from the implant in his brain. The light is accompanied by piercing jabs of sound.

88. Donovan in his quarters clutches his head in agony —- we hear the jabs of sound. Donovan staggers to his feet.

89. Donovan in travel tube.

90. Donovan bursts into Computer Room. The Computer Chief has just finished loading the new tape. Donovan pushes him aside and starts the machine. Donovan is in a terrible state. Alarmed, the Computer Chief contacts Helena.

91. Helena says: 'The asteroid is killing you, Donovan. Can't you make the asteroid understand that?'

Donovan: 'The asteroid understands.'

Helena: 'Then it must let you rest.'

Donovan: 'The transmission of information must not be interrupted.'

Helena: 'If the asteroid kills you it will defeat its own purpose.'

Donovan: 'If I cease to function, I shall be replaced.'

Helena: 'Who by?'

Donovan: 'There are 300 people on Moonbase. Any of them can be used as a link. All of them will be used if necessary.'

ACT FOUR

92. Moonbase Computer Room. Donovan is in a state of near collapse. The doctor tries to give him a vitamin injection as a boost. Donovan refuses.

93. Commander and Helena are watching this scene from the Command Module. Commander tells doctor to leave Donovan. Commander asks Helena how much longer she thinks Donovan has got. 'A day, perhaps.'

'Then what?'

'Then someone else will have to take over… and be doomed to die.'

'Isn't there anything we can do?'

'Apparently not. The Professor hasn't come up with any answers.'

94. Commander calls up Professor in chart room, where he is busy trying to plot the position of Uralt, helped by an assistant. Why hasn't he found it yet? Because he hasn't got the use of the computer. Calculations are laborious.

'What's the point of locating Uralt, anyhow,' the Commander asks. 'We have no means of getting in touch with its inhabitants.'

'Intellectual curiosity,' answers the professor. 'And at a time like this one should try to keep busy…'

95. Command module. An emergency call from the computer room. It's Donovan. In a short time, he says, he will cease to function. The Commander must immediately arrange for him to be replaced. Someone must be sent to the space vehicle to be taken to the asteroid for processing. What if the Commander refuses? Then the space vehicle will seek out someone itself . . . . . .

96. Command module. Commander addresses all personnel. 'I'm not going to ask for volunteers. I'm going to draw lots. Everyone has an equal chance of being chosen.'

The lots are drawn. (Presumably by some kind of electronic scrambling device). The 'victim' is one of the Technicians. He is ordered to prepare to board the space vehicle.

97. Chart room. The Professor has located the position of Uralt. A section of the sky chart is projected on a screen. The assistant magnifies the picture. Magnifies it further. But there is no trace of a planet. It seems that Uralt does not exist.

98. Decompression chamber. The technician, in a spacesuit, prepares to go to the space vehicle.

99. Commander is watching him from Command module. Then an emergency call from the Professor. 'Hold everything!'

100. Professor asks to be linked up with Computer Room via Command module. Professor tells Donovan: 'Uralt does not exist; inform the asteroid.'

101. Alien computer room. Asteroid rejects the information.

102. Three way link up. Can the asteroid see through Donovan's eyes? Yes. Then look at this star chart.

103. Large star chart. This is the galaxy. Asteroid agrees. Detail: this is the sector in which Uralt once existed. Does exist, the asteroid corrects. Closer detail: Here is Uralt's sun. It is a super nova. All its dependent planets have been destroyed. Among them, Uralt.

104. Intense activity in the alien computer room. All lights on. Then a total cessation of all movement. The lights glare brighter and brighter. A high-pitched whine.

105. Donovan falls unconscious to the floor. What's happening?

106. Look at the asteroid! On the screen. It's glowing. It's incandescent. It explodes. The moon lurches out of orbit.

107. Emergency stations! Close the airlock!

108. The space vehicle vaporizes in a burst of its own light.

LATER

109. Sickbay. Donovan recovers consciousness. He's weak. But his voice is

normal. 'What happened?'

'The asteroid destroyed itself.'

'Why?'

'It discovered that it had no reason for existence. It therefore acted logically, as it had been designed to do.'

110. Donovan will recover.

110. The moon voyages on.

(Editor's Note: Line 111 mis-numbered)

112. Command module. Commander and Professor watch the procession of stars. Out there are other asteroids, busily collecting information and transmitting it to a world which died millions of years ago...

END

ANALYSIS

Though this outline is credited to Donald Jonson, Edward Di Lorenzo received sole screen credit for the episode it developed into, 'Ring Around the Moon'.[19] The final story as aired replaces 'victim-of-the-week' Donovan with Helena. This creates much more sympathy with the viewer as her link with the alien probe may kill her as it did with technician Ted Clifford in the pre-credits teaser. Di Lorenzo tightens the plot pace by adding teleportation between the Moon and the alien probe, rather than the tedious rocket transport. Wisely, he also omitted the lottery for the next 'sacrificial lamb', which would have doubtlessly made the crew of Moonbase Alpha appear to be a pretty callous lot.

Interestingly, Bergman's somewhat odd ability to discover the fate of the probe's home planet came from Jonson's original outline. This obviously troubled author E C Tubb when he novelized the story so he changed the planet Uralt (later Triton) to a moon of Neptune. (DH)

---

[19] 'I cannot recall the name Donald Jonson. I certainly don't recall ever meeting him and it would be far more likely I would remember a face-to-face encounter than a name on a storyline. Eddie de Lorenzo worked very closely with Johnny and I in the script department. Both Johnny and I did a lot of re-writing, most of it under pressure, but I honestly can't remember whether I did re-writes for 'Ring Around the Moon'. – Christopher Penfold

'THE EARTHBOUNDERS'

Story Outline by Anthony Terpiloff[20]
Undated (1973)
Filmed as 'Earthbound'

SYNOPSIS

An alien ship performs a controlled crash on the Moon. Upon entering the vessel, the Alphans discover an alien crew in suspended animation. Dr Russell attempts to revive one, but the alien dies. Automatic systems engage and the others safely revive.

The creatures are from a peaceful race seeking refuge on Earth and hold Russell no ill will at the death of their colleague. Once their ship is repaired, they intend to continue on their journey and offer to take one human along.

Johnson, a malcontent, plots to force his way aboard, despite Koenig's plan for a fair lottery. Unfortunately for him, his actions prevent anyone from testing if the suspended animation equipment can even work on a human. As the alien craft continues its 74-year journey to Earth, Johnson finds himself awake, with no food or water.

HOOK

The superstitious would know that something was about to happen. Reports from department heads at the Executive Meeting in progress are far too optimistic. Helena sums it up when she says that morale is at an all-time high. People on Alpha are no longer simply resigned to their fate, they are actively adapting themselves to their condition.

But since the members of the Executive are scientists and not

---

[20] 'Anthony Terpiloff had written a brilliant play for the BBC called *Poet Game* about the last days of Dylan Thomas in New York. It was memorable, amongst other things, for a brilliant performance by a young Anthony Hopkins as Dylan Thomas. So, I got in touch with Anthony Terpiloff to see if he would be interested in writing for *Space: 1999* because he was a very good American writer who was actually living in the UK. In fact, he was connecting with Dylan Thomas's Welsh roots by living in the Brecon Beacons and I visited him at his house there where we first kicked around the story that was to become 'Earthbound' and it was probably Anthony's enthusiasm for Dylan Thomas that gave rise to the title 'Death's other Dominion' after Thomas's famous poem 'And death shall have no dominion'. If you don't know it, check it out. It's the first book of poetry I bought with my history prize money at school and I still have it!' – Christopher Penfold

superstitious, they don't knock wood in the midst of all this self-congratulation. The meeting is abruptly halted by an alert.

Sensors report a large alien craft approaching at speed. Moreover, its attitude is unquietingly erratic. It does not behave as if it were approaching for a landing. And to the consternation of all, it does not land. It crashes after only a last-minute attempt to pull up.

ACT ONE

Koenig leads an expeditionary force out to the Alien ship. They are suspicious of it, although there appear to be no signs of life. Although it crashed, the ship was obviously under some kind of control.

They decide to break inside with laser cutting gear. They reach a passenger compartment. Humanoid space people, male and female, lie dead in their seats. Obviously advanced technology. They explore the ship, its equipment. Its drive power. But what they really want to examine are the aliens themselves. Koenig summons Helena Russell. Together they arrange for one of the aliens to be transported into the Medical Section for a very thorough examination.

In the Medical Section, only minor variations in biological and anatomical structure are noted from the human species. But the basic biochemistry of the cell structure does appear to be different. And certainly it is dead.

Meanwhile Koenig has summoned Professor Bergman and the Head of the Technical Section, Murneau. Together they have made a thorough examination of the technical qualities of the ship, some of which they come near to understanding in principle, if not in detail. But there is one piece of equipment that they are very puzzled by. It seems to be still working away in some fashion. They are not sure what it is, or how it is working. But they retire to a safe distance — except Bergman who wants to stay and watch. To his amazement he soon becomes aware of what it is — an animator. He calls Koenig and Helena. Together they watch the revival of the aliens.

But now Helena is worried. Because the alien she examined was so definitely dead. By taking it away from its animator she has killed it forever. And a vastly superior people is awakening — to discover what the Alpha people have done to their colleague. Koenig decides on secrecy…

ACT TWO

Koenig meets the Alien Commander who tells him their story. They've come from a dying planet many light years away. Their ship is one of several dispatched to various planets in an effort to keep their race alive. They were placed in suspended animation aboard a ship operated by autopilot. This particular ship was bound for Earth and set for a preliminary Moon orbiting situation while the crew were re-animated in preparation for an Earth landing. But the Moon's unorthodox situation has played havoc with the alien auto computations and now they have crashed on Moon still many years of traveling away from Earth.

Now the aliens are introduced to Alpha. They are amazed at the primitive living conditions that the people appear to have accepted. They have no wish to stay here. But they need help and equipment to repair their ship and to prepare for the last stage of their journey to Earth.

Koenig and the Alien Commander fence around a bit, suspicious of each other's intentions. Koenig withholds the news of the alien death in the Medical Section, but the Alien Commander of course notices that one of their number is missing but refrains from asking questions. Koenig cautiously offers Alpha help.

But Johnson, a brilliant malcontent from the Service Department, is reluctant. He and his companions, not being dedicated scientists, and their jobs being more menial and tedious, have been slow to adjust to life on Alpha. Now Johnson turns passive resistance to the Aliens attempts to repair their ship, into active sabotage.

Until the Alien Commander slyly lets Johnson know that one of their number has disappeared on Alpha and that there is now room for one Alpha person in their spaceship who wishes to make the return journey to Earth.

Going home, going home. It becomes a refrain on Alpha, while the repair work now proceeds apace. For the first time it's a feasibility. One of them will be allowed to go. A wave of homesickness sweeps the base. Rumor and speculation distend their hard won 'normal' existence. Koenig is plagued with requests for private interviews with personnel who plead their special circumstances, beg to be chosen. It begins to grow ugly...

Chief among the early pleaders is Johnson who becomes obsessed with the idea of a return to Earth. So obsessed that Helena is concerned about his mental stability.

And Helena has another problem. how will the animator work for Earth people? She has considerable faith in the alien technology but a more profound sense of guilt at having been responsible for the single alien who died. So she insists that for medical reasons, she should be the guinea pig for an experiment. She is de-animated...

ACT THREE

Johnson claims to speak (and he does so powerfully) for a considerable following in all departments who insist on an early choice of candidate for the return. And he insists on an active role in making that choice. Moreover, he argues, it's unjust that only one Earthman can go home. Why not take all the alien's places? What do they owe these strangers going to invade their Earth? Koenig's authority comes into question, A rebellion in imminent.

Which is made the more likely by the successful re-animation of Helena Russell. But she wakes to a situation which she doesn't like at all, and she attempts to reason with Johnson, and makes a suggestion to Koenig.

At a public meeting Koenig counters Johnson's threat. Any actual or suggestion of violence will be dealt with summarily. Harsh security procedures throughout the base are instituted. There is only one opening on the earthbound ship and that is that. He wants each of them to listen carefully. When the one Earthman gets home he'll find himself in the year 2074! No one he knows will be alive. Those who are imagining themselves restored to the bosom of their family can forget it. Who knows what has happened on their Earth in their absence? Like the other aliens aboard, he will be a curiosity — a 20th century man thrust into the late 21st Century. Any family remaining to him will be his great grandchildren. Sternly, Koenig warns them to think seriously before submitting their names for volunteers.

Koenig's speech is temporarily successful. Requests for a lottery here and now are rejected. The one to go will be chosen, neither by lottery nor election, but by the most rational means at their disposal — by computer.

This is too much for Johnson, who successfully hi-jacks Alpha's electrical power station and begins to make his demands.

ACT FOUR

But Helena will not chance Johnson. She realizes that he is the focal point of the homesickness and the restlessness that they have worked to eliminate. She feeds these informations into the computer, knowing that it will be influenced by them.

But now Johnson demands the Alien Commander as hostage.

Koenig restrains the aliens from immediate force and tries to negotiate with Johnson. No deals.

Koenig decides to announce the computer's choice now so that Johnson can be confronted with the person whose place he is usurping. But the computer's choice is Johnson.

And now he doesn't believe it. Thinks it is a trick. Nothing Koenig says or does will convince him otherwise.

And now Johnson uses the Alien Commander as a means of getting on board the Alien ship and of ordering the crew to prepare for take-off.

Under these difficult circumstances Koenig says good-bye to the Alien Commander, who is still under Johnson's control as the door of the spaceship is closed and the main motors made ready for blast off.

Alpha people gather to watch the Alien ship leave, with Johnson on board, for earth. Most are relieved to see Johnson go, but most are now confused about their feelings for Earth.

Koenig confidently questions Helena about rigging the computer. Bergman questions whether the aliens will not soon tire of Johnson.

The alien spaceship lifts off, and they watch it set course for home.

EPILOGUE

Inside the alien spaceship, everyone is de-animated. Except Johnson, futilely holding his weapon. He realizes that they have left him alive for a journey that will take 74 years. And that he has no fodder, no drink, and no power to do anything about it at all. Helena confesses that the alien animator was alright as far as it went — but it couldn't hold her down for long. They hope it's doing the trick for Johnson.

ANALYSIS

Despite being killed off in E C Tubb's novelization of 'Breakaway', Commissioner Simmonds survived in all drafts of the opening episodes. This allowed his character to return as the main protagonist in this story, which elevates his dark fate in a way a one-shot villain could not. He's an established character, albeit unlikable, yet we can sympathize with Koenig's pain in knowing how Simmonds with die alone among the stars.

One theme that appears in many early drafts is the potential of some Alphans rejecting life on Moonbase. This threat of unrest was toned down over most of the series, replaced by an acceptance of their fate to wander space, though any new planet would still offer hope of a 'normal' life. On screen, Moonbase Alpha became a much more pleasant place to live, rather than a potential powder keg of revolution. Here, this episode rolled all that into one man, Simmonds, who clearly had no place in the somewhat idyllic community.

Other minor changes, from storyline to screen, saw the first alien die in Medical Center, as opposed to aboard their ship, and the visitor's names and backstory were fleshed out.

It is not known if Tubb was aware this episode was not to be novelized, or was it omitted because he killed off Simmonds? When viewed early in the series run (it really should be watched soon after 'Breakaway'), the story is an emotional tale of the fate of two races in space, and one man who refuses to accept his. (DH)

UNPRODUCED EPISODES

'PLANET OF THE EYE'

Story Outline by Victor Pemberton
Undated (1973)

SYNOPSIS

A series of meteorites bombards the Moon and a specimen from one is analyzed by geologist Alex Danilov, but soon begins expanding in size. A rogue planet is discovered, engulfed in a sinister reddish mist. An MTU sent to investigate the planet is crushed. A second MTU is sent out and successfully passes through a gap in the red mist and lands on the alien planet's rocky reddish surface where its two pilots discover a series of statue-like skeletons cocooned in a web-like mass.

Danilov has been acting increasingly erratic and Dr Russell alerts Commander Koenig that Danilov's personal data shows inconsistencies. Upon further examination, she confirms that his mind is split in two parts and is transmitting information back from the alien planet. Danilov, under electro-hypnosis, tells Helena the planet is a living center feeding off the best brains of space travelers.

On the planet, the MTU pilots are sucked into the ground and killed, and Alpha is bombarded by missile-like lumps of clay, cocooning Alpha in a red mass. The Professor determines that the planet is the nerve-center of the bombarding meteorites.

Danilov steals an MTU and goes to the planet. Koenig pursues him, despite Helena's warning that it is his brain the alien planet wants. On the planet, Koenig sets up a laser device to fire into the rock surface of the planet. Meanwhile, the red mass enveloping Alpha converts into foam which threatens the base. Danilov appears, without his spacesuit, and attempts to convince Koenig to surrender to the hypnotic pull of the planet. Koenig fires the laser, Danilov is sucked into the abyss, and the proverbial 'eye' of the nerve-center is destroyed.

WRITER VICTOR PEMBERTON

Author Victor Pemberton enjoyed a long and prolific career in British television and radio, as well as writing numerous novels. He is particularly well remembered for his contributions to *Doctor Who*, which included inventing the Doctor's trademark sonic screwdriver.

INTRODUCTION

'Planet of the Eye' was written by Pemberton in 1973 as a storyline for *Space: 1999*, based on concepts he had earlier pitched to *Doctor Who* as 'The Eye in Space'. While it wasn't developed beyond this point for *Space: 1999*, Pemberton subsequently expanded some of these concepts in *Space Watch* (aka *Starlab Zero*), an unproduced two-part radio play. Pemberton's 5-page outline for 'Planet of the Eye' was acquired by Shaqui Le Vesconte, who graciously shared it for inclusion in this book.

CHARACTERS & TECHNOLOGY

Commander Koenig is referred to here as ALCOM (Alpha Commander) KOENIG.

Professor Bergman is un-named and referred to simply as 'the English astrophysicist PROFESSOR'.

Likewise, Alan Carter is referred to as the 'Italian space reconnaissance CHIEF'.

Central Control would soon become Main Mission; MTU's became Eagles, and TSLA's became Stun Guns.

SPACE: 1999
PLANET OF THE EYE

By Victor Pemberton

(Idea for Storyline)

MOONBASE ALPHA on full alert, as they are rocked by a series of meteorites, bombarding the surface of the Moon.

A specimen taken from one of the meteorites is analyzed in the Geology Section by ALEX DANILOV, who tells ALCOM KOENIG that the small, rock-like specimen bears a close parallel to mineral formations around caves in the Sahara Desert on Earth. The rock specimen is sealed beneath a glass cover to await further experiments. Only when it is left unattended do we become aware of a living mass, with a pulsating movement and sound like a heartbeat...

In Central Control, the tele-scanner picks up a strange phenomena on the monitor. It is an unidentified planet, almost completely engulfed in a sinister reddish mist. All indications are that the mist is some kind of protective, radioactive shroud. KOENIG orders an immediate TV probe.

ALEX DANILOV's report that the meteorite specimen may have increased in size brings a skeptical response from KOENIG and DR HELENA RUSSELL, who have always regarded the likeable ex-Soviet geologist as something of a screwball. DANILOV, however, is beginning to do things which others find uncharacteristic of him. Whilst back in his laboratory, the meteorite specimen has clearly expanded more than when we had last seen it…

Information fed into the Central Computer shows that the unidentified planet contains no oxygen, water, or vegetation. As KOENIG and his staff watch the deep television probe on the monitor, we see a terrain consisting of weird, indefinable rock formations, of a reddish color. The English astrophysicist PROFESSOR theorizes that the planet could be one that has left its solar system, which does not revolve, and has no light. KOENIG, still curious about the meteorite bombardment earlier, orders his Italian space reconnaissance CHIEF to send an MTU craft up to the planet for an exploratory probe.

In the Geology Section, DANILOV studies microfilm slides of frescoes in the Tassili Caves, on the fringe of the Sahara Desert. He is absorbed by the ancient figures which could have been pre-historic space-travelers, and also the background rock formations, reddish in color. During this, DANILOV becomes aware of the pulsating sound, and the weird snatches of indistinct voices. He turns on the light, rubs his eyes, and decides to return to his living quarters.

The MTU approaches the protective red mist surrounding the unidentified planet. And as KOENIG and his staff listen in at Central Control, both PILOTS scream for help as they find their craft being crushed around them, to the accompaniment of a deafening, pulsating sound…

In his Living Quarters, ALEX DANILOV sits up with a start from his sleep. He rushes to the mirror to look at his face; it is bathed in perspiration. Looking at his hands, he finds one of them shaking, but the other quite still. The pulsating sound approaches, and builds to a climax… In the Geological Laboratory, the meteorite specimen expands rapidly, breaks out of its glass cage, and starts to spill over onto the floor…

KOENIG calls a meeting of his MTU Pilots. With the PROFESSOR's help, a plan is worked out to send one of the MTU's through a gap in the cloud of red mist surrounding the alien planet.

DR RUSSELL calls on ALEX DANILOV, who deliberately keeps her away from his Geology Lab. DANILOV is now wearing dark glasses, which he explains are a protection from the glare, the reason for his current headaches. DR RUSSELL suggests to DANILOV that he visit the Medical Section for treatment.

In Central Control, KOENIG and the PROFESSOR watch on TV the approach of the MTU towards the cloud of red mist. With the help of the computer, the craft finally succeeds in locating a gap large enough to get through. Now, there is to be an anxious delay before the PILOT's first report from the surface of the alien planet.

In the Alpha Commander's Office, DR RUSSELL asks Koenig for permission to take DANILOV into the Medical Section for psycho-analysis check, as the personal data gathered from DANILOV's sleeve doesn't seem to make sense. KOENIG checking on what DR RUSSELL has been saying, examines DANILOV's personal data, via the IDX and Central Computer, to his own videoscreen. The result is astonishing. The information is showing two sets of data, one of which is totally incomprehensible. KOENIG is called back urgently to Central Control.

The two MTU PILOTS have made a successful landing on the alien planet. The terrain, a reddish landscape of rock formation, has no dust as on the moon, and is dark. But everyone in Central Control stares in horror and bewilderment at the videoscreen. The two PILOTS are sending back pictures of a series of statue-like skeletons, some of human shape, others weird, sinister, & unfamiliar. All the skeletons contain remnants of the physiological structure, and are cocooned in a web-like mass...

In the Medical Section, DR RUSSELL puts DANILOV under electro-hypnosis, and it is soon clear to her that the young geologist's mind is split into two parts, with one side gradually dominating the other. And to DR RUSSELL's puzzlement, the alien side of DANILOV's mind is transmitting information back from the alien planet, where the two MTU PILOTS are now exploring.

Hindered now by communication static, KOENIG and THE PROFESSOR watch the progress of the two MTU PILOTS on the videoscreen. Gradually they become troubled by the now familiar pulsating sound...

DANILOV, under electro-hypnosis, tells DR RUSSELL the real objectives of the alien planet. It is a living center, gradually building in super-intelligence, feeding off the best brains of space travelers, human or otherwise. It is a magnet, drawing the brains of the Moonbase towards it, just like it has always done. Ever since those first meteorite landings in the Sahara Desert in pre-historic times... DR RUSSELL leaves DANILOV in the charge of a MEDICAL ASSISTANT, whilst she goes to inspect the specimen in DANILOV's laboratory.

The pulsating sound on the alien planet grows louder and louder, echoing throughout Central Control. With the video picture now breaking up, we hear the shouts and screams of the trapped MTU PILOTS on the surface of the planet. The ground beneath them... the rock-hard formations are becoming soft... it's like mud... it's sucking them down...! We see the two PILOTS in their spacesuits, toppling over into the substance, struggling to free themselves, but to no avail. Simultaneously, the Central Computer sounds the alarm. Another Meteorite Bombardment. The Base is under attack from missile objects which are like lumps of clay, thrown at the surface of the Moon and to the Base Observation Windows. And the noise which accompanies the bombardment is deafening, pulsating... like a heartbeat... it's everywhere... in the corridors, Central Control... and in the Geology Section, where DR RUSSELL is breaking down the door of the Laboratory. Inside – the cocooned skeleton of ALEX DANILOV...

All is now silent on MOONBASE ALPHA, its buildings cocooned in the red mass which has bombarded it. KOENIG confers with his Base Chiefs. Between them, they decide that for some reason or another, the substance is only active for short periods at a time. DR RUSSELL hurries in as news is received that ALEX DANILOV has broken out of the Medical Section.

DANILOV, like a frightened animal, hides in the dark of the deserted Solarium. There follows an extraordinary moment, when someone enters, switches on the Solarium lighting system. DANILOV, protecting his eyes from the glare, screams out in pain, attacks the man. But the attack is only half-hearted; one of DANILOV's hands tries to throttle the man, the other tries to stop it.

DR RUSSELL tells what she knows about the connection between DANILOV and the alien planet. The PROFESSOR talks of the planet as being like the eye of an octopus, which exudes the red mist to protect it. The eye is clearly the nerve-center of the bombarding meteorites. The Solarium attendant rushes in to tell what had happened with DANILOV. Simultaneously, DANILOV is seen on the videoscreen, now in space-gear, making his way by travel tube towards the MTU launch pad.

Breaking his way through all the IDX barriers, DANILOV warns Central Control to launch his craft, or he will destroy the entire MTU Section with his TSLA. Reluctantly, KOENIG gives the go-ahead for DANILOV's launch. To everyone's objections, KOENIG says he will go after DANILOV. But DR RUSSELL tries to tell KOENIG that this is exactly what the alien intelligence wants him to do. It is KOENIG's brain that is needed. He must not be drawn into the web. But KOENIG replies that this is precisely the reason why he must go to the planet. In a matter of hours MOONBASE ALPHA may be completely engulfed by the invading substance. If they are to survive, the substance must be attacked at the nerve-center – the eye of the space-octopus itself. But with what do you attack? With KOENIG and the PROFESSOR to stimulate the theories, they recall the reasons why DANILOV's eyes had been susceptible to any form of glaring light. Why was he in such pain in the Solarium? The reason must be that the alien planet is never subjected to the sun's rays. They must attack the nerve-center of the octopus planet with an infra-red detonating device, which will be set up to ignite the moment the organic matter surface becomes active again. But although such a solution may not work, KOENIG assures everyone that if it is his brain the alien planet wants, then he alone must take the risk of acting as decoy.

After many tense moments, KOENIG's MTU finds its way through a gap in the protective cloud of red mist surrounding the alien planet. But the moment he is through, the gap in the mist closes up behind him.

Watched by everyone on the videoscreen of Central Control, ALCOM KOENIG sets up the infra-red laser beam device on the surface of the alien planet. The whole operation, which is to be electronically ignited from MOONBASE ALPHA, is a slow and tense job, with KOENIG clearly fighting for time, before the organic matter becomes active again. But suddenly, MOONBASE Control report that the foam-like matter on the surface of the Moon is beginning to move, that they can hear the start of the pulsating sound.

KOENIG moves quickly to finish the infra-red wiring system, with its laser-rod aimed directly down at the rock-surface itself. But then, he too becomes aware that the organic rock is becoming active again, he too is fighting for breath as he is nearly deafened by the pulsating sound. From Central Control, there are shouts from HELENA RUSSELL for KOENIG to hurry, as they can feel the pressure building up all around them. Now the ground on which KOENIG is standing starts to soften. He calls to Central Control to ignite the infra-red laser detonator. But simultaneously, we hear a cracking sound in Central Control, and the whole MOONBASE is plunged into darkness by the force of the alien matter. Contact is now severed between MOONBASE ALPHA and KOENIG. The organic matter starts to bubble with life. KOENIG steps from one spot to another, trying desperately to avoid the approaching slide of foam-like matter. But then suddenly, ALEX DANILOV, his spacesuit discarded, appears. He calls to KOENIG to give up his useless efforts to destroy the alien intelligence, to allow himself to be drawn towards a far greater type of civilization than travelers from Earth have ever known. But KOENIG desperately keeps trying to make contact with MOONBASE Control, where now the personnel are beginning to feel the real impact of the invading intelligence on their own minds. Down the Observation windows of the Central Control Area, the foam-like substance gathers in momentum…

KOENIG, now himself gradually being drawn mentally into the nerve-center of the alien planet, struggles to find another way of igniting the infra-red laser rod. His hands reach for the TSLA, and by use of the chain ray selector, he activates the infra-red ignition. The effect is tremendous, with the laser beam piercing through the now susceptible organic matter. To the accompaniment of deafening pulsating sounds, during which the planet surface hardens again, and the organic matter recedes from MOONBASE ALPHA, DANILOV is sucked into the abyss, the eye of the space octopus nerve-center destroyed, the living cloud of red mist disappears…

THE END.

ANALYSIS

There are numerous similarities in 'Planet of the Eye' to other produced episodes of *Space: 1999*, most significantly 'Space Brain', where the brain itself takes the place of the planet and surrounding cloud of 'red mist' featured here. Other similarities include: a meteorite specimen being brought into the base for examination, and the later reference to the skeletons being 'cocooned in a web-like mass' sounds quite a lot like the organic matter that coats the surface of the meteorite (actually a crushed Eagle) in 'Space Brain'.

The subsequent image of a 'rock specimen sealed beneath a glass cover' corresponds to 'Space Brain', in which Koenig and Bergman study the alien foam contained within a glass/Perspex box, and would also be reflected in 'End of Eternity'.

The planet described here is a rogue planet, 'one that has left its solar system, which does not revolve, and has no light.' The other rogue planet encountered in *Space: 1999* is Meta, in 'Breakaway'.

The scene when 'KOENIG and his staff listen in at Central Control, both PILOTS scream for help as they find their craft being crushed around them, to the accompaniment of a deafening, pulsating sound' is duplicated in 'Space Brain', as an Eagle with astronauts Wayland and Cousteau aboard is crushed by the brain then hurled back to the Moon.

The medical condition described, 'the young geologist's mind is split into two parts, with one side gradually dominating the other' is similar to what would happen to Regina in 'Another Time, Another Place'.

Another connection to 'Space Brain is when, 'the alien side of DANILOV's mind is transmitting information back from the alien planet'. In 'Space Brain' Computer transmits data to Kelly's brain, and through him to the brain. This scenario is also utilized in 'Ring Around the Moon' with both Ted Clifford and Helena Russell being taken over and their minds being used to transmit data. Additionally, 'Ring Around the Moon' features the depiction of the Triton probe as a one-eyed brain ('We are the eyes of the planet Triton.')

The scene where 'DANILOV, under electro-hypnosis, tells DR RUSSELL the real objectives of the alien planet. It is a living center, gradually building in super-intelligence, feeding off the best brains of space travelers' is also paralleled in 'Space Brain' as Koenig discovers the brain's objectives. Koenig's mind is linked to Kelly's (which is connected to the space brain) in order to read his thoughts and discovers 'It's a living organism... like a brain... pulsating with life, and light... It's the center of a whole galaxy...' The space brain doesn't want to feed off of their minds, but the general scenario is essentially the same.

The scene where Alpha undergoes another meteorite bombardment and 'is under attack from missile objects which are like lumps of clay, thrown at the surface of the Moon and to the Base Observation Windows. And the noise which accompanies the bombardment is deafening, pulsating… like a heart-beat… it's everywhere…' is also paralleled in 'Space Brain' as the Moon enters the brain and is bombarded by its 'anti-bodies'. These anti-bodies then expand as a massive quantity of foam, covering and invading Alpha, like in 'Planet of the Eye' which finds Alpha's 'buildings cocooned in the red mass which has bombarded it.' Indeed, toward the end of the 'Planet of the Eye' story outline, there is even specific reference to 'the foam-like matter on the surface of the Moon'.

Another element that made it into 'Space Brain' is the idea that they 'must attack the nerve-center of the octopus planet with an infra-red detonating device'. In 'Space Brain' an Eagle is launched toward the brain loaded with nuclear charges in an attempt to weaken the brain's crushing effect.

As the climax is reached, 'From Central Control, there are shouts from HELENA RUSSELL for KOENIG to hurry, as they can feel the pressure building up all around them.' This scenario also plays out in 'Space Brain' as the external pressure of the foam builds and is countered by increases to Alpha's internal pressure.

A further 'foam' reference appears when, 'Down the Observation windows of the Central Control Area, the foam-like substance gathers in momentum…'

In the end, 'the eye of the space octopus nerve-center destroyed, the living cloud of red mist disappears…' rather like in 'Space Brain' when, having torn through the brain 'like a bullet' and exited again into normal space, it is presumed that the brain has been killed.

While Victor Pemberton's 'Planet of the Eye' was clearly the basic inspiration for Christopher Penfold's 'Space Brain', the most significant concept – that of the benevolent space brain itself – was Penfold's. By re-framing these specific elements of Pemberton's story within the larger 'Space Brain' context, Penfold made the episode wholly his own.

Pemberton's 'Planet of the Eye' also contains notable similarities to 'Dragon's Domain', including its seemingly metaphorical references to the alien planet as a 'space octopus' and the need to attack it in its 'eye'. In addition, an Alphan steals a ship to go out and confront or attack the enemy, and Koenig pursues. Characters feel themselves 'drawn mentally into the nerve-center of the alien planet' (rather like the hypnotic pull the Dragon exerts), the Alphan is 'sucked into the abyss' (a description not unlike people being sucked into the Dragon's maw), and Koenig ultimately prevails in his struggle to destroy 'the eye of the space octopus'. Indeed, these appear to have been the seeds from which Christopher Penfold grew his science fiction-horror classic, 'Dragon's Domain'.

Although 'Planet of the Eye' was not produced, Victor Pemberton made an indelible impact on *Space: 1999*. (REW)

'ALPHA PEOPLE'

One-Hour Format Script
By Jerome Coopersmith
October/November 1973

INTRODUCTION

As detailed in the Correspondence section of this book, George Bellak wrote to Abe Mandell on October 15, 1973 informing him that, 'we have this day commissioned a script from Jerome Coopersmith for Alpha People.'

He then summarized the story, and ended his letter with the comment, 'A good story. And can be a fine show.'

Christopher Penfold has read the letter and said, 'I note that George's letter is addressed from his wonderful apartment in what we know as the *Ghostbusters* building on Central Park West. This script would have been part of the deal with Abe Mandel that there would be a slew of American writers on *Space: 1999* and that proved to be a curse that was very difficult to live with as time went by. This, of course, pre-dates email, and toll call communication between Pinewood and Los Angeles and New York across differing time zones was a real problem (NOTE: As well as very expensive). Art Wallace was the one who stayed the course longest, but in the end we had to give up on him and Johnny wrote the episode ('Matter of Life and Death') that he had originally been commissioned to write. Jerome Coopersmith was a name that I don't believe ever reached our script department in London. So whether Abe Mandell poured cold water on this storyline or not, I certainly never discussed it with George.

'I'm surprised, though, that George says he has actually commissioned a script from this guy, and surprised, too, that we hadn't discussed the storyline. It may be that George was working "remotely" and that this was something he decided to do while he was back in New York without discussing it with me. Perhaps he was responding to pressure from Gerry to get some actual scripts commissioned!'

Bellak's references to 'Alpha People' are fairly clearly a reference to the series itself, rather than the title of the script he was commissioning from Coopersmith. What the episode title would have been is unknown, but for the purposes of this article it will be referred to as 'Alpha People'.

WRITER JEROME COOPERSMITH

American writer Jerome Coopersmith authored over one hundred scripts for television movies, specials, and various series including *The Streets of San Francisco* and *Hawaii Five-O*. He also wrote numerous theatrical plays and taught screenplay and television writing as an Adjunct Professor at Hunter College and Brooklyn College from 1970 to 2009.

ALPHA PEOPLE

By Jerome Coopersmith
Summarized by George Bellak

The story concerns itself with a mission that Koenig and Helena are on in space. Their vehicle falters, fails – they zero in on a small planet they have never even charted before and manage a crippled landing.

Astonishingly, they find themselves in an earth-like atmosphere with an extremely advanced people. So advanced, in fact, that no one does any work at all. Machines are at everyone's beck and call. Thinking is done by the computers and tapes, so no one has to think. It is all done for them, and has been for untold generations.

To amuse themselves, these beings are involved in all sorts of pleasures… some involving wild machines, some only themselves.

It is all somewhat head-spinning to the Alpha people but they find themselves under a strange kind of attack, a series of attacks, subtle and overt, by these people, which imperil the possibility of their getting off this planet. And to complicate this, beings with whom they have made certain contact seem to vanish, disappear, to be replaced by others. When our people inquire, they are told that there is yet another community on the other side of the planet, much more advanced – that they here are, basically, only children. And at a certain time, people go there to truly begin their lives. But they never let Koenig see this place or fly over it – even if he could.

And now, open sabotage takes place against their MTU just as they think they have it repaired. This rises the action to a moment when Koenig is approached by certain of the beings who say they will work it out for him to go, if he takes them along. This is a curious request, but Koenig agrees.

At the last moment, the secrecy of the agreement is broken… And as hordes of beings descend upon Koenig's MTU, he learns the stunning truth. There is no other community. This is a planet upon which the beings exist for a terribly short span of time – exist in pleasure – but for, perhaps five earth years. The mythology has developed that there is 'another community'. In reality, when their time comes, the non-living are spirited away. Period. But the secret has broken loose, and, hoping to escape this inevitable fate, the population storms the air vehicle. Koenig gets away but only as the beings drop down to their own planet – there to go on with their myths and pleasures. Koenig knows this is no place for the Alpha People.

ANALYSIS

Due to this short summary being the only extant documentation of Coopersmith's script it is difficult to judge in detail.

While this could perhaps have made an interesting episode, if handled well, it doesn't quite feel that it would have fit in *Space: 1999*. Like 'A Breath of Death' it required the depiction of an alien society with a relatively large number of beings living in it, which is something the series avoided.

The opening, in which an MTU 'falters, fails' and manages 'a crippled landing' is similar to the opening of the *Space: 1999* episode, 'Missing Link', but it's unlikely to be more than mere coincidence. One might also perceive a vague connection to 'Guardian of Piri', a planet of pleasure and no work, if the Alphans had found others on that planet beyond the Servant of the Guardian.

No other specific elements of this story summary found their way into the series, but it can be noted that the general concept of a highly advanced alien race was something *Space: 1999* would deal with on a number of occasions. As was the melancholic note at the end of the summary that this is 'no place' for them, and the Alphans have yet to find a new home. (REW)

'A BREATH OF DEATH'

One-Hour Format Script
by Irving Gaynor Neiman
Fall 1973
Unfilmed

SYNOPSIS

Tensions flare on Alpha as an alien planet is sighted, perhaps offering hope of a new home. Probe One discovers a primitive civilization exists on the planet and upon landing and investigating, Catani and Paul learn the planet's name is Medli and that the people seem inherently nice.

Koenig proposes establishing a colony on Medli and leads another exploratory flight to the planet in an MTU, and soon witnesses a murder: the Medlians may not be as nice as they first appeared. The Alphans learn that Medli is a moon of planet Med and is actually an insane asylum housing aberrant citizens born without aggression. There are two peoples here: the peaceful Medlians and the warlike Meds who guard the asylum and soon arrive in a spaceship demanding the Alphans leave.

Back on Alpha, a debate rages over what to do, and the decision is made to return to the planet to retrieve a Med and a Medlian specimen for Dr Russell to examine. Upon return to Alpha, the command staff argue whether or not they should settle on the planet through use of force, while Helena determines the Medlians represent the best of the human personality and the Meds represent the worst. The decision is made to proceed with settling on Medli using a newly developed oxygen weapon to ensure their superior force. In the subsequent process of proving their technological might over the Meds, the Alphans also realize that they are merely becoming an occupying force and the new masters of the Medlians. They choose instead to return to the Moon and continue their journey.

WRITER IRVING GAYNOR NEIMAN

'A Breath of Death' was written by American Irving Gaynor Neiman, who had worked extensively in television but had no apparent background in the science fiction genre. His closest relevant experience was writing three episodes of the short-lived 1961 anthology TV series *Way Out*, which was a chilling companion to *The Twilight Zone*. Coincidentally, he also wrote the 1971 TV movie *Murder Once Removed*, which starred Barbara Bain.

REFERENCE MATERIAL

The 'Working Draft' of 'A Breath of Death' is the only copy known to be in existence.

TECHNOLOGY

Neiman appeared confused about Alpha's ships. Reference is made to them as 'MTU's', as well as 'large MTU' (from which 'a smaller module detaches from the large ship and starts a gliding descent to the surface'), as well as 'Probe One' (and generic references in the script to 'Probe Ship' and 'Probe Cockpit'). This demonstrates the evolving state of the series during the time period in which Neiman was working on the script.

Considerable use is made throughout of characters peering into 'scopes' to view visuals and data, which had been used to great effect on *Star Trek* with Mr Spock but would undoubtedly have appeared derivative if prominently featured in *Space: 1999*.

The use of 'direct injection oxygen' to enable the Alphans to function in the lower-oxygen atmosphere of the planet is unique, but never ended up appearing in the series.

CHARACTERS

Professor Bergman's name has finally been settled on, after previously being known as Prof Penmarric and before that as Prof Danilo Sabatini.

Capt Catani, who was formerly called Grayson, and would soon become Carter.

Murneau, head of Tech Section, was a central character at this stage of development.

Paul is introduced as 'Catani's assistant' and proceeds to essentially shadow Catani and do his bidding throughout the script.

Numerous characters behave in ways that are entirely contradictory to their eventual on-screen personas, including Commander Koenig, Dr Russell, and Capt Catani. One of the only characters viewers would recognize in this script is Prof Bergman, who seems to be an island of humanity amidst other harsh, irrational, and mean-spirited characters.

MOONBASE ALPHA SETS / LOCATIONS

Central Control is the name used throughout 'A Breath of Death' for what would become Main Mission.

IN-SCRIPT NOTES

Neiman made several notes within his script, indicating his uncertainty with the technological aspects of writing for *Space: 1999*. These include:

On page 2 Neiman both questions Murneau's position on the base ('head of Tech Section?'), and how Murneau would get from his elevated desk overlooking the area down to the work area below him ('in whatever swift way that is available to him… like a platform elevator?')

On page 34 Neiman inserts a note questioning the functions of the Alphan's laser guns. Koenig fires a short laser burst from across the street and drops a Med soldier. Neiman then writes, '<u>Short</u> burst doesn't dissolve… just kills nicely. Okay?' This question was directed toward George Bellak, story consultant during early development, as is the next one. It's doubtful that either of those descriptions of the function of Alpha's laser guns (that they could 'dissolve' or 'just kill nicely') would have been 'okay' with Bellak. Christopher Penfold adds, 'We really tried to downplay the military in the series. We had lots of discussions before we got underway about guns. Mine and George's whole approach was that Moonbase Alpha was a non-military operation, a research establishment. We were about science rather than space militarism. My own feeling was that in any given situation of escalating conflict the moment a gun is produced is the moment the real drama evaporates. I know this is not a commonly held belief, but I felt that, with good writing, most conflict situations are more dramatic the more equally the protagonists are matched. The moment when one party produces a gun, is the moment when the balance – and the drama – are gone. It was, and is, my view that the easy resort to guns is, more often than not, indicative of lazy writing. Of course, there was not universal acceptance of my view and we did end up with the stun gun. And although we did try to hold onto the notion that Alpha was a research rather than a military establishment, compromises were made and the kind of unisex uniform that Rudi Gernreich designed – and which has proved so enduringly popular with fans of the show – was one very positive result.'

On page 47, in reference to Koenig's dialogue about the methane in the planet's atmosphere combining with oxygen to form an orgon layer that would then hold a mass of oxygen below it, Neiman wrote: 'NOTE: GEORGE, I didn't get your scientist-friend's mumbo-jumbo straight. Will you fix the language above?') This is interesting as it is a direct reference to George Bellak. Bellak had begun working with Christopher Penfold in the studio offices at Elstree Studios in late August 1973. The version of the Writers Guide issued on 3 September 1973 included references to MTU's but didn't include a name for Bergman. Bellak continued working on the series throughout September, then left in October. Bellak continued working on the development of stories at least until October 15 (see the 'Alpha People' section of this book), and likely until sometime around the end of October (as per the Gerry Anderson letter of 15 November 1973 discussing the resolution of the 'Bellak situation'). Based on that timeline, it would appear that 'A Breath of Death' was likely developed in the month of September and then subsequently abandoned.

ANALYSIS

References in the script (to Bergman, Catani, MTU's, etc...) tell us that 'A Breath of Death' was developed after 'Siren Planet' but judging from its content it was always destined to remain unproduced.

From its opening sequence of Alphans harshly fighting amongst each other, 'A Breath of Death' strikes an ongoing series of discordant notes to the series *Space: 1999* was becoming.

The script's use of narration by Bergman is notable as this technique was only employed twice in the as-aired series (in Christopher Penfold's 'Dragon's Domain' and Johnny Byrne's 'The Testament of Arkadia'), and in neither instance was Bergman the narrator. He was originally intended by Bellak to be the narrator in 'The Void Ahead' and here, which is perhaps the only stand out element in 'A Breath of Death' that one wishes had ended up on screen.

Neiman does delve into some noble questions of morality, such as whether or not the Alphan situation on the moon is sustainable even in the short term, and the degree to which they would consider sacrificing their humanity and forcing themselves on to an inhabited planet. This is in keeping with some of the early concepts in which the Alphans themselves were considered to be invaders in space, and potential titles under consideration for the series included *The Intruders* and *Space Intruders*. Notably, those moral issues are confronted later in the series in Christopher Penfold's 'War Games'. But in Neiman's script the characters themselves don't agree on the precariousness of life on Alpha, with Bergman seeming comfortable in their ability to survive, while Helena and Koenig are stressed to their personal breaking points. This dichotomy undermines both the drama of the story and the integrity of the characters.

Another appealing element of the script concerns the fact that the Medlians are judged 'mutants', 'aberrant', and 'insane' and have been sent to live on this moon, which is a large-scale insane asylum. Their mutation? Being born without aggression and love of war. A wonderfully pacifistic concept that would indeed have been very much at home in *Space: 1999*.

The Medlian characters limited vocabulary and slow speech patterns would likely have seemed tediously slow on-screen. (A similar species of plodding aliens called Pakleds later appeared in *Star Trek: The Next Generation*'s 'Samaritan Snare'.) The presentation of their village would also have been difficult, requiring the construction of multiple buildings – indeed, most of a village, a factory, a barracks, and a landing pad (with an alien rocket ship, as well as the Alphan's oxygen bomb missile) – flanked on at least two sides by hills that the Alphans would need to climb. It is difficult to imagine how that could have been achieved either within studio soundstages, or on location, within the series budget.

As it stands, the script's flaws run deeply through the motivation of several key characters (Koenig, Helena, and Catani), and the central plot point that the Alphans are literally behaving as an antagonistic invading force, driven by their own conflicted and debatable motivations. They are not redeemed by Koenig's half-hearted question on the final page, 'We always have intended only good, haven't we…?' No! In this script they clearly haven't, and their morality has been highly questionable, particularly Koenig's as Commander and Helena's as a doctor whose prime motivation should be the preservation of life. All life, not just their own.

Could the script have been salvaged? Probably. There are some noble concepts that could have made a worthwhile episode. The Alphans would need to have been re-cast from their role as aggressive invaders to one where they would have been saviors assisting in freeing the Medlians from their Med overlords and convincing them that they are not mutants or insane due to the accident of birth which created them as peaceful beings. Koenig and Helena's roles would have needed a major re-write. The Medlian village could have been re-imagined in a way that would have been easier to convey on screen. And the Medlians themselves would need to be changed from slow, seemingly dull-witted beings in order to resonate on screen and not adversely affect the episode's pacing.

Ultimately its worst sin is that 'A Breath of Death' is a ponderous, frustrating slog of a script, but that is due to the fixable flaws outlined above. It required re-imagining from a different perspective.

It is perhaps most surprising that it got as far along in the development process as it did, while going down the proverbial wrong road. Neiman would have had to make an initial story pitch, which would have then been accepted, resulting in his being commissioned to do a First Draft script. The existing copy is labeled Working Draft (most likely a Second Draft under revision), and includes numerous hand-written edits on virtually every page, and – it should be pointed out again – the note written directly to George Bellak referencing a discussion Bellak had arranged between his 'scientist friend' and Neiman in order to work on technical details in the story. It seems a strange waste of time to devote so much energy to working on a script that – after so much work – remained so clearly unsuited to the series. But as such it is a piece of our puzzle; part of the 'Lost Universe of *Space: 1999*'. With a little imagination one can envision what might have been. (REW)

WRITERS & ACTORS

By Robert E Wood

SCIENCE FICTION WRITERS

As part of the overall effort to tailor *Space: 1999* to appeal to the American market, significant effort was made to attach American writers to the series, both to write scripts and to fill the role of script editor. As with several other sections of this book, the extensive collection of paperwork related to the search for writers and actors has come from the collection of Martin Landau.

The first piece of correspondence on the subject of writers is dated January 3, 1973, when Abe Mandell wrote to Gerry Anderson, 'As per our conversation while you were in New York I am enclosing attached resume from D C Fontana, for your information and guidance.'

Accompanying her credits and personal references (which included Gene Roddenberry, Samuel A Peeples, Harlan Ellison, and Douglas Trumbull, among others), Fontana wrote a fulsome cover letter dated December 29, 1972, in which she outlined her history as a science fiction writer. Excerpts from her letter include, 'Between 1966 and 1968, I wrote eight scripts and two stories for *Star Trek*, a series with which I was associated since its inception. I also served as script consultant a season and a half (November 1966 to January 1968) …

'"Script consultant" is a euphemism for story editor. In my case, the position involved reading all assigned scripts as they came in, giving written comments on them, rewriting and polishing of scripts as needed, meeting with writers at all stages of script progression, writing my own originals, and reading and evaluating all unsolicited material submitted through agents. All my duties were related to the writers, the scripts, and their progression from story outline to shooting script.'

Fontana then detailed her involvement with the TV series *The Sixth Sense* (1972), two scripts she had written in the past year for *Ghost Story* (aired in 1972 as *Circle of Fear*), a series she was developing at the time called *The Winds of Space*, 'based on a concept by Douglas Trumbull and Michael Gruskoff, respectively the director and producer of the feature, *Silent Running*.' She also detailed being involved 'in the development of a science fiction format for a half hour animated cartoon series for youngsters,' adding, 'I am not under exclusive contract and I feel free to accept any other offers that interest me.'

She went on to relate her personal association with Gene Roddenberry and the recent assistance she provided him for his science fiction genre projects *Genesis II*, *Questor*, and *Spectre*.

Fontana then brought the letter back toward the topic at hand, adding – with regard to the recent Roddenberry projects, 'none of these are 'space adventure' science fiction projects, while all my scripts, with the exception of the *Ghost Story* pieces, have been in that area of the field.

'Personally, I am a devotee of science fiction in all its forms, from horror to fantasy to "hard" SF. I feel it is one of the most exciting types of literature published, and it allows a broad freedom of theme and thought within the context of an interesting, entertaining story. In the past ten years, filmmakers have begun to realize the genre's potential, and we are finally seeing some intelligent science fiction on our motion picture screens. With the exception of *Star Trek*, *Outer Limits*, and now *UFO*, TV has not done as well, largely because people conversant with science fiction have not been hired to write and produce the projects. This year, I know most of the proposed SF projects developed and written for TV were done by experienced and knowledgeable writers in the field. I'm looking forward to a surge of more quality science fiction on television, and I deeply hope to contribute to it.'

The date of Fontana's letter and her reference to *UFO* make it clear she was approaching the series when it was a continuation of that earlier Anderson production, while her emphasis on her experience with 'space adventure' science fiction projects tells us she knew that this new series was going to be a space adventure as opposed to being set on Earth, as *UFO* had been.

Gene Roddenberry recalled that an offer was made for him to take the job as story editor for *Space: 1999*, but said, 'I didn't even consider it. I was *not* a producer-for-hire; I was a creator/producer with numerous properties of my own in development, and, at that particular time, I was especially busy.'[21] Nevertheless, Roddenberry was helpful in ITC's search for an American story editor and writers.

On April 4, 1973, Arnold Friedman – Director of Creative Services at ITC – wrote to Abe Mandell on the subject of 'Science Fiction Writers'. He said, 'Today I spoke with Art Wallace. He wrote some *Star Trek* scripts, and is an established TV writer, generally. He has worked with Gene Roddenberry on other properties ... I will have more names for you tomorrow.'

The following day, April 5, 1973, Friedman again wrote to Mandell

---

[21] Cushman, Marc. *These Are the Voyages: Gene Roddenberry and Star Trek in the 1970s - Vol 2 (1975-1977)* February 2021, 199.

with 'a partial list of writers of *Star Trek*':

Gene L Coon	Art Wallace
Don M Mankiewicz	Jerome Bixby
Robert Hamner	Theodore Sturgeon
Steven W Carabatsos	S Bar-David
D C Fontana	George Clayton Johnson
Harlan Ellison	Paul Schneider
David Gerrold	John D F Black
Lee Cronin	Adrian Spies
Norman Spinrad	Barry Trivers

On June 25, 1973, Leonard S Kramer of the William Morris Agency wrote to Abe Mandell, 'Attached are credits on George Lefferts, Art Wallace and George Bellak, each of whom we represent and each of whom might fit the bill and be interested.'

Leonard S Kramer again wrote Abe Mandell on June 27, 1973, 'Re: Head Writer – Science Fiction Show', offering 'another prospect – Joe Stefano.'

And on July 2, 1973, Robert H Goodman of the William Morris Agency wrote to Abe Mandell, with 'credits on Richard Landau, who could well fit the needs of your series. Look forward to hearing from you on all of our submissions.'

In each case extensive biographical and credits lists were forwarded to Abe Mandell.

The next piece of correspondence related to the search for writers is dated July 13, 1973, from Arnold Friedman to Gene Roddenberry:

'This is a note to thank you for your help and courtesy on the phone today. I spoke with Art Wallace, who wants to think about it. He'll call me early next week. I remember liking Art when we first spoke a few months ago. Now that your reaction to his name is so enthusiastic – and especially since you have told me of his talents in the areas of production – I think it would be an excellent idea for him to meet with Abe Mandell. It doesn't sound as though Art is ready for a fast move to London just now – but we'll see how he feels next week, when I hope to get them together.

'I mentioned that you had recommended him, and in turn he had lovely things to say about you – so I began to feel as though I had stumbled into a meeting of The Outer Space Mutual Admiration Society. I hope that when our new series goes into production we will be able to develop the same sort of camaraderie you and your unbelievable staff did during the making of *Star Trek*.

'Thanks again for your interest – and I will be anxious to hear from you about anyone else you feel would make a sensational story editor.'

Arnold Friedman then wrote to Abe Mandell on July 16, 1973, with the subject '*Space: 1999* / Story Editor', stating:

'I spoke to Gene Roddenberry and he is as friendly as reputed. He wants to think over a recommendation before he makes one – and said he'd call me this week. In the meantime, I tried out a few names from my list (see memo to you dated 4-5-73).

'Theodore Sturgeon: Roddenberry says he is a good novelist but may not adapt very well to week-to-week requirements of television writing and production.

'Art Wallace: Roddenberry is very high on this man – and said he would like to bring him to California to work for him, but Wallace won't come. However, Roddenberry said London may be his bag – Hollywood is not. Roddenberry feels that a story editor's job may be less than what Wallace would consider since, in addition to being a top writer, he is also a producer. Apparently they have worked together on some projects. Roddenberry suggests Wallace might be more valuable to us in some kind of producer post, or consultancy.

'I called Wallace and he wants to consider it before meeting with you. He will call me back 'early this week' he said. He wanted to know how eminent the assignment was and I said very. If he is interested in pursuing it further I suggest you get together with him and see what comes of it. I don't know any more about Wallace than this – but we can check him out further later.'

On July 23, 1973 an internal piece of correspondence at William Morris from Martin Dubow to Bob Goodman, copied to Leonard Kramer and Sam Weisbord, under the heading 'ITC – London – Science Fiction Series – Joe Stefano' stated, 'I noticed that Gerry and Sylvia Anderson, who will produce the above will be out here on July 29th. There has not been any specific reaction to Joe Stefano. In order to get the above for Joe – would suggest we set up a meeting with Joe Stefano and the Andersons when they are in town. Please advise if the above can be accomplished before they arrive in town here.'

That same day, July 23, 1973, internal correspondence at William Morris from Mike Peretzian to Robert Goodman noted, 'Please advise Abe Mandell that I have cleared Joe Stefano to meet with him and the Andersons on Monday afternoon at the Beverly Hills Hotel. The same for Richard Landau on Tuesday afternoon. Confirm with Mandell that he will call me Monday morning and advise the specific times for each meeting.'

William Morris wasn't the only agency submitting lists of writers for *Space: 1999*. Jay Sanford of IFA (International Famous Agency) wrote to Abe Mandell on June 22, 1973, 'Here are some more suggestions for your science fiction project in addition to Gene Coon:'

Alan Armer	Irving Elman
Richard Collins	Milt Gelman
Jerry De Bono	Lionel Siegel
Meyer Dolinsky	Robert Stamler

Information was provided on all of these writers. Another list of names put forth by IFA repeated most of those names and also included Robert Dozier.

In the end, George Bellak and Art Wallace were brought on board the series, though neither lasted long.[22] Wallace worked long-distance and wrote 'Siren Planet', which Johnny Byrne then re-wrote as 'Matter of Life and Death', on which the two share credit.[23] Bellak worked partly from his home in New York City and partly on-site in England serving as story consultant, working closely with Christopher Penfold on the Writer's Guide, and writing 'The Void Ahead', which Penfold then re-wrote as 'Turning Point' and refined into 'Breakaway'. Penfold has credited Bellak with bringing 'enormous humanity' to the series as well as insisting on 'a powerful role for a woman at the head of the show.'

SEARCH FOR A COMMANDER

By mid-July 1973 the search had expanded to find an actor to play Commander John Koenig. Various agencies submitted lists of actors for the role. Martin Landau also retained a copy of these lists in his collection, enabling us to share them here.

Accompanying the lists are several pieces of 'Inter-Office Correspondence' from the William Morris Agency. The first, on July 19, 1973, from Leonard S Kramer to a lengthy list of recipients, reads as follows:

'RE: ITC – LONDON (GRADE'S COMPANY) – SCIENCE FICTION SERIES

Relative to my June 20th note wherein this company was looking for a head writer and we submitted several people whom they are interested in, they are now looking for a lead

---

[22] 'I had such a bad experience trying to script edit Art Wallace remotely that I would not have been keen to repeat the experience. Long distance phone calls were not good news.' – Christopher Penfold

[23] 'Johnny Byrne had written a BBC *Play for Today* which had a sci-fi dimension to it and which I had greatly admired. So, when we moved into Elstree and began work on *Space: 1999* proper, he was the first writer I called in. We hit it off straight away, became firm friends and Johnny's contribution to the show needs no further embellishment from me.' – Christopher Penfold

for the series which would be a commitment for 26 films for a one-hour science fiction series similar to *Star Trek* to be produced in London. It would mean living in London for a full year.

They are looking for someone like William Shatner.

This is a co-production deal to be produced by Lew Grade's company with RAI, the Italian government television network. There would be no percentage of profits but the salary and living expenses could be very substantial.

The series will be offered for sale on a network basis in the United States but nevertheless will definitely go into syndication. It is being produced by Gerry and Sylvia Anderson who produced *UFO*, *The Protectors*, a science fiction feature for Universal entitled *Journey to the Far Side of the Sun* and 7 science fiction puppet series, among other productions.

These producers will be in New York starting Wednesday of next week and will be ready to sit down and meet with us with respect to the head writer situation and the star and make a deal as quickly as possible. They will then go to California and will be at the Beverly Hills Hotel commencing Sunday, July 29th, with Abe Mandell of ITC's New York Office, to meet with any people we have to suggest.

Bob Goodman has been channeling this in New York so he will continue to handle it from this end and make arrangements to set up the contacts with Casting. However, someone should pick this up on the California end so it can be followed through from there by contacting Abe Mandell next week when he arrives on the Coast.'

The second is dated July 20, 1973, addressed to Bob Goodman from Sandy Littman, copied to Leonard Kramer and Stan Kamen. It reads, 'Per your memo, please discuss Patrick O'Neal for the lead. If you need any help, I will be glad to call Abe Mandell, as I have a long relationship with him.'

Handwritten notes on that memo also follow up with a list of appointments for writers: '11am George Lefferts', '12am Art Wallace', and '3pm George Bellak.'

The next William Morris memo is dated July 23, 1973 from Ron Myer to Leonard Kramer and copied to Bob Goodman, stating, 'Abe Mandell called to see about setting meetings with Robert Conrad, Chris George, Larry Hagman, Doug McClure and Hugh O'Brian for the ITC science fiction series in England. I explained that these clients would not take a meeting unless he was prepared to make a firm offer for one of them subject to a meeting. He seemed rather indignant so I wanted you to be aware of our conversation.'

Here are the complete lists of actors:

CMA

Stuart Whitman
Vince Edwards
Lloyd Bridges
Robert Goulet
Robert Lansing

Robert Culp
Christopher Jones
Brian Kelly
Adam Rourke

ROBERT HUSSON

James Drury

IFA

Martin Landau
Vince Edwards
Robert Horton

Michael Landon
Roy Thinnes

GENE SCHWAM

Ross Martin
Carl Betz
Gary Conway

Martin Landau
William Shatner

WILLIAM MORRIS

Patrick O'Neal
Robert Conrad
Chris George
Larry Hagman
Doug McClure
Hugh O'Brian
Michael Tolan
Richard Mulligan
George Maharis
Dean Jones
Barry Nelson
Noel Harrison
Robert Forster

Paul Burke
George Chakiris
Bert Convy
Paul Richards
Barry Newman
Tony Roberts
John Phillip Law
Tom Hunter
Robert Lansing
Carl Betz
Allen Case
Earl Holliman
David Hedison

So, based on the William Morris memos we know that – of their clients –

Abe Mandell was interested in and expressed a desire to meet with actors Robert Conrad, Chris George, Larry Hagman, Doug McClure, and Hugh O'Brian. Whether meetings ended up taking place with any of those actors is unknown. And despite William Morris's interest in pushing Patrick O'Neal there is no evidence that suggestion was met with interest on the part of ITC.

It has long been known that Robert Culp was considered for the lead role. Gerry Anderson recalled, 'Robert Culp was interviewed. We met in Beverly Hills. I'm a great fan of his because he's a very, very competent actor and has a very great charisma. He arrived and I said, "Right, I'll tell you, what the series is about..." And he said, "Look, before you tell me what the series is about, may I say a couple of things?" So, I said, "'Certainly." He said, "First of all, I am a superb actor." And I said, "Yes, that's why we've invited you over here." He said, "Fine. But what is not generally known is that I am also an outstanding writer." So, I said, "Well that, I must confess, I didn't know." And he said, "Finally, I am an even better director." Now all of those statements may well be true. But, knowing what television production means, where you've got one picture a fortnight going through – one hour every ten days -- in my view the lead artist hasn't got the time or the physical strength to cope with leading the series and be involved with the writing and also criticize the direction.

'I felt that this would be a great danger and so, very politely, I said, "Thank you very much and goodbye." And, equally politely, he said, "Thank you very much. Goodbye." We didn't have any kind of argument. I respected his point of view. Whether he respected me, I don't know. But the interview terminated there.'[24]

Sylvia Anderson also recalled, 'We were interviewing lots of actors to play the leads when we got a call from Lew Grade saying we really needed someone that was very well known, like *Mission: Impossible* people. I wanted Robert Culp. We met him. He was quite outrageous, but he would have given the series a very interesting angle, He would not have been the stereotyped hero; he would have been scared at times, he would have made the wrong decisions. But we had to cast Barbara Bain and Martin Landau, whom I freely admit I did not want. I battled very hard and stood up to Lew Grade and said, "I don't think they're right. They were okay in *Mission: Impossible* but having seen them, I don't think we're going to get what we should get." But he said that they were very popular in *Mission: Impossible*, and that they were a good commercial bet, and that was that.'[25]

Despite Sylvia Anderson's negativity, her account makes it clear that Lew Grade made the decision to cast Landau and Bain, and his decision came while the Andersons were in the United States interviewing actors. In an

---

[24] John Fleming, *Starburst* number 8 (April 1979).
[25] Steven Turner, *Time Screen* number 18 (1992).

interview in *The Space: 1999 Documentary*, Gerry Anderson also related Lew Grade's insistence that, 'you've got to get these people.'

And thus *Space: 1999* not only cast the role of Commander John Koenig, but Doctor Helena Russell as well.

GEORGE BELLAK

By Christopher Penfold

When Gerry and Sylvia Anderson were in production at Elstree Studios with *The Protectors*, I was working on a series called *Pathfinders*. Money had been committed to it very late in the day and the schedule was so punishing that many people in the studio expected the series to fold, and I'm sure Gerry was one of them. But I had a motor caravan at the time and I parked it on the studio lot and lived in it while writing scripts through the night that were virtually taken out of my typewriter straight to the production floor. Under those circumstances the results were, to say the least, inconsistent – although there are individual episodes of which I still feel quite proud – but the important outcome as far as Gerry was concerned was that the doomsters were confounded, and the series did not fold.

It was not long afterwards that I had a call from Gerry who asked me if I would consider working with him to develop his new series of *UFO*. I spent many productive hours with Gerry and Sylvia at their house, Whiteplains, in Gerrards Cross until the day when *UFO* was transformed into *Space: 1999* and we moved back into production offices at Elstree Studios. Charged now with expanding the writing team, my first call was to Johnny Byrne whose contribution to the series was to become so crucial. Johnny and I began working together on the transformation but it was not long before a technicians' union strike caused Gerry to move the whole production from Elstree to Pinewood Studios where he came under pressure from Abe Mandell, in the interests of securing a US network sale, to 'Americanize' the writing team by hiring an experienced American script editor.

Gerry had been very appreciative of the work I had done to date and was apologetic about having to bring in an American writer to run the script department in my place. He was keen to keep me on as a member of the team and assured me that when he went to the US to interview potential candidates, he would be looking for someone with whom I could work successfully. And when he had eventually offered the job to George Bellak, Gerry phoned me to say he was sure we would get on well together.

He was quite right. Although George was a generation older than me and vastly more experienced in the TV scriptwriting trade, it was apparent from the moment he arrived in the UK that there was excellent chemistry between us. And beside a strong personal connection the basis of our good working relationship was a shared ambition for the direction the show should take.

People read and write science fiction for a variety of reasons but, for me, it has always been a genre for examining the way we live now with the benefit of foresight rather than hindsight. And that accorded strongly with the humanity with which all of George Bellak's work was endowed. Like so many others, George had arrived in the US as a child of parents fleeing the pogroms of Eastern Europe. He had grown up in very difficult circumstances in the human melting pot that was the Bronx and he poured all of that experience into the humanity of his writing. He was a brilliant observer of the quirks of human behavior; he was fiercely intelligent, quick-witted, generous and endowed with a scintillating and irreverent sense of humor and I don't think it is well appreciated just how many of those qualities George left as his legacy after what was to prove a very brief tenure as head of the writing department of Series One of *Space: 1999*.

For although Gerry was absolutely right in his hunch that George and I would get on, it became quickly apparent that the chemistry between George and Gerry was never going to be fruitful. With his background as a playwright, George's approach to series television was that each episode should work as a single play. His focus was on character and on the often-unpredictable interaction between complex human beings, and the characters he created were very far from being puppets manipulated by a puppet master's plots. George and Gerry quickly discovered that they were speaking to one another across a cultural divide and the relationship was never going to last.

But in the work George did in developing the writers' guide for the series and in writing the first drafts of what was to become the pilot script, George left his imprint on the series in ways which came to mark out *Space: 1999* as very different and distinctive space fiction. Much of the drive for ethnic diversity and gender equality in the population of Moonbase Alpha derived from George's vision of a humanity devoid of prejudice and unafraid of difference. And if there was one character in the show who most reflected those characteristics which so illuminated George Bellak himself as a human being, it was Victor Bergman. Bergman was quintessentially George's creation and in Barry Morse, Gerry and Sylvia cast an actor who was in every way so well-equipped to make the character his own.

The timeline tells us that George left the series long before it went into actual production on the studio floor and although much of the episode which became 'Breakaway' was actually my work, it was infused throughout with the lingering influence of George Bellak — as, indeed, was the whole of Series One. And, of the many things for which I came to be grateful to Gerry Anderson, the greatest of all was the accidental gift of my friendship with George Bellak which lasted until the end of his life and which will continue until the end of mine.

Christopher Penfold – December 2020

Award-winning screenwriter and novelist George Bellak's impact on *Space: 1999*, its themes, and its characters, extends far beyond his credit as screenwriter on 'Breakaway'. Of the key writers who most substantively influenced the series – including of course Christopher Penfold and Johnny Byrne – Bellak's role is fascinating in both its impact and its brevity. His active involvement ended before 'Breakaway' began filming, but in the spirit of the theme of this book, "To everything that might have been," and our focus on the genesis and evolution of the series and in glimpses of alternate possibilities had that evolution taken just slightly different turns, it's fascinating to consider what might have been had George Bellak remained with the production. We see from the series itself what stories came from the minds of Christopher Penfold and Johnny Byrne, but imagine what a second, third, or fourth George Bellak script for *Space: 1999* would have looked like, and where he might have taken the Alphan characters. (REW)

SPACE: 1999
CORRESPONDENCE

By Robert E Wood

INTRODUCTION

Martin Landau maintained an extensive collection of items related to *Space: 1999*, including a significant number of letters documenting the production of the series. I was able to acquire this collection of correspondence, which has enabled us to share it here. Additional correspondence has come from David Hirsch's collection. We are grateful to be able to reproduce the content of many of these letters in this book in their entirety thanks to generous permission granted by the estates of Martin Landau, Gerry Anderson, Sylvia Anderson, Barry Morse, and George Bellak.

Correspondence from the Landau collection written by people other than Martin Landau, the Andersons, Barry Morse, and George Bellak is quoted here in part.

The correspondence is covered here in chronological order. In most cases the authors' words will be left to speak for themselves, while I will provide sufficient establishing information to set the narrative stage. Together, this collection forms an amazing glimpse into the behind-the-scenes production of *Space: 1999*.

BEGINNINGS

The first three letters in the collection are all dated 22nd August 1973 and are from Gerry Anderson to Martin Landau and Barbara Bain (and reference Landau & Bain's company Bellaroma Productions). Two of them are formal business letters referring to 'the Heads of Agreement between Bellaroma Productions Incorporated, Martin Landau and Barbara Bain of the one part, and Independent Television Corporation of the other part, dated 10th August 1973. We wish to confirm that the period of first call shall commence on Monday, 29th October 1973 and it therefore follows that Martin Landau and Barbara Bain should be in London and available on that date. We further wish to confirm that the principal photography will commence on Monday, 26th November 1973.'

The third letter struck a more casual tone, in which Gerry referred to the 'formal letters':

group
three
productions
limited

marsham lane
gerrards cross
bucks.
SL9. 8HD.
GA/SI

Mr. Martin Landau and
    Miss Barbara Bain,
1240 Benedict Canyon Drive,
Beverly Hills,
California,
U.S.A.   22nd August 1973

Dear Martin and Barbara,

Enclosed please find our formal letters confirming dates for first call and commencement of principal photography.

I am sure that you will be pleased to hear that everything is progressing well in London, and we all look forward to your arrival.

We are making every effort to ensure that a Rolls Royce is ready for you and have a driver that we can recommend from every point of view.

I am also enclosing a photostat of a letter that was sent to Sir Lew Grade relating to a house in London that may interest you. If you wish, Sylvia and I will gladly look at it and report. Alternatively, you may prefer to pursue the matter direct.

We will shortly receive the first draft script of Episode One and I will arrange for a copy to be sent to you.

Looking forward to seeing you both soon.

With kindest regards.

Yours sincerely,

Gerry Anderson   Encs.

DIRECTORS — GERRY ANDERSON · SYLVIA ANDERSON · REG HILL
REGISTERED IN ENGLAND No. 904890 · REGISTERED OFFICE · 4 GRAYS INN SQUARE, GRAYS INN, LONDON WC1R 5AU

WELCOME TO LONDON

On his arrival in London, Gerry Anderson wrote to Martin Landau at his hotel:

**group
three
productions
limited**

**marsham lane
gerrards cross
bucks.
SL9. 8HD.**

GA/EM   7th September, 1973.

Mr. Martin Landau,
c/o A.T.V. Suite, (71),
Grosvenor House Hotel,
Park Lane,
LONDON, W.1.

Dear Martin,

Welcome to London.   It was my intention to meet you at London Airport, but I was assured by Dick Blodget that all the necessary arrangements had been made; which I must say was a help since, by the time you read this letter, I will be travelling to Cambridge to inspect a brand new miniature monitor television set with a 2" screen which I am hoping will form part of the futuristic communications equipment that people like yourself will be carrying on their person in the year 1999.

If you made the trip non-stop from L.A., you must be reading this letter feeling like death and so, rather than call you, I suggest that you call me when you have slept it off.   My home number is Gerrards Cross (49) 83357 and the Studio number is 953-1600.

Sylvia and I realize that you are here to house-hunt, fix up schools and generally attend to your personal affairs, and so there may be days when you prefer to be left alone.   Would you, however, take it that we will be delighted to hear from you day, or night, and look forward to meeting you as soon as it is convenient, and are at your disposal to offer you whatever assistance or advice you may need.

If the hotel is as efficient as I think it is you will find a bottle of Dom Perignon, which is far better than any sleeping tablet that I have yet come across.   Good health, kindest regards from Gerry and Sylvia and Reg Hill, our other partner who is looking forward to meeing you.

GERRY ANDERSON

DIRECTORS — GERRY ANDERSON · SYLVIA ANDERSON · REG HILL
REGISTERED IN ENGLAND No. 904890 · REGISTERED OFFICE · 4 GRAYS INN SQUARE, GRAYS INN, LONDON WC1R 5AU

Martin not only kept that letter from Gerry, but along with it he kept the very small – and quite delightful – gift card that accompanied the bottle of Dom Perignon in his hotel room. Here is that card:

SPACE ELIXIR

Dose: three to four glasses
before retiring.

Welcome to England

Gerry & Sylvia Anderson.

ALPHA PEOPLE

Shifting gears now to the only letter in the collection written by story consultant George Bellak. This letter is dated Oct 15, 1973 and is addressed to 'A M' (Abe Mandell), in which Bellak wrote, 'For your information, with the concordance of everyone in London and NY, we have this day commissioned a script from JEROME COOPERSMITH for Alpha People.'

Bellak went on to describe the storyline in detail (which is presented in full in the Story Outlines section of this book), and then summed it up by adding, 'A good story. And can be a fine show.'

Bellak's references to 'Alpha People' are fascinating. No evidence of the Jerome Coopersmith script is known to exist, apart from the description in this letter, but Bellak's mentions of 'Alpha People' are fairly clearly referring to the series itself, rather than the title of the script he was commissioning from Coopersmith. Regarding this, Christopher Penfold said, 'I think that "Alpha People" must have been a typical piece of George shorthand. He was never enthusiastic about the title *Space: 1999* because, like me, he felt it too derivative of *2001* and because it invited critics to see us as the very poor relations to Kubrick's masterpiece.[26] At the time we were still trying to persuade Gerry of the virtues of a number of other titles, but he wouldn't budge so I'm sure this was George's subtle way of registering his objection to the title to Abe Mandell!'

---

[26] MGM did attempt to sue over the title, but lost.

Oct. 15,1973
300 CPW NYC.

Dear A.M.

For your information, with the concordance of everyone
in London and N.Y., we have this day commissioned a script
from JEROME COOPERSMITH for Alpha People.

The story concerns itself with a mission that Koenig
and Helena are on in space. Their vehicle falters, fails--
They zero in on a small planet they have never even charted
before and manage a crippled landing.

Astonishingly, they find themselves in an earth-like
atmosphere with an extremely advanced peoples. So advanced,
in fact, that no one does any work at all. Machines are at
everyone's beck and call. Thinking is done by the computors
and tapes, so no one has to think. It is all done for them,
has been for untold generations.
To amuse themselves, these beings are involved in
all sorts of pleasures...some involving wild machines, some
only themselves.
It is all somewhat head-spinning to the Alpha people
but they find themselves under a strange kind of attack, a
series of attacks, subtle and overt, by these people, which
imperil the possibility of their getting off this planet.And
to complicate this, beings with whom they have made certain
contact seem to vanish, disappear, to be replaced by others.
When our people inquire, they are told that there is yet
another community on the other side of the planet, much more
advanced--that they here are , basically, only children. And
at a certain time, people go there to truly begin their lives.
But they never let Koenig see this place or fly over it--even
if he could.
And now, open sabotage takes place against their MTU just
as they think they have it repaired. This rises the action to
a moment when Koenig is approached by certain of the beings
who say they will work it out for him to go, if he takes them
along. This is a curious request, but Koenig agrees.
At the last moment, the secrecy of the agreement is
broken...And as hordes of beings decend upon Koeing's MTU,
he learns the stunning truth. There is no other community. This
is a planet upon which the beings exist for a terribly short
span of time--exist in pleasure--but for, perhaps five earth
years. The mythology has developed that there is "another
community". In reality, when their time comes, the non-living
are spirited away. Period. But the secret has broken loose,
and , hoping to escape this inevitable fate, the population
storms the air vehicle. Koenig gets away but only as the beings
drop down to their own planet--there to go on with their myths
and pleasures. Koenig knows this is no place for the Alpha People

A good story. And can be a fine show.
Take care...

Seorge

186

THE GEORGE BELLAK SITUATION

George Bellak's time working on *Space: 1999* was short. Sometime later in October of 1973, after writing the 'Alpha People' letter, Bellak left the series. Gerry Anderson sent a letter to Abe Mandell on 15 November 1973, which dealt with a number of subjects; among them he updated Mandell on what he referred to as 'the George Bellak situation'. Gerry wrote, 'The George Bellak situation, as I am sure you can imagine, put us on the spot, but with much burning of midnight oil I am confident that we have pulled through and if our plans work out we will have restored the script position by the end of the first week of shooting.

'Always bearing in mind that you are a long way away, I am most anxious to give you the "good news" as well as the "bad news". Bellak was the "bad news" and here's the good –

'Had we have gone through with Bellak our total commitment would have been $88,000. The settlement however is going to be somewhere around $25,000. We are utilizing the balance by taking on our permanent payroll two additional writers to work with Chris Penfold. One is an Englishman, Johnny Byrne, who recently re-wrote *Cold War In A Country Garden* for Harry Saltzman. This picture, if shot, will be the biggest science fiction extravaganza since *2001* (NOTE: The film was never made). The other writer, Edward di Lorenzo, is an American residing in England who has been recommended to us by Lee Katzin. Of course we have to try this team out, but the first indications are that it could work very well. In fairness I must tell you that the head writer will be Chris Penfold, whose efforts were largely responsible for getting us through the recent crisis.'

Gerry went on to add, 'Main Mission (the Control Room) is now nearly completed and looks sensational. To sum up therefore, we have had a pretty rough time. We are very tired but despite all it looks like we are going to achieve what we set out to achieve.'

SCRIPTS

Continuing to quote from the same Gerry Anderson letter of 15th November 1973 to Abe Mandell, Gerry discussed several scripts. Regarding the first episode, he wrote, 'Herewith the <u>final</u> shooting script of the first episode now re-titled "TURNING POINT". We still have a few ideas to incorporate but basically this is it. We have now completely visualized the first episode taking into account Special Effects, the Settings and the Optical Overlays together with the believable people that are being created and we are all quite confident that it is going to be a smash (we all includes Lee Katzin).'

Anderson then discussed 'Siren Planet', and that material is included in the 'Siren Planet' Analysis chapter of this book.

Discussing 'Black Sun' he then wrote, 'Enclosed also you will find a photostat of a First Draft entitled "THE BLACK SUN", an English script which we feel contains every element that you will require for your second presentation to the Network. I do hope you agree. We are, as a result of writing this script, going to establish the Talking Computer in Episode One although we will not feature it too heavily. "THE BLACK SUN" requires some modifications, mainly in terms of some of the production problems, but we hope to put it on the screen basically as is. Other episodes are in various stages of writing and we will keep you advised.'

LETTER TO SIR LEW GRADE

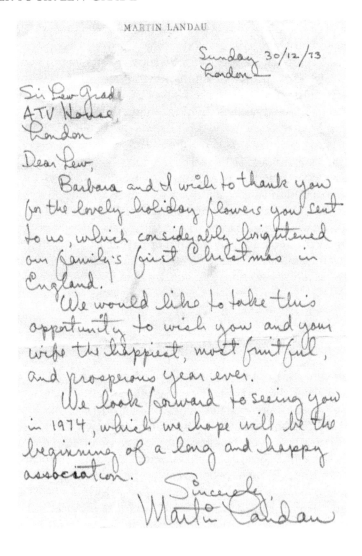

On Sunday, 30th December 1973, Martin Landau sent a letter to Sir Lew Grade in which he wrote, 'Barbara and I wish to thank you for the lovely holiday flowers you sent to us, which considerably brightened our family's first Christmas in England.

'We would like to take this opportunity to wish you and your wife the happiest, most fruitful, and prosperous year ever.

'We look forward to seeing you in 1974, which we hope will be the beginning of a long and happy association.'

FIRST PHOTO SESSION

In an ITC 'inter-office communication' dated 19th November 1973, Martin and Barbara were advised that a 'photo session has been arranged for the afternoon of the 21st November at 2pm in Pinewood's Photographic Studios with Barbara Bain and Martin Landau. David James is the photographer. It will start with a portrait session and then costumes. Make-up, hairdressing and wardrobe will be in attendance.'

This was the first photo session for Landau and Bain in their *Space: 1999* costumes.

CREATIVE INTEGRITY

Gene Schwam, of Hanson & Schwam Public Relations in Los Angeles, California, wrote to Martin and Barbara on January 18th, 1974. Part of the letter discussed *Space: 1999*. He wrote, 'I have spoken with Abe Mandell again this week, we speak regularly about your show's progress, and so I am up to date on ITC's side. Abe tells me that it took quite a lot to get the first show completed. If that makes the future ones better, then, from his point of view, it was time and money well spent.

'I am in touch with Bob Broder at IFA, Peter Bennett and Stanley Bushell and we are working on the areas of importance you expressed, particularly the need to preserve the creative integrity on the show and not to try to make up the extra time through the loss of production values and quality.

'My feeling, after speaking with Abe Mandell, is that we do stand a good chance with the networks who are eager to see the film and that there is no plan to compromise the quality of the show now or in the future.'

Schwam's reference to the American networks being 'eager to see the film' began to demonstrate the level of optimism that existed at the time.

GOING THEATRICAL & NETWORK!

In the next letter from Gene Schwam, dated February 4th, 1974, he mentions an enticing possibility, 'There have been some preliminary discussions about the possibility of going theatrical on the first *Space: 1999* but nothing definite. I think, when the film is put together, we will know more about the direction.

'When Abe returns from London, we will discuss which film or films to show the network; also whether we will have it screened in New York or invite them to London. With some additional prime time access being given back to the networks, this could be a very encouraging sign.'

SYLVIA ANDERSON   SYLVIA ANDERSON

Gene Schwam's letters are not the only ones to make reference to the US networks, or indeed to make reference to the potential for a theatrical release. In an undated letter – and the only letter from her that was in Martin Landau's collection – Sylvia Anderson wrote, 'Am planning on being in London on Monday & thought I would "drop in" at ATV & have an impromptu chat with Sir Lew – perhaps by that time I would have spoken to Dick & seen the script that Gene mentioned – I would then be able to talk about the future of *Space: 1999* (forgive the pun!) & production between now & decision time in November. – I am deliberately making my visit an informal one & not a planned appointment – What do you think?'

Sylvia signed off the letter, then wrote 'PTO' (Please Turn Over) and added in an additional note on the back side of the second page, 'Have spoken to Yvonne re: the publicity points & she will be in touch with you before going away on Sat. – I think the EXPRESS should do a follow up

Have spoken to the Yvonne re: the publicity points & she will be in touch with you before going away on Sat. – I think the EXPRESS should also a follow up article on you both nearer transmission time which is now SEPT. I believe – NETWORK! Also I think CANNES Film Festival in April ought to be well represented by SPACE 1999 don't you?

article on you both nearer transmission time which is now SEPT. I believe – NETWORK! Also I think CANNES Film Festival in April[27] ought to be well represented by *Space: 1999* don't you?'

Those are some astonishing references! First, Sylvia states that she believes the series will begin airing in September, 'NETWORK!' She is obviously referring to September of 1974, which was the original target date for *Space: 1999* to debut. Optimism was running very high, and they clearly believed the show was going to get picked up by an American network.

Sylvia's references to 'the future of *Space: 1999*' and 'decision time in November' in conjunction with her 'impromptu chat with Sir Lew' indicate that at that point they were anticipating a decision to be made about moving forward on a second season of *Space: 1999* in November 1974, two months after they anticipated the network broadcasts to begin. 'Decision time' still ended up being anticipated in November the following year, as in September 1975 Martin Landau said, 'If it works, then sometime this coming November, Sir Lew Grade will decide if he wants to make another 24 episodes. If he says he wants to shoot more, then it will be our turn to decide if we want to do the next group.'[28]

Sylvia's mention that the 'CANNES Film Festival in April ought to be well represented by *Space: 1999*' is amazing. This reference serves to establish the timeframe for Sylvia's letter, which must have been sufficiently in advance of April 1974 to be able to have adequate time to consider launching *Space: 1999* at Cannes that year, while also tying in with Gene Schwam's mention of a potential theatrical release. It establishes – from Sylvia Anderson herself – that they were not only considering a theatrical release for the first episode, but that Sylvia was thinking of debuting it at the

---

[27] The Cannes Film Festival is typically held in May, not April, and was held in May throughout the 1970s.

[28] Dick Kleiner, *Killeen Daily Herald*, 'Husband-Wife Team Star In *Space: 1999*' (September 28, 1975).

Cannes Film Festival!

If this timeline were to have transpired, *Space: 1999* would have premiered at the Cannes Film Festival in May 1974, with the potential for wider theatrical release over the summer of 1974, prior to its American network TV debut in September 1974.

Of course, none of that happened. *Space: 1999* was not picked up by an American network for the Fall 1974 season, and a theatrical release never materialized.

Conventional wisdom, based on accounts told by Gerry Anderson in later years, informs us that both he and Abe Mandell hated the first cut of 'Breakaway'. From Gerry Anderson's biography: 'The New York office assured me that Lee Katzin was "the best pilot director in America,"' remembers Gerry. 'The schedule to shoot the first episode was ten days, but it overran and we were soon tens of thousands of pounds over budget.' Katzin finished editing his footage and screened the completed 'Breakaway' for Gerry. 'It ran for over two hours,' he remembers, 'and I thought it was awful. He went back to America, and I sent a cutting copy of the episode to Abe Mandell. Abe phoned me in a fit of depression, saying, "Oh my God it's terrible – what are we going to do?" I wrote a lot of new scenes myself, and these were filmed over three days. I'm pretty sure I directed them myself. I then totally recut the episode to 50 minutes, integrating the new footage.'[29]

However, that's not true. When Gerry said, 'I wrote a lot of new scenes myself, and these were filmed over three days,' he is referring to the scenes that were actually shot over four days and filmed on February 21-26 1974 (February 23 and 24 being the weekend, the filming took place on Thursday and Friday, February 21 and 22, and on Monday and Tuesday, February 25 and 26). As documented in this book in shooting schedule notes meticulously maintained by Martin Landau (as they affected how much he would be paid, specifically for overtime days), those four days of added scenes were directed by Lee Katzin, not Gerry Anderson. The additional scenes began shooting the same day that 'Black Sun' (also directed by Lee Katzin) was completed, February 21, with 'Black Sun' finishing in the morning (AM) hours, and the additional 'Breakaway' shoot beginning in the afternoon (PM) hours.[30] Whether or not Anderson wrote those new scenes himself is doubtful; it's more likely they were written through a collaborative effort by Christopher Penfold, Martin Landau, and perhaps others. Anderson may well have had a hand in writing them, but there is no

---

[29] Simon Archer and Marcus Hearn, *What Made Thunderbirds Go* (BBC Worldwide Limited, 2002).
[30] Additional pick-up shots were filmed for 'Breakaway' on Tuesday May 7 1974 featuring Carter in the Eagle Command Module. It is possible that Gerry Anderson directed these and conflated them in his memory with the four days of additional scenes directed by Lee Katzin in February 1974.

evidence to confirm his claim that he wrote them himself. Of course, the fact now established through Martin Landau's notes that Anderson did not direct the additional scenes shot over those four days also casts further doubt on the veracity of his claim to have singlehandedly 'totally recut the episode to 50 minutes' himself.

Lee H Katzin had a tremendous reputation as a director. Most relevant in the case of *Space: 1999*, he had previously directed eleven episodes of *Mission: Impossible* (between 1967-68) starring Martin Landau and Barbara Bain, so had an established working relationship with them. He had also directed feature films, no less than ten television movies, and nearly thirty episodes of other television series such as *The Wild Wild West* (in 1966), *Mannix* (1967), *The Mod Squad* (1968), and *McMillan & Wife* (1974). Prior to that he had been an assistant director on numerous other series including on nine episodes of *The Outer Limits* (1963-64). Put simply, Lee H Katzin knew what he was doing. He knew the demands and requirements of filming network television programs. A highly experienced director does not just randomly go wildly over-schedule. The suggestion that Katzin didn't know the difference between delivering a 50-minute episode, and a two-hour feature-length cut, is not believable considering his experience. There is also no evidence that a feature-length script was ever written as all known copies of the first episode all follow a four-act format with a pre-title and trailer.

As has been well documented, Katzin shot a lot of film for 'Breakaway'. There is no doubt, as Gerry Anderson said, that the first cut of 'Breakaway' that Katzin delivered was feature-length. Indeed, audio recordings of some of those excised scenes have subsequently been re-discovered.

But what has not been considered before, and which can now be reasonably assumed based on the content of the letters included here from Sylvia Anderson and Gene Schwam, is the likelihood that Katzin was *under instructions* to deliver a feature-length cut!

That Gerry Anderson or Abe Mandell may not have liked the feature-length cut Katzin delivered is a separate matter.

It would logically follow that due to Anderson and Mandell's unhappiness with the feature-length cut, plans for a theatrical release were abandoned. Of course, regardless of the quality of the feature-length cut, with no network sale for the fall of 1974, there would have been no reason to push forward with a theatrical release at Cannes Film Festival in May (or elsewhere in the summer) of 1974.

The point is, the perception that Katzin was somehow entirely to blame for shooting too much film, running wildly over schedule, and delivering a cut that ran *twice* as long as what he was supposed to deliver – according to Gerry Anderson's (at least partly incorrect) re-telling of events – is difficult to believe.

In light of these letters from Sylvia Anderson and Gene Schwam, it seems more likely that the feature-length cut was indeed a consideration from the time of filming, and Katzin delivered precisely what he was asked to deliver: a feature-length cut of 'Breakaway' that had the potential to go theatrical.[31]

Gene Schwam wrote to Martin and Barbara again on March 29th, 1974, and once again referenced the American networks. He wrote, 'It is almost impossible to accurately speculate what the television networks would do at this time for next season. The enclosed is certainly a positive indication to me of the tremendous enthusiasm that Abe Mandell and ATV have for you both and your project.' It is unknown what Schwam had enclosed with his letter. Shwam's reference to 'what the television networks would do at this time for next season' reflects the uncertainty at that point over whether the series would be picked up by a US network for the 1974 fall season.

In the end, it wasn't. The network that was supposed to have picked up *Space: 1999* was CBS. To give a little background, when *UFO* had premiered to strong ratings on CBS network stations in September of 1972 ITC and CBS discussed continuing the series. In October, Sylvia Anderson, Christopher Penfold, and Keith Wilson began development work on *UFO 2*, but when ratings dropped off in later 1972, ITC cancelled development. Gerry Anderson then suggested to Lew Grade and Abe Mandell that the development work not go to waste and that he could turn it into a new series. By the beginning of August 1973 CBS gave verbal agreement to broadcast the new series, tentatively titled *Space: 1999*, conditional on the casting of American stars in the lead roles. Martin Landau and Barbara Bain were then cast.

CBS aired the TV broadcast premiere of the film *Planet of the Apes* as the *CBS Friday Night Movie* on September 14, 1973, to hit ratings, and followed it up on October 26 with *Beneath the Planet of the Apes* and then *Escape from the Planet of the Apes* on November 16. On the strength of the ratings for those films, CBS ordered a *Planet of the Apes* series to premiere in the Fall 1974 season. (Coincidentally from a *Space: 1999* point of view, the *Planet of the Apes* debut episode, 'Escape from Tomorrow', was written by Art Wallace and premiered on September 13th, 1974.) It can be presumed that CBS network executives felt they had one science fiction series in *Planet of the Apes*, so they didn't need a second one in *Space: 1999* and cancelled their order, but precisely when CBS rejected *Space: 1999* is uncertain.

Martin Landau has given a different account of *Space: 1999*'s encounters with American networks. He recalled for his autobiography, 'We made

---

[31] 'I was intrigued to see the correspondence related to Sylvia's enthusiasm for the prospect of taking a feature-length cut of "Breakaway" to the Cannes Festival. I suspect that there might have been a little bit of dispute in head office about whether that was going to be a good thing or a bad thing. I suspect that Lee Katzin and Sylvia probably had one notion in mind, and Gerry another. I did my best to stay clear of the somewhat volatile politics between Gerry and Sylvia.' – Christopher Penfold

Space: 1999 for ABC and they rejected it. We had about ten finished episodes so they could see the series, not just a pilot and a hope, but we were on course to produce twenty-four for our first season and ABC said, "We'll put thirteen on." I was involved in the discussions because I was a part owner of the series, and Lew Grade and ITC said, "Wait a minute. Why should we agree to a commitment for only thirteen? Put the twenty-four on," but they'd only take thirteen. We wondered what would happen to the rest of the episodes if they were to cancel it, so we decided not to take their offer.'

ITC then decided to syndicate *Space: 1999,* and Abe Mandell began selling the series at the NATPE (National Association of Television Program Executives) Conference on January 20, 1975. On March 12, 1975, ITC published a four-page spread in *Variety* including a letter from Abe Mandell and Pierre Weis (Executive Vice President-Syndication at ITC-New York) stating that the response of the broadcasting community to *Space: 1999* was 'unprecedented' and 'completely overwhelming, even to a pair of syndication veterans with over half a century of experience between us. In the 19 working days since programming executives returned from the NATPE Conference in Atlanta, 48 stations bought *Space: 1999* – many within hours of our original announcement – with more stations signing up every day. At this rate, we fully expect to have 150 markets in our network by June.' The *Variety* spread also included an announcement that *Space: 1999* would have a 'simultaneous world-wide premiere in 101 countries in September 1975.'

PIRI

The next correspondence from the Landau collection that is relevant for inclusion in this book was dated just over five months later, on 5th September 1974. Gerry Anderson wrote to Martin and Barbara concerning the episode 'Guardian of Piri', 'I mentioned to you that we were a little disappointed with "PIRI" and of course conveyed the same sentiments to Charles Crichton.

'Reg Hill has now screened the first colour print at the laboratories and surprise, surprise, all the boys there thought that it was great – and they're pretty tough critics – so maybe I was wrong.

'We'll screen the picture for you in the near future so that you can judge for yourselves.'

Concerns over 'Guardian of Piri' were not restricted to this letter from Gerry Anderson, as will be shown later in this book in Johnny Byrne's Critical Commentary.

DEMANDS OF THE SCRIPT

On 7th November 1974 Gerry Anderson sent Martin and Barbara a letter along with the Shooting Schedule for episode eighteen, 'The Last Enemy', explaining, 'You will see that the attached Schedule is for nine days, eight "A" Unit and one "B" Unit. I thought that I would drop you this note simply to explain that this is not an endeavor to cut down the quality of the shows but is simply this way because the picture has a high special effects content and the story presents us with an opportunity of shooting with two Units simultaneously on the same day.

'All future pictures will be scheduled according to the demands of the script but I think it most unlikely that we will be lucky enough to have another one like this.'

A WINNING SHOW

On December 5th, 1974, Gene Schwam wrote to Martin and Barbara with praise for *Space: 1999* and continued hope for an American network sale. He said, 'Everybody who has seen your show appreciates the quality of your performance as well as feeling that the canvas also reflects a similar quality.

'Though ITC hasn't lost their enthusiasm for the show as a network presentation and feel that there is a good chance that intelligence at the network level will prevail and give them what they need desperately, a winning show with talented performers as their stars.'

THANK YOU

Special effects director Brian Johnson wrote Martin and Barbara on 6th January 1975, to thank them for the Christmas gift they gave to all members of the cast and crew that year: personalized, embossed address books.

CALL FROM SIR LEW...

Gerry Anderson wrote the following to Martin and Barbara on January 14, 1975:

GERRY ANDERSON

14th January, 1975.

Dear Martin and Barbara,

Further telephone call from Sir Lew...

He would like to meet you some time this week.

I have asked Ron Fry to see if he can re-jig the schedule one night inorder to get you both away a little earlier...if this is not possible Sir Lew will see you whatever time you arrive at A.T.V. House.

Could you please call him with your answer soonest.

Luv,

GERRY

A HUGE SUCCESS

The next time Gene Schwam wrote to Martin and Barbara was on January 21, 1975. His letter is filled with promise, but notably is the last letter from him in Martin Landau's collection. He wrote, 'I have some good news for you and I believe that one way or the other your *Space: 1999* show definitely will be a huge success, both in the United States and around the world.

'I have had some conversations with ATV and am laying the groundwork and developing a formula which would allow for all to be together in future business projects as well as an extension of the present relationship …

'Keep the relationship an important one, particularly with Lew Grade and associates and the pay-off will be a major one for you both.'

THE FUTURE OF SPACE

Gerry Anderson wrote Martin Landau on April 11, 1975, 'Hope you and Barbara had a good trip. Dave Lane requires you both for post-synch and since it is urgent I wondered if you would be kind enough to ring him at his home … some time over the weekend so that the necessary arrangements can be made.

'Later on in the week perhaps we can get together to discuss the future of "SPACE". Why don't you call me too.'

PUBLICITY TOUR

Filming on Year One concluded at the end of February 1975. Martin Landau and Barbara Bain stayed in London until the end of June, and then returned to Los Angeles. On July 8, 1975, they were sent a 'revised itinerary' for their US tour to promote *Space: 1999*, which was now due to premiere in syndication in September. The itinerary was as follows:

PHONERS TO 40 TOP MARKETS
(2 calls per hour for each = 16 daily x 5 days = 80 calls)
Monday, July 14 – 7:00am – 11:00am
Tuesday, July 15 – 7:00am – 11:00am
Wednesday, July 16 – 7:00am – 11:00am
Monday, July 21 – 7:00am – 11:00am
Tuesday, July 22 – 7:00am – 11:00am
Wednesday, July 23: DINAH! (5:15 call; 6:00 tape) – air 8/21-29
Saturday, July 26: Tape promo spots/Monday, July 28 'stopover'
Monday, July 28 – Friday, August 1: LA Shows, Press
Saturday, August 2: KHJ-TV Party

Monday, August 4: To San Francisco
Tuesday, August 5: Work San Francisco; to Portland
Wednesday, August 6: Work Portland; to Chicago
Thursday, August 7: Work Chicago
Friday, August 8: Work Chicago
Saturday, August 9: Rest in Chicago
Sunday, August 10: To Miami
Monday, August 11: Work Miami; to Atlanta
Tuesday, August 12: Work Atlanta; to Philadelphia
Wednesday, August 13: Work Phil.; to Boston
Thursday, August 14: Work Boston; to New York
Friday, August 15: Work New York
Saturday, August 16: Rest in New York
Sunday, August 17: Rest in New York
Monday, August 18: Work in New York
Tuesday, August 19: Press Party
Wednesday, August 20: To Los Angeles

Also in conjunction with the publicity tour, Martin and Barbara received a letter from Dolores Finlay, the Director of Publicity at KHJ-TV in Los Angeles, dated July 10, 1975, detailing various meetings beginning with, 'On Monday, July 14th, I will see you here at KHJ-TV at 11:30am and we will go directly to Mr Lionel Schaen's office, the Vice President and General Manager of the station.

'Then, I would like to have you meet Mr Walt Baker, the Program Manager, and Mr David Pina, Director of Advertising and a couple of other key executives at our station.

'Then, we will go to the Hollywood Brown Derby for a 12:30pm lunch with Morton Moss of the Herald-Examiner. As you can see by the enclosed article he wrote in April, the editors are really enthused over the *Space: 1999* series.

'Tuesday, we will have a luncheon interview with Bob Martin, TV Editor of the Long Beach Press Telegram which is a very important Sunday supplement distributed throughout Long Beach and Orange County. You will have the cover feature for Sunday, August 17th. Time will be 12 noon but the place is yet to be confirmed for the lunch.

'Friday afternoon, July 18th, Gregg Kilday, Los Angeles Times, would like to come to your home at 3:00pm and do an interview.

'As I said, these are directly tied in with the Sunday TV magazines for the week of August 17th.

'We are very excited about having the series in Los Angeles and I look forward to meeting you in person on Monday, July 14th.'

Space: 1999 premiered on KHJ-TV on Saturday August 23, 1975 and would continue to debut in various other US and worldwide markets in September 1975.

GLOWING REVIEWS

national space institute

September 5, 1975

Mr. Abe Mandell
President
Independent Television Corp.
555 Madison Avenue
New York, N.Y. 10022

Dear Mr. Mandell:

The National Space Institute welcomes Independent Television Corporation's new series SPACE: 1999.

SPACE: 1999 imaginatively captures the excitement of living in the incredible age of space.

Freeing the creative imagination -- so effectively accomplished in SPACE: 1999 -- characterizes mankind's exploration of space.

The National Space Institute is concerned with what comes next in our space program; what our Country's long range goals are; and how we can make space exploration benefit mankind.

Presented on the mass medium of television, SPACE: 1999 will stimulate the public interest in the potentials of space technology in such fields as energy, environment, natural resources and food production.

It is for this reason that we recommend viewing SPACE: 1999, for the series can only make the public more enthusiastic and concerned with the further exploration of our universe.

Sincerely,

NATIONAL SPACE INSTITUTE

Wernher von Braun
President

WvB/mem

P.O. Box 23527, L'Enfant Plaza • Washington, D.C. 20024 • Phone 202/554-2654

Gerry Anderson sent Martin and Barbara a short Western Union telegram on September 4, 1975, which said, 'Congratulations on Los Angeles Preview. Looks like we will be seeing you soon. Love Gerry'

On September 12, 1975, Abe Mandell wrote to Barbara Bain, 'It was a pleasure talking to you on the telephone last night and, as promised, I am enclosing a couple of copies of the letter just received from the National Space Institute which so glowingly endorses *Space: 1999*.

'I will in due course be sending you Photostats of all of the press which is coming in by the ton and is all absolutely glowing and marvelous.'

Of course, we know the reviews were not 'all absolutely glowing and marvelous,' but rather were a mix of positive and negative responses.

FREDDIE FREIBERGER

The next letter, dated October 10, 1975, must be framed in the context that *Space: 1999* had only premiered approximately one-month prior. Various American stations debuted the series on different dates, the earliest being August 23 in Los Angeles (KHJ-TV). Other premiere dates included September 5 in San Francisco (KRON), September 10 in Miami (WTVJ), September 13 in Phoenix (KTAR) and Washington, DC (WMAL), and September 20 in New York City (WPIX). It's also important to note that the early ratings for *Space: 1999* in most major markets was strong, and while the ratings did decline after the first twelve weeks (which would take the series through to early or mid-December) they were still respectable.

That said, on October 10, 1975 Gerry Anderson wrote to Martin and Barbara. See next page for the letter.

There is quite a bit to unpack from this letter. First, by October 10, 1975 Gerry was in the United States on the hunt for a new American story editor for *Space: 1999*. He was obviously anticipating a renewal to be forthcoming while striking a cautious note (*'should* the show be renewed'; emphasis added). October 10 was too early for the series to have been renewed, but the ratings were doing well, particularly with key 18-49 age demographics.

Gerry was also consulting Landau and Bain and seeking their approval of Fred Freiberger's credentials prior to hiring him. Gerry wanted to 'secure his services' immediately.

Anderson also asserted that there was 'no question' he would produce the second series. Of course, Freiberger ended up in that position.

Space: 1999 was publicly renewed in a press release by ITC on December 15, 1975, which stated 'that due to the extraordinary success of *Space: 1999* in the United States and the rest of the world, we have decided to make another series of twenty-four one-hour episodes. This production will commence at Pinewood Studios in the middle of January 1976.' Behind-the-scenes, the renewal notice had come much earlier than that …

GERRY ANDERSON productions ltd.

pinewood studios · iver heath bucks.
SLO.ONH. telephone iver 651700

telex no. 847505
cables. takeone iver

October 10, 1975

Dear Barbara and Martin,

Herewith is the rundown on Freddie Freiberger. You will see that his past credits are excellent and I am not in the least put off by his three and a half years with Hanna Barbera, for I know that Joe Barbera wants to break into the live action field, and it is my view that he chose the best man to help.

Perhaps you will be kind enough to check with the people listed on Tuesday of next week (after the holiday), and call me in New York at The Regency Hotel, for I think we have found our man and would like to secure his services before leaving the country, probably Wednesday night.

I would also like to confirm Space 1999 is my top priority and that should the show be renewed, there is no question about my producing it... I will.

Will be in touch over the weekend.

Love,

Gerry

DIRECTORS — GERRY ANDERSON · TERENCE C CONNORS
REGISTERED IN ENGLAND No. 1190027 · REGISTERED OFFICE · 4 GRAYS INN SQUARE, GRAYS INN, LONDON WC1 5AU

I WANT TO WISH YOU WELL

As extensively detailed in my book *Destination: Moonbase Alpha – The Unofficial and Unauthorised Guide to Space: 1999*, Barry Morse maintained personal diaries throughout his time working on *Space: 1999* and noted on December 4, 1975, 'Lesley De Pettitt makes offer re: B.M. *Space: 1999* to Michael Whitehall. Derisory. Equivalent of 33% plus <u>CUT</u> – AND No Transport!' (Lesley De Pettitt was the casting director for Year Two and Michael Whitehall was Barry's agent.)

Clearly the series had been officially renewed (although not publicly announced) sometime prior to December 4, when the 'derisory' offer was made to Morse, cutting his pay by '33% plus' and removing the transportation to and from Pinewood Studios which he had been provided during Year One.

Morse attempted to negotiate through his agent, as well as by attempting to speak with Gerry Anderson directly, for the next thirteen days to no avail. Lesley De Pettitt refused to improve the offer, and Gerry Anderson failed to return Barry Morse's phone calls. On December 17, Morse instructed Michael Whitehall to call Gerry Anderson to accept the original offer, only to be informed as Morse noted in his diary, 'Other plans made.' The actor added, '<u>Space: 1999</u> all over!'

Martin Landau and Barbara Bain had returned to the United States from June 1975 through December 1975, and then returned to London in January 1976. On January 20, 1976, Barry Morse wrote to them, 'My dear Barbara and Martin – It was so good to talk to you on Sunday and most kind of you to think about my headaches when you've only just touched down.

'If it turns out that I'm not to be with you in *Space*, I want to wish you well with it all.

'If I do stop being an Alphan (and become an Omegan?) one of the things I shall most keenly and genuinely miss will be the joy of working with two such warm chums and good pros.

'One way or another I shall hope to see you 'ere long.'

Morse was clearly holding out hope that he might yet return to the series when he wrote, '*If* I do stop being an Alphan' (emphasis added), but the decision had been made, and filming began on 'The Metamorph' on January 26, 1976 without his character, Professor Victor Bergman.

20
—
1
—
'76

FLAT THREE
41 PALL MALL
LONDON SW1Y 5JG

01-930 0592

My dear Barbara and Martin –
It was so good to talk to you
on Sunday and most kind of
you to think about my
headaches when you've only
just touched down.

If it turns out that
I'm not to be with you
in Space, I want to
wish you well with it all –

If I do stop being an Alphan (and become an Omegan?) one of the things I shall most keenly and genuinely miss will be the joys of working with two such warm chums and good pros.

One way or another I shall hope to see you ere long.

Love to you both –

MAYA TRANSITION SEQUENCES

While 'The Metamorph' had entered production on January 26, 1976, it wasn't until February 3 that an internal production memo detailed the following about how her transformations would be achieved. The memo read:

MAYA TRANSITION SEQUENCES

1)   ZOOM IN to M.C.U. MAYA's face – make Zoom as fast as possible.
2)   Special effects to ZOOM IN to MAYA's eyes – copying exact angle and speed of Zoom as Studio.

3)   Cut or Mix two Zooms together.

Studio – No Contact Lenses
Special Effects – Contact Lenses

Final Effect – The feeling that MAYA's eyes have changed just before the point of transition.

Note: If all the above works and the eyes are found to be attractive, then further tests can be shot to establish whether additional use of the Contact Lenses should be made or not.

A TOKEN APPEARANCE

Gerry Anderson wrote to Martin and Barbara on March 23, 1976, 'You have asked that you should have a token appearance in the episode scheduled to be shot during your vacation.

'We really need to talk about this and I suggest that you come over to the office one evening after shooting so that we can fix a date and make the necessary arrangements.'

The episode in question is 'The Beta Cloud', which filmed from July 20 – August 6, 1976. Landau and Bain did end up appearing in the episode.

ATV PROMOTIONAL FILM

An apparent lack of UK media coverage in the summer of 1976 led Gerry Anderson to write Dennis Davidson of Davidson Dalling Associates Ltd in London. Anderson sent a copy of Davidson's response to Martin Landau and Barbara Bain on June 21, 1976 with a short note stating, 'Following our recent discussion I have taken action which has resulted in the receipt of the copy letter attached hereto. It looks as if we have started the ball rolling.'

Davidson's letter to Anderson was dated June 18, 1976 and read, 'Concerning our lack of involvement with getting *Space: 1999* Year Two UK media breaks.

'Unfortunately, our brief from ITC precludes our working with the British press as this is solely the responsibility of the ATV Network press office.

'In fact, we have been pushing lots of material through to the European, Australian and Middle/Far East countries as well as supplying vast amounts to ITC New York for dissemination there. As you know, Pam has been quite active in bringing overseas journalists to the Studio, but we really cannot bring UK journalists down unless there is a change in our instructions.

'We have, however, taken the point up very strongly with David Withers and as he agrees completely he is trying to arrange an early meeting with ATV Network to find a solution to the present embargo on our work.

'I hope that this clears up the matter as far as you, Barbara and Martin are concerned.'

This effort successfully kicked ATV Network into action to promote the series. On July 27, 1976 Mike Jackson of ATV's Promotion Department wrote a letter to Gerry saying, 'I should now like to outline our plans for a short promotional film on *Space: 1999*.

'On the morning of Thursday, 5th August, we intend to shoot sequences of Brian Johnson talking about some of the special effects models and techniques as used in the show. Location – Bray Studios.

'In the afternoon, we would like to film short pieces to camera from yourself, Fred Freiberger, Martin Landau, Barbara Bain, and Catherine Schell.

'The form of our film will be a voice-over linking people involved in the series talking to camera about various aspects of the show.

'We would like to talk to you about the whole business of science fiction on television … its scope, development and history… and, in particular, how the subject will evolve on to a new high plane with the new series of *Space: 1999*. That is, now the superbly accurate special effects, and logically futurized technology format will combine with strong story material concerning interaction with life forms from other galaxies.

'We should like Fred Freiberger to talk about some of the new elements in the new series of *Space: 1999*. In particular, the areas of story development and new characters featured in the series.

'We would like to talk to Martin Landau about taking part in a science fiction drama. How does it compare to acting in contemporary or historical settings? How seriously does he take the role? Can he identify with the problems generated in the *Space: 1999* stories?

'To Barbara Bain, we would like to talk about her relationship to Martin in both real life and the series. What is it like to be the first featured lady of space? What will we see her doing in the new series?

'We would also like to talk to Catherine Schell about her role in the new series. We should like her to tell us about her character, and what happens to her in the show.

'We intend shooting in a free corner of one of the stages, preferably the stage that is not in use for *Space: 1999* shooting in the afternoon of 5th August 1976.'

Jackson went on to further detail various arrangements for the shooting.

Then, on July 29, 1976, Frank (F Sherwin) Green sent an inter-office memorandum regarding the 'ATV Special Promotional Film' to shoot on August 5th, stating in part, 'It so happens that the chosen shooting date for this promotional film coincides with the commencement of our double-up episodes and life will be difficult enough for our survival, without added problems. Therefore it must be explained to Mike Jackson that we shall obviously give him the fullest cooperation, but his work will have to be shot "off the cuff" – especially with the artists' interviews.

'I mention this in view of the fact that Mike is asking to shoot on a stage that is not in use, which would obviously affect our building programme and require an additional studio floor shooting crew to arrange and light whatever is required. This problem can be sorted out at our meeting, but this is an advance warning.'

(NOTE: This material was eventually shot during the live filming of 'A Matter of Balance' and the SFX shooting for 'The AB Chrysalis'.)

A SERIES WHICH WILL LONG BE REMEMBERED

On Tuesday October 19, 1976, the day after filming had begun on episode twenty of Year Two, 'The Seance Spectre', Gerry Anderson wrote the following:

TO ALL MEMBERS OF THE SPACE: 1999 UNIT

ITC have decided not to proceed with a third season of *Space: 1999* for the time being. It would appear that 48 pictures is a viable number for continued syndication, taking into account the general state of this country's economy and the high interest rates that at present exist.

I feel that it is only fair to transmit this information to you immediately so that you can all plan your futures accordingly. It is of course in all our interests to ensure that the remaining pictures are completed to the highest possible standard and I know that you will all continue to give of your best.

Whilst ITC's decision is a disappointment, the enthusiasm and expertise of all concerned has produced a series which will long be remembered. Work is already in hand on other projects and it is my hope that our excellent team will be working together again in the not too distant future.

Fred Freiberger received the news one hour before taking off on a pre-arranged visit to Los Angeles and was most anxious that he should join with me in this message to you; he will be back at the helm next Monday.

Tuesday 19th October 1976.

TO ALL MEMBERS OF THE "SPACE 1999" UNIT

I.T.C. have decided not to proceed with a third season of "SPACE 1999" for the time being. It would appear that 48 pictures is a viable number for continued syndication, taking into account the general state of this country's economy and the high interest rates that at present exist.

I feel that it is only fair to transmit this information to you immediately so that you can all plan your futures accordingly. It is of course in all our interests to ensure that the remaining pictures are completed to the highest possible standard and I know that you will all continue to give of your best.

Whilst I.T.C.'s decision is a disappointment, the enthusiasm and expertise of all concerned has produced a series which will long be remembered. Work is already in hand on other projects and it is my hope that our excellent team will be working together again in the not too distant future.

Fred Freiberger received the news one hour before taking off on a pre-arranged visit to Los Angeles and was most anxious that he should join with me in this message to you; he will be back at the helm next Monday.

Sincerely,

GERRY ANDERSON
Executive Producer.

WHAT I HAD HOPED THE SECOND SERIES WAS TO BE

Martin Landau retained a rough draft copy of a letter he wrote to Gerry on November 12, 1976, in which he said, 'Gerry – Received this article in the mail today from a fan from Los Altos, Calif. – who said in his accompanying letter that it "documents my (his) feelings about the show quite clearly." –

'It is very much in keeping with what I said in your office earlier this week – as to what I had anticipated the second series was to be.

'No! Michael Muyell is not a penname of mine – nor is he a relative or friend – Interesting! Just wanted you to see it.'

Unfortunately, while Landau kept his rough copy of the letter he wrote to Anderson, he didn't keep a copy of the accompanying article that had been forwarded by Michael Muyell, the fan in California. However, some details are clear, or quite clearly implied. First, the article in question was written about Year Two, which had premiered in the US in September. It could not have been written too close to the date of Landau's letter in order to account for postal transit time for the fan's letter from California to reach Landau in England. It would reflect a negative perception of the series, as implied by the fan's comment and by Landau's own comments. And, as the fan was from Los Altos, California, the article could have come from a California-based publication rather than a national publication.

With those criteria – and particularly that timeline – in mind, one article seems to be a match: a critical review of 'The Metamorph' published in *Daily Variety* (a publication Landau would naturally have been concerned about) on September 27, 1976, which read in part, 'One of the things to be said in favor of maligned primetime network television is that if it had ITC's syndicated *Space: 1999* to kick around there is no way this plastic invader from outer nonsense would have lasted the first year, let alone gone into annum two.

'That, if nothing else, would have rescued those interplanetary prisoners, Martin Landau and Barbara Bain, and returned them to the world of real acting …

'All basic space ingredients are present as the new season goes into fitful orbit. There is the good planet and the bad planet; a forest of test tubes; canyons of computers; an overkill of push-buttons; papier mâché performances; listless direction, and a sterile world polluted with space platitudes and clichés.

'The only redeeming feature about this over-peopled and overdrawn epic is that it is frequently interrupted for long commercials and is forced to go into a week's remission at the end of an hour.

'*Space: 1999*, in renewal, is only a continuing embarrassment for Landau and Bain …

'John Byrne's script is a melange of interplanetary space junk hooked up to a larger than life pinball machine gone berserk. Fred Freiberger, late of *Star Trek*, is on board this year as the new producer and story editor, which sure gives him a lot to answer for. Gerry Anderson still is around as executive producer ...

'Britain's ITC boasts that the now $300,000 an episode show spins out for a claimed record series expenditure of $7,200,000 – making impossible to resist a Churchillian paraphrase that seldom has so much been spent on so little.'

A harsh review, to be sure. But it is very easy to imagine Martin Landau in Gerry Anderson's office expressing his well-documented displeasure with the direction Year Two ended up taking, and his concerns that he and Barbara should get back 'to the world of real acting', and that '*Space: 1999*, in renewal [was] only a continued embarrassment' for them.

SPACE: 1999 COMPETITION

Martin and Barbara received a letter (c/o Pam Godfrey at Dennis Davidson Associates, London) dated February 8, 1977 from Mike Smith at London Weekend Television concerning the program *Saturday Scene*, which included, 'Many thanks for your continued interest in our *Space: 1999* competition. As I told Pam, and Gerry Anderson when he phoned me, the response, to put it politely, has been ridiculous!

'To date we have had over 11,000 entries, and to be honest to say that we have picked the best 24 in each category would be stretching our work force here in the office to the limit! So we have selected the best entries out of the first 2,000 that arrived in the post and have had to throw the others away, as we could hardly move in the office!

'I would appreciate it if you would ring me as soon as possible ... with the name of a winner for the medical bag and another winner for the laser gun ...

'We really enjoyed having you here for the day and the reaction certainly warranted the time you spent with us on that Friday afternoon. The ratings were excellent.'

Also, on February 9, 1977, Pam Godfrey wrote to Barbara and Martin, 'I enclose the competition entries (final selection!) for you to choose the most appropriate.

'Many thanks for your cooperation with this programme. Mike Smith would like you to make a return appearance before you finally leave for America, perhaps you could let me know what you feel about this.'

TO EVERYTHING THAT WAS

Some recollections of my episodes of *Space: 1999*.

By Christopher Penfold

The Scripts

In putting together the amazing material they have researched for this book, Robert and David asked me to comment on the running of the script department as Story Consultant and on the scripts for which I was wholly or in part responsible as writer. Bearing in mind that I am now recalling events which took place nearly fifty years ago and after what has been a varied and very busy life as editor and writer of TV and film, the recollections that I have been able to produce here are subject to the vagaries both of memory loss and of memory regained. What follows are some quite random thoughts that have come to the surface as David and Robert have taken me down that rocky road of memory.

The script department was in the main house at Pinewood and the pressures we were under meant that visits to L&M stages and the production departments were all too infrequent — a lasting regret.

Space: 1999 was produced long before the days of the photocopier and the scripts were typed and Gestetnered[32] by a marvelous elderly couple called Steve and Elly Sice. They lived in the East End and had a tiny office on the first floor of premises in Percy Street, Fitzrovia on the North side of Oxford Street. They were an incredible resource.

I would either take personally, or send in a car, a script that was a nearly indecipherable bundle of pages of typescript, some overwritten in barely legible handwriting (Johnny's was notorious!), others cut and stapled together with arrows indicating intended insertion points, bits stuck on with Sellotape here and there. I would hand this shameful bundle to Elly Sice sometime during the day and often on my way back from Pinewood in the evening. She would never flinch at the chaos, never complain, but flawlessly type it all up either late into the evening or early the following morning and her husband, Steve, would then crank up the old Gestetner and churn out the necessary fifty or so copies. I can still smell the toxic fluid Steve used to repair the skins where they had been corrected by Elly. Together they would

---

[32] *Gestetnering* is a verb created to signify the use of a duplicating machine patented in 1879 by its inventor David Gestetner (1854-1939).

then hole-punch the pages, print out the front cover and bind them all together. Next day, miraculously, this pristine bundle would arrive at the production office in Pinewood by car.

Steve and Elly Sice were unsung heroes of the production of pretty much all the film series that were made from Elstree or Pinewood at that time. I only hope that the coming of the word processor and the photocopier enabled them to take a hard-earned and long-overdue retirement!

'Black Sun'

One memory has long been etched in my cerebral hardware -- because it was a major challenge at the time, and I was so relieved to have successfully dealt with it. David Weir was a very interesting writer, and he had a quirky imagination which played well with his undoubted erudition. He was very much my choice and we spent many enjoyable hours at his house overlooking Hampstead Heath developing the story that was to become 'Black Sun'. I liked David very much and I think we were complementary in our aspiration for the episode and for the series as a whole. But he was also quite a wayward writer for whom the exigencies of series production were of secondary interest to his determination to write a good story. Lee Katzin had so massively overrun, both time and budget, on Episode One that resources for his second episode were severely constrained. As pre-production was just days away, we had a script that was way too long and too demanding of production resources and I remember Gerry calling me over to his office on a Friday afternoon to tell me as much -- and to tell me what we could and could not achieve. We spent the afternoon with Gerry doing what he often did so well which was to play the 'What if' game. And while the discussion went on, the bones of a revised and cut-down version of the story began to take shape in my mind.

I left the meeting late afternoon and drove back into central London where I lived and I remember so clearly watching the stream of traffic going in the opposite direction and thinking, 'They are all done for the day and are on their way home for the weekend and I am just about to get down to work.' I retired to my writing shed at the bottom of my garden, stuck my feet into a sleeping bag to keep them warm and went to work. The task was well beyond cutting and pasting, so I rolled a blank sheet of paper into the typewriter and began at the beginning. I had rehearsed the conversation between Koenig and Bergman and the voice of the female mystery being as they endured the big freeze as I was driving back along Western Avenue and it went down on paper like a dream.

By Monday morning, I had a completed draft of the new script and, still full of black coffee, I drove back to Pinewood and dumped it on Gerry's desk. I waited while he read it and, about thirty minutes later, he looked up, breathed a sigh of relief and blessed me with the renowned Gerry Anderson beatific smile. I know it wasn't the script that David Weir had wanted but I like to think that his inspiration is all over it and, to this day, I am privately proud of what I had achieved. With the possible exceptions of 'Dragon's Domain', 'Guardian of Piri', and 'War Games', I still think of 'Black Sun' as one of my best achievements on the series.

I often went home with Martin and Barbara after the day's shooting and they may well have had input into the re-writes on 'Black Sun', possibly also with notes from Lee Katzin. But it would have been me that eventually put pen to paper for the Sice-produced blue/green/pink/yellow pages of amendments.

I greatly enjoyed recently being able to re-read David Weir's original typescript and it certainly was a reminder of everything that might have been! What a treat! It's wonderful; all the elements are there and the character writing for Koenig, Bergman and Helena is so vivid. But you can see why it freaked Gerry out, especially after Lee Katzin's overspend on Episode One. It's twenty pages too long and David's note on the back page about spending a fortune on SFX might have been a bit of an understatement. I also remember Lee Katzin saying audiences just wouldn't tolerate dialogue speeches of more than three lines!

After reading David's original, I wanted to read my re-write version just to compare – but that went years ago to auction, so I did the next best thing and watched it. Although there's a lot of what must be my original stuff there, it seems the major contribution was in cutting it down to size and making the production of a really good story possible. There's much more of David Weir's original there than I imagined, so memory does play funny tricks. But it certainly does retain the spirit of David's original and the fact of having done the re-write that enabled us to get that on the screen is good enough for me. What a brilliant memory trip!

'Guardian of Piri'

I don't recall a David Weir storyline called 'Nobody's Perfect' but I certainly did write 'Guardian of Piri', and the lack of an on-screen credit is probably an indication that I did take over the script from someone else. But the person who deserves a proper mention here is Charles Crichton. Charles had begun his film career, as I had done, as a film editor and, as a director, he was an absolute stickler for getting the script right in terms of its inner logic and characterization. He encouraged me – maybe even insisted – that I should attend rushes screening every day and he would sit me down afterwards and go through any lessons we had learned from what we had just seen and how they might play out favorably in what was left to shoot. In my opinion Charles was in a league of his own amongst the directors who worked on *Space: 1999* and I am eternally indebted to him for all that I learned under his wise aegis.

I don't know who suggested my play *Spawn* might have been an inspiration for the planet Piri but it featured a young, avant-garde sculptor who littered his father-in-law's vicarage garden with what the press described as 'giant fibreglass mushrooms'. I guess it's a possibility that Keith Wilson saw the show on television and may have taken his cue from there.

As a footnote to 'Guardian of Piri' I might mention an incident that occurred years later. My stepdaughter was a student at the Central St Martin's College of Art and hers was a brilliantly talented cohort. She brought a gang of them around to our house one day and we were all sitting around the table in the garden, and I realized they were talking about a fashion shoot that was getting a lot of attention (unknown to me) in the press. And that they were talking about 'Guardian of Piri' as being the inspiration for this prizewinning show. My stepdaughter then dropped the bombshell that I had actually written that show and they reacted as though they suddenly had a superstar in their midst! They were complete fans of the show and were quite convinced I must have been on acid when I wrote it. I wasn't, but the adrenaline was pulsing at pretty high pressure.

'Alpha Child'

The genesis of 'Alpha Child' is quite difficult to recall. I'm pretty sure that the idea of a child being born on Alpha, and the kind of celebration of that event, being then undermined by the anxiety of the child's pace of development, was one that came from Gerry. I have pretty clear recollections of sitting in Gerry's office at Pinewood and us talking about that as an idea. I think that a lot of the actual plot of 'Alpha Child' was probably straight from Gerry. And whilst acting, I hope, as something more than Gerry's amanuensis, it remains a story that I would not, in all probability, have come up with myself.

'The Last Sunset'

'The Last Sunset' has, at its core, an epic idea – the idea of the human Diaspora that is Moonbase Alpha actually finding a home. A homecoming. That's a pretty powerful notion and the history of Israel was not far from my mind. The possibility of finding a place in which all of those things that had been left behind on Earth would be rediscovered, was something that engaged me. The whole sense of an imperfect humanity being given a second chance was as attractive as it was ultimately unachievable.

'War Games'

I had long been a member of the Campaign for Nuclear Disarmament and, as a student at Cambridge, had protested loud and long outside American Air Force bases in East Anglia and participated in the huge demonstration in the Market Square at Cambridge at the time of the Cuban missile crisis. I was also unhappy about the proliferation of civil nuclear power stations and the failure to solve the problem of radio-active waste. At the time, there were lunatics who proposed that we should load it all into rockets and fire it off into space. Which was probably the origin of the idea of a nuclear waste dump on the Moon. But the real inspiration for 'War Games' was a dramatized documentary film that was made for the BBC by Peter Watkins called *The War Game*. It was made in about 1966 and was promptly banned by the BBC. It was later released in cinemas where audiences were treated to the utter horror of a nuclear war on the civilian population. The idea that a species capable of such self-harm might take with them that sickness into space was one which played into my own sense of the function of science fiction as being to look critically at the way we live now with the benefit of foresight.

'Space Brain'

Mostly I was in awe of what Keith Wilson and Brian Johnson were able to achieve in the way of sets and special effects but the one show that disappointed me in that department was 'Space Brain'. It was what now would be called a high concept show and it never really got to where I hoped it would be. Maybe it was just *too* high concept.

That fire-fighting foam may have been where the production answers to the problems posed by the script came from, but I can certainly say that detergents weren't seriously engaging my mind as a writer. Microbiology was the idea behind 'Space Brain': the notion that microbiologists spend their time looking at smaller and smaller particles. We spend billions of dollars building particle accelerators and looking at, and looking for, smaller and smaller particles. It seemed to me that it might be quite interesting to turn that around and head off in the other direction. To think of the entire planet Earth as a very small particle; and that it was itself a particle within a very large entity – which might be the universe – and that we might think of the universe as a brain.

'Dragon's Domain'

Mythology and metaphysics have always been territory that science fiction has profitably inhabited, and 'Dragon's Doman' was inspired by the mythical contest between St George and the dragon. It was also an attempt to take on the whole issue of monsters in Space in what I hoped was a creative and constructive way. At the time, I had a house on the Welsh borders near Ludlow which, because of the pressure of work on *Space: 1999*, I couldn't get to all that often. Whenever I did get there, the spiders' webs over the kitchen windows would be full of moths and flies that had had the life blood sucked out of them and I wanted to tell a story in which belief in the monster would turn out to be real. Charles Crichton, ably abetted by the design and SFX departments, did a brilliant job and I am still quite pleased with the result.

I think Cellini was a replacement for Carter in 'Dragon's Domain'. I think it was a nod towards the Italian network RAI who had finance in the show.

'Dorzak'

'Dorzak' was a joke. I think it might have been through Johnny's good offices that Freddie Freiberger asked me to write a script for Series Two. I did. But when the production script eventually dropped through my letter box the only thing that I recognized from my own work was my name on the front cover. I have never seen the show.

It wasn't a happy experience and whatever the original concept was, it certainly didn't survive Freiberger's take-over of the script and has been entirely erased from my conscious memory.

JOHNNY BYRNE'S CRITICAL COMMENTARY

By Robert E Wood

INTRODUCTION

If there is one document that could be regarded as holding legendary status amongst many literary-minded fans of *Space: 1999* it would likely be the Critical Commentary that Johnny Byrne wrote of the first series. As Byrne himself recalled, 'I was asked by Gerry to write a Critical Commentary on Year One, probably as a way of keeping me around and out of mischief. They were trying to get the second series going, so I wrote a very detailed thing. It was very critical, including of stuff I'd written myself. I was taking a very hard look at everything and trying to find the point of departure to move what we had – the considerable achievement I felt we had managed – forward, on the same path, but correcting obvious anomalies … We had been finding our way. Now it was time to really go for it.

'I was very hard on everyone. I was particularly hard on myself – I was feeling very sorry for myself. But I looked at some of the difficulties or the disadvantages of the system that we had evolved – Chris and I particularly. There were lessons to be learned about what Chris and I and the other writers had left in our wake – we had not been aware of the larger implications of what we were doing. But there is a good deal of truth in the notion that, as the Alphans were struggling to come to terms with that dangerous and threatening and different universe out there, they were echoing the state of mind and the state of being of the writers. So out of it had emerged what we now call a story arc, as such. And I think in the commentary I wrote I did pick up on this and said, "There is a very large theme here, that we can project forward. We can ask ourselves, 'What is Space: 1999? What is the basic nature of its appeal in the largest universal sense?'" And the idea was that it was an epic story. It was humanity condensed to a small number of individuals, with all their hopes and expectations, going out there. And for me particularly, with my background in Celtic history, it was an origin story – a great epic story of a people in search of a destiny, trying to fulfil a destiny, and a home. All of those things could have picked up from the point we left it at episode 24.'

Sadly, in the ensuing years following production of the series Johnny

Byrne had lost any copies of his critical commentary, and his recollections at convention appearances and in interviews became the only evidence of its existence. Byrne's critical commentary became part of *Space: 1999* folklore… until now.

Two original copies surfaced in November 2019 at an estate sale for Martin Landau, who had preserved them in his collection.

It is indeed a fascinating document, particularly looked at with the benefit of hindsight. Byrne's critiques must be viewed in the context of the time he wrote them. Many will elicit nods of agreement, while some will prompt incredulity and intense disagreement.

Without further ado, here is Johnny Byrne's Critical Commentary:

CRITICAL COMMENTARY ON
SPACE: 1999 (1st SERIES)

By Johnny Byrne

RATING VALUES:
*****Excellent
****Good
***Average
**Fair
*Poor

Ep. 1: 'BREAKAWAY'

CRITICAL COMMENT: Sub-plots slow the build-up in the first half, which is also heavy on technical dialogue. Performance uncertain. Direction poor. However, main characters strongly established and good action sequences throughout, building to a spectacular finale.

GENERAL COMMENT: Spectacle overcomes the picture's inherent weaknesses, and the ongoing dramatic theme of the series is strongly established at the end.

RATING: ****

Ep. 2: 'MATTER OF LIFE AND DEATH'

CRITICAL COMMENT: An intriguing story with good performance and direction and a strong guest artiste. The show suffers from a lack of pace but should maintain the viewers' interest into the last act, where this weakness is largely redeemed by an exciting planet surface sequence.

GENERAL COMMENT: Good average episode with considerable female interest.

RATING: ***

Ep. 3: 'BLACK SUN'

CRITICAL COMMENTARY: Subject matter now of compelling interest to science fiction fans and the scientific community. The picture is a well-directed off-beat episode, with good all-round performance and strong human interest. However, it suffers considerably from lack of pace, but given the above comments, plus good production values it should maintain interest.

GENERAL COMMENT: The slow pace and off-beat treatment of the picture does not recommend it for early transmission, however it will be an interesting show to transmit once the series has become established.

RATING: ****

Ep. 4: 'RING AROUND THE MOON'

CRITICAL COMMENT: A good story, efficient performance and direction, with good up-beat pacing. The story however is badly plotted, and this makes it somewhat confusing to follow in places. However, the picture is well staged and builds to an exciting climax.

GENERAL COMMENT: Good production values and the telling use of special effects, largely overcomes the picture's script weaknesses.

RATING: ***

Ep. 5: 'EARTHBOUND'

CRITICAL COMMENT: Strong story, featuring interesting sympathetic aliens. Very competent direction and performance. Slow pacing, however, mars the general excellence of the picture.

GENERAL COMMENT: The picture features two very strong guest artistes, one with a wide international appeal. Their presence, plus the other positive qualities, make this a good average picture.

RATING: ***

Ep. 6: 'ANOTHER TIME, ANOTHER PLACE'

CRITICAL COMMENT: A story with strong, human interest and special appeal to the female audience. Direction good, with telling use made of special effects. However, the general pace is marred by the lethargic performance of Barry Morse.

GENERAL COMMENT: The story embodies intriguing scientific notions, which should have a wide general appeal. A good average picture that could be transmitted anywhere in the schedule.

RATING: ***

Ep. 7: 'MISSING LINK'

CRITICAL COMMENT: A well-staged picture with a guest artiste of international standing. Sadly, it is marred by the confusing nature of the story, which is too subtle for the general audience, the story points being open to too many interpretations.

GENERAL COMMENT: The good direction and performance are so badly affected by the story treatment, that the picture should be put towards the end of the schedule.

RATING: **

Ep. 8: 'GUARDIAN OF PIRI'

CRITICAL COMMENT: The credibility of the picture is destroyed by a serious error in the planet surface set design, which is too abstract for audience believability. A pity since the show is well-directed and performed with an exciting guest artiste, whose starring role in the new Peter Sellers *Pink Panther* feature, will add a big plus to our picture.

GENERAL COMMENT: The importance of credible set design has been brought home to us by our failure with this picture.

RATING: **

Ep. 9: 'FORCE OF LIFE'

CRITICAL COMMENT: This picture embodies all the elements we want in a science fiction series. It has a strong, clear story, a good guest artiste, good performance and direction. It is well paced and has a spectacular ending.

GENERAL COMMENT: The successful fusion of the dramatic and visual elements have made this an exciting picture.

RATING: *****

Ep. 10: 'ALPHA CHILD'

CRITICAL COMMENT: An absorbing story, well-paced, with good action and strong human interest. The picture is flawed however by the comic strip treatment of the last two acts.

GENERAL COMMENT: Had the development of the alien characters been maintained, this would have been an excellent picture. Apart from missed opportunity, this is a good average picture.

RATING: ***

Ep. 11: 'THE LAST SUNSET'

CRITICAL COMMENT: An ambitious story, with good action, strong performance and direction and wide human interest. However, the picture never measures up to its full potential, owing to its weak technical realization. Disappointing for us, but a good episode which could be very well received.

GENERAL COMMENT: A good average picture except for the technically discerning audience.

RATING: ***

Ep. 12: 'VOYAGER'S RETURN'

CRITICAL COMMENT: A well-plotted science fiction notion, with strong guest artiste. The picture is marred by the floor direction and claustrophobic atmosphere which weakens the overall effect.

GENERAL COMMENT: The relevant nature of the story plus good

production values just about overcome the basic directorial weaknesses. A good average episode.

RATING: ***

Ep. 13: 'COLLISION COURSE'

CRITICAL COMMENT: A good story, well-paced, with spectacular action and story climax. The production values are excellent, and the guest artiste is a famous marquee name – Margaret Leighton.

GENERAL COMMENT: An all-round excellent picture in which all the elements work.

RATING: *****

Ep. 14: 'DEATH'S OTHER DOMINION'

CRITICAL COMMENT: A well-written story, superbly directed, with excellent performances and outstanding production values. This is a beautifully realized picture and a good episode to screen for the discerning critics.

GENERAL COMMENT: From a mature, critical point of view, our best episode.

RATING: *****

Ep. 15: 'THE FULL CIRCLE'

CRITICAL COMMENT: A good basic story idea that was spread much too thinly throughout the picture. The overall effect is also marred by poor direction, but the intriguing nature of the story idea helps to balance these negative qualities.

GENERAL COMMENT: An average picture with special appeal to younger viewers.

RATING: ***

Ep. 16: 'END OF ETERNITY'

CRITICAL COMMENT: A good story idea, marred by bad casting in the main guest spot. (The artiste in question was very competent, but wrong for the part.) The picture maintains story interest for the first two acts, but thereafter suffers from a lack of believability, which weakens it considerably.

GENERAL COMMENT: The intriguing story notion, and good production values never quite recover from the effects of bad casting in the guest spot.

RATING: **

Ep. 17: 'WAR GAMES'

CRITICAL COMMENT: Our most spectacular picture, with quite outstanding action sequences. Performance and direction are superb, and the story maintains interest throughout. However, the script suffers from a major lack of effective plotting in the sense that it opens on such a high point of spectacular action that the rest of the picture, though excellent and exciting, seems anti-climactic by comparison.

GENERAL COMMENT: The construction faults are overcome by the spectacular nature of the episode.

RATING: *****

Ep. 18: 'THE LAST ENEMY'

CRITICAL COMMENT: This picture is one of our failures. It went seriously wrong on the floor and needed extensive reshoots. Performance and direction are extremely poor, and even the high special effects content fail to rescue it.

GENERAL COMMENT: The high special effects content might just make it acceptable to the undiscerning viewer.

RATING: *

Ep. 19: 'THE TROUBLED SPIRIT'

CRITICAL COMMENT: An unusual story that combines a good science fiction notion with the ghost story. It is well directed with good atmosphere and performance. The pacing, however, is a little slow.

GENERAL COMMENT: An above average picture that could go anywhere in the transmission schedule after the first six episodes.

RATING: ****

Ep. 20: 'SPACE BRAIN'

CRITICAL COMMENT: A complicated story notion that fails to measure up effectively in visual terms. The picture is well directed and performed and has some spectacular sequences. It suffered from lack of visual credibility however, and required major surgery in the cutting room.

GENERAL COMMENT: Despite major faults, this is now a reasonable episode, with good production values.

RATING: ***

Ep. 21: 'THE INFERNAL MACHINE'

CRITICAL COMMENT: A strong story, somewhat slow in pace, with excellent performance and direction, and a distinguished guest artiste. This is a thoughtful picture, with strong human interest, marred somewhat by the claustrophobic setting.

GENERAL COMMENT: The picture is strong on performance but weak on action. Nevertheless, it is a first-rate episode.

RATING: ****

Ep. 22: 'MISSION OF THE DARIANS'

CRITICAL COMMENTARY: A very ambitious episode in terms of story, sets and number of artistes involved. Performance and direction are excellent, the pace is fast, and the controversial subject matter is delicately handled. This is a picture with high screen value.

GENERAL COMMENT: A strong picture excitingly realized – one of our best.

RATING: *****

Ep. 23: 'DRAGON'S DOMAIN'

CRITICAL COMMENT: An excellent picture, well-paced with good performance and direction. The picture has as its villain a believable B.E.M. –

bug-eyed monster – and as a result has a wide-ranging appeal. Excellent story, and outstanding production values.

GENERAL COMMENT: An ideal picture in many ways, but sadly too expensive to repeat.

RATING: *****

Ep. 24: 'TESTAMENT OF ARKADIA'

CRITICAL COMMENT: A strong story of profound human interest. The picture is marred by weak direction and indifferent guest performance. Had the story material been fully exploited this would have made an excellent picture. As it now stands, this is a good average episode.

GENERAL COMMENT: A thoughtful picture, down in pace, and basically unsatisfactory due to its missed opportunities.

RATING: ***

DISCUSSION

In Johnny's comments on 'Another Time, Another Place' he is notably harsh on Barry Morse, describing the actor's performance as 'lethargic'. Since Byrne himself was the writer of this episode, it may have been a case of Morse's performance choices not matching up with the concept Byrne had envisioned in his mind while writing the script. It is also worth noting that this is the only instance in which Byrne calls out a specific actor by name to criticize their performance, and this perception of Morse's performance will arise again in the next section of this book discussing the Summary of Executive Meetings.

Looking back on it now, Byrne's clearly stated opinion of the time is not in keeping with any of his subsequent public references to Morse made over the years until his death in 2008. In one particular subsequent quote about Morse, Byrne stated, 'The particular cleverness of Barry Morse's portrayal of Bergman was that when he said, 'I don't know', what he was really saying was, 'I might know, but I'm not telling you' … I could watch Prentis and Barry Morse and Martin Landau talking forever while they're waiting for the black hole to swallow them up. It doesn't matter that it's slow and people are not running around and bashing each other on the head. It's important that they're in that situation, they're sharing something warm and human, and they're also discussing interesting philosophical thoughts, as they occur.'

Byrne's critique of Morse is also discordant with audience reaction to the actor, who has always been warmly regarded as a fan-favorite amongst the cast. Obviously, Johnny's own initial opinion of Morse's performance evolved, and we might surmise that Johnny himself would have been surprised by what he wrote if he had had the opportunity to re-read his Commentary again in later years.

Second, regarding 'Guardian of Piri', Byrne felt, 'The credibility of the picture is destroyed by a serious error in the planet surface set design, which is too abstract for audience believability.' He added, 'The importance of credible set design has been brought home to us by our failure with this picture.'

We know that Byrne's opinion was not an isolated assessment, as Gerry Anderson had previously relayed similar concern about the episode to Martin Landau and Barbara Bain in a letter on 5th September 1974 (as previously discussed in the Correspondence section of this book).

These negative opinions are completely at odds with decades of audience response to the episode, which largely regards the Piri set as a masterful, mind-blowing example of alien planetary design, and rather than a 'failure' it is arguably considered the finest in the entire series.

Apart from those areas of obvious discord, Byrne's Critical Commentary largely stands the test of time. One may agree or disagree with specific elements of Byrne's critique, but the document as a whole provides an invaluable glimpse into the contemporaneous thoughts of one of *Space: 1999*'s most influential writers. And as Byrne looked back on Year One, he also began to shape the narrative on where the series would go next …

SUMMARY OF EXECUTIVE MEETINGS

By Robert E Wood

INTRODUCTION

Although the 'Summary of Executive Meetings Relating to *Space: 1999'* document is undated, the reference to 'March and June of this year' is referring to 1975 (production on Year One had concluded at the end of February). And although the author is not specified, we can confidently conclude that these notes were written by Johnny Byrne due to consistencies in spelling, punctuation, and word choice with his Critical Commentary.

It has long been known that executive meetings took place between Year One and Year Two, but the content of those meetings had never been revealed, and by this point in time – forty-five years later – it was doubtful that any documentation survived. Gerry Anderson had nothing. ITV have nothing. Once again, we are grateful to acknowledge that the following document came from the estate of Martin Landau. It is reproduced here in full, and minor typographical errors have been corrected.

SUMMARY OF EXECUTIVE MEETINGS
RELATING TO SPACE: 1999

Once the good sales news on the first series of *Space: 1999* was received, immediate planning began on ways and means of improving a possible second series. With this end in view, numerous meetings, too many to document here, took place between March and June of this year. Among those consulted, singly and in groups, were the regular writing team, potential new writers, science fiction authors who had written books based on the scripts, artistes and technical crew. The widest possible spectrum of opinion was canvassed, and all this activity culminated in a day-long meeting at Pinewood Studios to define the precise nature of the improvements that could be made. Those present at this meeting included the Executive Producer, Gerry Anderson, Story Editor, Johnny Byrne, Martin Landau and Barbara Bain, regular writers, special effects Director Brian Johnson, and Floor Director Charles Crichton. After intensive discussion and analysis, certain conclusions were reached. These conclusions are summarized as follows:

SCRIPTS: It is generally true that scripts are the heartbeat of any series. Should difficulties arise in this area, the reverberations are quickly felt throughout the entire production. The script position on the first series, prior to shooting, very quickly went wrong because there was no clear sense of direction. There were too many opinions as to what the network wanted, with the result that the early scripts were trying to please a number of people with conflicting views of the series. Thus, once in production, logistics took over from the creative element and the early lack of unanimity of purpose produced the following results.

1. Due to time pressure, scripts which had not had the necessary detailed study and analysis, got onto the floor. Correcting the resulting faulty shows involved unnecessary waste of human and financial resources. Clearly these resources should have gone towards making good shows better rather than having to make bad pictures acceptable.
2. The late delivery of scripts imposed unnecessary limitations on the directors, since it was not possible to choose story material most suited to their individual talents.
3. With no finished approved scripts in hand, there was a serious failure to capitalize on the re-use of expensive one-off sets.

CONCLUSION: If this situation is to be avoided in a possible second series, the following conditions must prevail. We have to:

1. Establish a clear line of direction for the series and rigidly adhere to it.
2. Commission a number of scripts – at least six – prepare these scripts to the point where they are ready to go on to the floor at a moment's notice.

These two vital conditions must be met if the objective of really first-class scripting is to be achieved. Their acceptance would eliminate most of the errors in the first series since it would:

i. Allow time for more careful scrutiny and selection of story material.
ii. Allow time to develop difficult, but very promising stories.
iii. Allow time for effective liaison to take place among the departments concerned in getting shows on the screen.
iv. Eliminate the inevitable wastage that occurs on having to rush shows onto the floor.

A script situation thus established, would also allow time to improve the quality of the story content by devising means to include – at nominal expense – the expertise of established science fiction authors. An effort of this kind is necessary since experience has shown that:

1. Not many screenwriters are capable of originating good science fiction ideas.
2. Science fiction authors are rarely competent at writing for the screen. A promising pilot scheme has already been launched, aimed at fusing these quite separate skills to the undoubted benefit of the series.

Also, an important omission in the preparation of the scripts in the first series would be rectified. Due to time pressure, it was not always possible to research and check out errors and inaccuracies in the factual scientific content of the stories. This is obviously undesirable if we are to avoid criticism from the scientific community and the more knowledgeable section of the viewing audience. With this in view, Professor John Taylor, Professor in Mathematics at Kings College, London, has already been approached and has expressed willingness to act as scientific censor on the scripts. His role would simply be to make sure that the factual scientific concepts employed in the stories, if not accurate, were at least acceptable to the more discerning viewers of the general public.

FORMAT: A lot of positive discussion took place concerning the existing format. The experience gained in producing the first twenty-four episodes pointed to areas where quite definite improvements could be made. The following is a summary of some of the weaknesses and suggested alterations to the format:

JOHN KOENIG

It was felt that the lead character had now established a commanding presence on the screen as a dedicated, intense, and very credible human being. No change was foreseen in his basic characterization, however care will be taken to maintain and extend, wherever possible, his involvement in action, personal conflict, and emotion. The more the character of Koenig is stretched, the better the results on the screen.

HELENA RUSSELL

Helena's character suffered from a major flaw in the series format, a fault directly traceable to her role as Chief Medical Officer on Moonbase Alpha. This role was found to be too restrictive for a lead character, whose presence in any one episode requires strong story involvement. The problem with Helena was that as a doctor it was necessary to devise plots with a strong medical bias. While in stories without a medical angle it was difficult to justify her involvement with any real degree of credibility. This situation was obviously bad for the artiste, bad for the writer and bad for the series.

In a second series, Helena will now be given a new position on Moonbase Alpha. Instead of being Chief Medical Officer, she will now be a Space Environmentalist. In her new position Helena will still be in overall charge of Medical Section, but in addition will be responsible for all aspects of survival in space. By this change, Helena will now be vitally concerned in the widest possible area of story involvement. She will be solely responsible for the life support systems on the base, in charge of prospecting for food and mineral resources on alien planets, evaluating alien environments, etc. In terms of story involvement, the possibilities are endless.

Also in a second series, careful provision will be made to involve Helena in more jeopardy situations. These are situations in which the artiste has proved most effective.

PROFESSOR BERGMAN

The general feeling was that though Bergman was a very important character, he has not always been as effective as he might have in many of the episodes. As he stands, Bergman is a humane father figure, fascinated by science and the mystery of space. Born just after the Second World War, he is a man who has seen phenomenal change in his life, and on Alpha his values reflect an older, more easy-going era.

Although his values provide welcome relief from the efficient clinical world of Moonbase Alpha, his fascination for science and space has weakened many tense scenes, especially act endings, by his too casual reactions. In general, there was too much agreement between Helena and Bergman, while any advice Bergman gave to Koenig on vital issues was on a 'take it or leave it' basis.

These performance points need to be revised to strengthen Bergman's character. Careful scripting in the future will ensure that Bergman will react in moments of stress or danger with real fear, anger or whatever other strong emotional response is required. Bergman's character potential will be further exploited since, as one of the two people Koenig heavily relies on, he is in a position to push harder for what he believes and in doing so, influence the vital decision-making process on Alpha.

To sum up, Bergman will continue to be his usual, easy-going self until under stress, when he will react like any other human being. He will also reveal a steadiness of purpose, a stubbornness in situations where he feels his solution to any one life or death dilemma, is the right one. There will be moments when, because of the deep emotional relationship between Koenig and Helena, Koenig's decision to side with Helena on some vital issue is open to a number of interpretations by Bergman, thus creating conflict by doubting Koenig's judgement.

These changes are largely concerned with the scripting of the characters. If the writers incorporate them into scripts, the artiste has the ability to bring them to life on the screen. They will make for much stronger interaction between the principal artistes, and in doing so will filter down to the rest of the supporting cast with beneficial results for the series in terms of character believability.

COSTUMES: The Executive Producer, artistes and Directors made several points concerning the Moonbase costumes. These points can be summarized as follows:

1. They are too unisex and generally fail to exploit the basic physical differences between men and women.
2. They limit the acting talent that can be used in guest roles, because they are unsuitable on people who are not in good physical shape.
3. In the clinical atmosphere of Moonbase Alpha, where to a certain extent the artistes have already been robbed of their individuality, the costume design was an added burden. Artistes deprived of their essential props – cigarettes, cigars, spectacles – found that they had no sleeves to roll up to show them setting to work, no jackets to take off at the end of a tough day, not even pockets to fumble with. Martin Landau described it succinctly when he said that he could play his scenes more effectively with both arms amputated.

These points were accepted and in the event of a second series, planned changes will take place to the costumes. These changes will include the addition of pockets, roll-up sleeves and use of occasional jackets to be worn around the base.

CASTING: One of the undoubted successes of the first series was the quality of guest artistes the show was able to attract. But the general high quality was rarely extended to the casting of the minor roles, which left a lot to be desired.

This was due in part to the limitation imposed by the costumes, hairstyles and an obsession with creating a so-called science fiction look (whatever that is). Another weakness in casting related to roles which called for physical toughness. These were too often filled by weak and unsuitable physical types, with the effect that believability suffered. The guiding principle in the casting of minor roles in a second series will be to populate Moonbase Alpha with the widest possible spectrum of human beings, making the show more interesting, more believable, and allowing most people to find physical types they are able to identify with.

MOONBASE ALPHA: In future stories set on Alpha, the writers will be instructed to open out more areas of the base. This will give viewers a wider view of the lifestyles of the personnel, their environment, their loves, hates, jealousies. The overall intention being to highlight wherever possible, the tensions of a community living on borrowed time, searching for somewhere to live. However, the feelings of optimism, usually reflected by Koenig, will be retained. To demonstrate this optimism, Alpha has extended its activities down into the lunar surface. Large subterranean areas have been excavated for the controlled growing of food, the discovery and replenishment of mineral resources and a quest for frozen water, which some believe to exist somewhere beneath the lunar surface.

CONCLUSION: The weakness and mistakes of the first series as seen from the production end have necessarily predominated in this summary. It should be noted in passing that the achievements and successes are taken for granted, since all the criticism and soul-searching represents a keen desire to improve.

In terms of sales, it seems the series will justify the work and expense that went into its creation. Shortly to come are the reactions of the viewing public. Should they share the belief that *Space: 1999* deserves a second lease of life and the 'start button' is pressed, the result of all this intensive effort will be a more creative and efficient product.

DISCUSSION

The content of this document is largely self-explanatory, but it is fascinating to point out several elements, which in some cases eventually made their way on-screen in Year Two, and in other cases did not.

Regarding scripts, we know that the production of Year Two was rushed (a matter which was of significant concern to the producers as subsequent documents in this book will reveal), which did not allow for increased care and consideration of scripts as advised in this document. Established science fiction authors were not brought in.

It is interesting to note the concern that 'there was a serious failure to capitalize on the re-use of expensive one-off sets' as there are numerous examples of sets and props being re-used in Year One (such as the 'Death's other Dominion' ice cavern being converted into the prehistoric cave in 'The Full Circle', and Arra's throne re-appearing as Companion's bed in 'The Infernal Machine'). That said, Year Two did make more frequent – and more obvious – re-use of sets and props. One notable example of economical set re-use appears in the first three episodes of Year Two, when The Grove of Psyche set from 'The Metamorph' is redressed and appears again in 'The Exiles' as the life-support center on planet Golos, and again in 'One Moment of Humanity' as the Garden of Vega.

The suggestions for changes to the character of Helena Russell were largely implemented in Year Two. Although her title remained Chief Medical Officer, she was often seen to be responsible for Alpha's life support systems, as well as prospecting for minerals on alien planets (such as Titanium on the surface of Psychon in 'The Metamorph'). Helena would undergo additional changes for Year Two, including her overall demeanor and hairstyle, in an effort to soften and warm her character. This effort was successful, but also resulted in a character often so strikingly different from her Year One persona that she might indeed have been a different person.

Unfortunately, Professor Bergman didn't fare as well. While it is heartening for fans to see that the intention was there for Bergman to continue into Year Two, references that the character had 'not always been as effective as he might have in many of the episodes' and 'weakened many tense scenes, especially act endings, by his too casual reactions' strike not only at the character, but at the actor who portrayed him. And taken alongside Johnny Byrne's negative comment about Barry Morse's performance in his Critical Commentary, the reference here that 'these performance points need to be revised to strengthen Bergman's character,' sadly portends the character's future. It must be stated that these perceptions are wildly out of synch with how audiences reacted to the character, and to Morse's performance. But this document indicates that when the new Producer, Fred Freiberger, would eventually be brought on-board and given a virtual blank slate to make changes to the series for Year Two, his decision to eliminate the character of Professor Bergman would not be met by strenuous objection, and Space: 1999 would lose a large part of its heart and soul in the process.

Costume changes were implemented largely as indicated, as was the desire to open up other areas of the base, as seen on-screen with the

Underground Research Area in 'The Exiles' and the subterranean tunnels in 'Catacombs of the Moon'. However, the need for a general standing Moonbase set meant that frequently used rooms, such as Medical and Crew Quarters, remained the same except for dressings. The freshest expansion of Alpha came in the sets built specifically for 'The Bringers of Wonder' (ie the destruction of the records lab).

The effort undertaken by all involved in these executive meetings was clearly admirable, and their conclusions in many ways appear to have been on the right track. If the same production team (including Johnny Byrne in the all-important role of story editor) had moved forward with Year Two, more or less in a consistent style with Year One, and if adequate time had been given in which to follow through with some of the more difficult recommendations concerning scripting, the results could very well have been an improvement over the first series.

The 'start button' was indeed pushed, but unfortunately it came too late…

SUGGESTED TRANSMISSION LIST

The following 'Suggested Transmission List' was stapled to the front of the Summary of Executive Meetings and is therefore presumed to be a product of those meetings, reflecting the prevailing opinion at the time (corresponding to Johnny Byrne's opinions in his Critical Commentary) on the strongest episodes to launch the series, as well as weaker episodes to schedule later in the run.

1. BREAKAWAY
2. FORCE OF LIFE
3. COLLISION COURSE
4. WAR GAMES
5. DEATH'S OTHER DOMINION
6. MISSION OF THE DARIANS
7. ANOTHER TIME, ANOTHER PLACE
8. DRAGON'S DOMAIN
9. ALPHA CHILD
10. TROUBLED SPIRIT
11. LAST SUNSET
12. THE INFERNAL MACHINE
13. SPACE BRAIN
14. VOYAGER'S RETURN
15. BLACK SUN
16. END OF ETERNITY
17. EARTHBOUND
18. RING AROUND THE MOON
19. TESTAMENT OF ARKADIA
20. GUARDIAN OF PIRI
21. MATTER OF LIFE AND DEATH
22. MISSING LINK
23. THE FULL CIRCLE
24. THE LAST ENEMY

Broadcast order would eventually vary in different markets around the world. It is notable that the first five episodes on this list match the original UK broadcast order on Granada, Yorkshire, ATV, LWT, Anglia, and HTV.

RENEWAL: 1975

By Robert E Wood

Filming on *Space: 1999*'s first series finished on February 28, 1975, and post-production continued through March and April. Year Two didn't begin filming until January 26, 1976, fully eleven months after completion of the first series. During that time Johnny Byrne wrote his analysis of the first season's episodes and the executive meetings were held analyzing the strengths and weaknesses of the first series and charting a path forward. Planning for a prospective second series looked to be on firm footing from a creative point of view as the production awaited word whether the series would be renewed.

Yet there were other considerations to take into account. The history of Anderson productions for ITC shows that Lew Grade very rarely commissioned second seasons of Anderson productions, even when a series had been highly successful, like *Thunderbirds*. Referring to his successful string of Supermarionation series, Gerry Anderson said, 'Lew always wanted to know what my next idea was.' That type of decision-making on the part of Lew Grade and ITC UK is quite different than the way most television has been produced since then, particularly in the United States, but those contemporaneous and cultural differences must be considered when looking at ITC's decision-making process with regards to the renewal of *Space: 1999* for a second series.

In addition, the first twenty-four episodes of *Space: 1999* had been in production since late 1973, and then were complete and sitting on a shelf for months until the series finally premiered in September 1975, fully a year after its intended debut. The investment of millions of dollars in a series that failed to sell to an American network and had to sit on the shelf for a year would likely not have been looked on favorably by those in charge of the purse strings.

It's clear that when the time came to renew *Space: 1999*, Abe Mandell and ITC New York would be making the decision.

Mere weeks after *Space: 1999* had premiered, Gerry was in New York and wrote to Martin and Barbara on Friday, October 10, 1975, with 'the rundown on Freddie Freiberger', and expressed his belief that, 'I think we have found our man and would like to secure his services before leaving the country, probably Wednesday night.' It is clear in Anderson's letter that a second series was not yet confirmed ('should the show be renewed') but it's also obvious that a new American story editor was being hired with the hopeful anticipation that a renewal order would be forthcoming. As Gerry recalled, 'After the completion of series one, the New York office of ITC Entertainment asked me to find an American head writer. I went to Hollywood to seek out someone who knew anything about SF and who was prepared to come to England immediately and stay for a year. It was quite a project to find someone like that who was available. When I found Fred I, of course, contacted ITC New York and they said, "Fine, but why is he available?" When you think about it, it was kind of silly since a person who wasn't available would be of no use to us at all.'[33]

While Johnny Byrne had been closely involved with the executive meetings planning for a second season, had written scripts for it, and would have been a natural choice as story editor for the second year, ITC New York and Abe Mandell were fixated on having an American in that position. In retrospect, Gerry Anderson said, 'It's very difficult to have ITC New York telling us to use as many American writers as we can and then have our American story editor say, "I could have used six writers, but I didn't want to work from 3,000 miles away." It's a point I can understand but for the same token, why have an American head writer then?'[34] Christopher Penfold had left the production prior to the end of the first series, but recalled, 'One of the, I think, destructive influences of ITC was to undermine the self-confidence that we as a team had built up amongst ourselves that we were actually making something that was exciting and original and new.'[35]

Freiberger was hired and then went to the UK and wrote his assessment of the first series on November 25. His memo stated that he watched eight episodes, but he later admitted to only watching three before passing judgement. Freiberger said, 'We had meetings with Abe Mandell and Gerry Anderson, and I went over to England for three weeks to discuss the feasibility of continuing the series... Barry Morse played a scientist in the series... Morse is an excellent actor, but I felt his part was all wrong... I said, "Gerry, if you're going to have anybody as a professor, he should be a young kid with a beard. Do something different. Another problem with the show is that you can't have people standing around and talking and being philosophical with these long speeches... nobody will hold still for it. Let's do some switches on the characters."'[36]

Freiberger's memo pushed characterization, humour, action, and the specific addition of a female space alien metamorph character who would become Moonbase Alpha's new science officer, Maya.

---

[33] 'Anderson Replies.' *Starlog* 42. January 1981, letters.
[34] 'Anderson Replies.' *Starlog* 42. January 1981, letters.
[35] *The Space: 1999 Documentary*, Kindred Productions, 1996
[36] Clark, Mike, and Bill Cotter. 'An Interview with Fred Freiberger.' *Starlog* 40. November 1980, 58-61.

The American ratings for *Space: 1999* were strong but despite that there was an uphill climb to get the series renewed. It's possible – as with many other Anderson series – that ITC simply didn't have a specific expectation of producing a second series. At that time, shortly before the arrival of *Star Wars*, science fiction was not yet a hot commodity, there were no other sci-fi hits to compare *Space: 1999* to, and ITC may have felt that one season of twenty-four episodes was sufficient. Perhaps Mandell lacked the excitement to pitch another season of the same series to syndication again, and like Lew Grade, was looking for 'the next idea' that would excite him. But it's also clear that the door wasn't shut to a second series since Mandell had Anderson go to the US in search of a new story editor.

It's clear during this time that Anderson was in close contact with Martin Landau and Barbara Bain during his search, and indeed sought their approval of Fred Freiberger, so it seems very likely that the drive to continue the series was coming from the three of them.

Freiberger said, 'We had to generate enough enthusiasm and confidence in Mandell and Lew Grade's organization to make it a viable series the second year … I was there to get a show back on the air again that would get ratings and would be entertaining in the American sense… Gerry and I sold them on continuing the series based on this new character, Maya. One of the reasons I was able to come up with Maya was part of my science-fiction background. I worked three years with Hanna-Barbera on their Saturday morning shows. Working in kid's television sparks your imagination; you can do some wild things.'[37]

Budgetary factors also played a role in the renewal, as Freiberger recalled, 'There was a big question of the budget. We made several trans-Atlantic calls to Martin Landau and Barbara Bain … would they take a salary cut? They wouldn't take a cut. People assume when you're making an offer that you're lying and that they're in the driver's seat. This show was on the edge for weeks … it looked like we were finished. I stayed an extra week, and then it looked like *1999* had a life when I came up with Maya.'[38]

Gerry and Johnny Byrne also both said that it was Freiberger's concept that convinced Mandell and ITC New York to greenlight the second season. Precisely when the renewal notice was given behind-the-scenes is unknown, but by the time the public renewal notice came on December 15, all of the key details and players were in place. The Year Two promotional brochure clearly shows what ITC was excited about, with its cover boldly proclaiming, 'Year 2' as 'Bigger, Better, More Exciting Than Ever!' and inside prominently featuring Maya and a list of 'New' attributes such as 'New

---

[37] Clark, Mike, and Bill Cotter. 'An Interview with Fred Freiberger.' *Starlog* 40. November 1980, 58-61.
[38] Clark, Mike, and Bill Cotter. 'An Interview with Fred Freiberger.' *Starlog* 40. November 1980, 58-61.

Exciting Roles!' and 'New Top Sci-Fi Producer!'

Martin Landau said, 'I guess to get the second season going they had to make some compromises, but I don't think should have. To this day I think that they could have stuck by their guns, had a second series, and I really feel that the series would have had a third and fourth season had they. I feel that very strongly. The style of our show was our own. We were not like *Star Trek*. There was no need to become more like it. That was giving up. I believe that, without question, you have to stick by your guns and go the way that the show is meant to go ... I was never happy with the second season.'[39]

Gerry had assured Martin and Barbara that there was no doubt he would be the producer of the second series, but when the time came and Freiberger pitched his changes, Gerry seemed perfectly agreeable to giving the producer role to Freiberger. Perhaps this was because Freiberger's changes were amounting to a quite radical revamp of the series and Gerry legitimately felt Freiberger should therefore be the producer, or perhaps it was due to the difficulties in Anderson's personal life at the time leading him to be more willing to take a backseat. As Zienia Merton recalled, 'Gerry was there, but Freddie was very much in charge.'[40]

Gerry remembered, 'It was claimed – again, by ITC New York – that we didn't understand the American market and how the American mind worked, and so on. And so, we had to have a younger woman in the show. Fred Freiberger, one of the first things he did, was to introduce this new character, Maya, [with] this ability to change into other creatures ... I didn't particularly like the second series and oddly enough when I've been to conventions in the States, to a man people prefer the first series, which sadly shows that we were badly misguided by, again, the American office [of ITC] ... I tried to be as far as possible Mr Nice Guy, who was recognizing other people's problems and trying to please too many people. I think if I had been much more ruthless and said, "Get the hell out of here, otherwise we stop shooting tomorrow," and had totally done it my way it would be very conceited to say it would have succeeded, but I honestly believe that it would have stood a much better chance.'[41]

---

[39] *The Space: 1999 Documentary*, Kindred Productions, 1996
[40] Wood, Robert E *Destination: Moonbase Alpha*. (Telos Publishing, 2014), 308.
[41] *The Space: 1999 Documentary*, Kindred Productions, 1996

SPIN-OFF SERIES

By Robert E Wood

INTRODUCTION

It has long been rumored that not only was a third series of *Space: 1999* under consideration, but that there were also plans for a potential spin-off series.

Actress Catherine Schell recalled, 'There were plans to do another series. There was even talk of a spin-off series … with – as I was told – Maya as the leading character. I don't remember Tony or Nick ever being mentioned, but I presume that they would have been featured in it … I would of course have gone on to make another series. Greed almost always wins over common sense, and I had been promised an American type contract, giving me residuals on all the foreign sales and repeats. It would have been an ideal form of a pension plan. As for Maya's character developing, that would have been entirely in the hands of the writers. I am sure I would have thought of something and made some suggestions, but this is now merely rhetorical … It wasn't only Freddy [who mentioned the thought that there might be a spin-off of the Maya character], it was also Gerry. [That] obviously would have been very interesting for me. The conversation was really about what would happen, what did I think, and would I want to do it? Yes, of course! … But, anyway, [the spin-off] never happened. It was in [just the early stages] of the planning system. There were no scripts involved. It was just a theory: there was some interest, and perhaps we could do this.'

However, apart from Catherine Schell's recollections, there was never any documentation to prove that a spin-off series was ever a serious proposition. Once again, Martin Landau's carefully preserved collection of documents has unearthed a treasure: two pages documenting proof of the spin-off series.

The first page is a letter dated 29 June 1977 from Lloyd H Evans, Group Solicitor at ATV Management Services Ltd, addressed to lawyer Peter C Bennett in Beverly Hills, California (and cc'd to Martin Landau). On the topic of *Space: 1999* Evans wrote, 'I have just returned from holiday and had a long meeting with Martin which you said you would not object to. Following this meeting I have now obtained instructions that the spin-off clause which Martin found acceptable is also acceptable to us. To stop any argument, I enclose a copy of this which is basically the introduction with the time limit, the agreed format, contents and your clauses 13.1 and 13.2 as amended by me. I believe we can now exchange the Agreement.'

The second page, in its entirety, reads as follows:

For the purposes of this Agreement the term 'spin-off' shall be deemed to mean any other series of television programmes which is based wholly upon or derived entirely from one or more elements of the format of the series and transmitted on or before the 31st day of December 1979 and for the purposes of this Clause the parties agree and confirm that the said format elements comprise the following:

1.   Set in a time period which contains a reference in the title to the year 1999, <u>or contains a reference in the opening narrative of the show to the year 1999</u>
2.   The principal characters living in a Moonbase built by earth people on the moon which is itself travelling through space having broken away from orbit and
3.   The principle or major continuing character being an alien being capable of changing its form but represented by a human female

Without in any way limiting the generality of the foregoing the term spin-off shall also be deemed to include any other programme or series of programmes

1.   based upon any character or characters whether the same or different names are applied to them who should from time to time appear as a principal character in the series
2.   which utilizes any of the special equipment, props, machinery and/or devices of any nature, <u>solely</u> readily and immediately identifiable with its prior usage in the Series (as distinguished from special equipment, props, machinery and/or devices of any nature of similar genre common to a programme involving science fiction and/or travel in space).

DISCUSSION

Intriguing information! But why did no one else – Gerry Anderson, Brian Johnson, or Johnny Byrne – ever remember there being discussion of a spin-off? The simplest answer is that they probably were not involved with it at that stage of development.

By late June 1977 Gerry was working with Reg Hill on *Thunderhawks* for

Japan, having completed the *Alien Attack* advertisement for Jif Dessert Toppings with Brian Johnson earlier that year.

Fred Freiberger had continued working with Gerry Anderson for a period of time after the production of Year Two, devising and unsuccessfully pitching new series concepts (*Rescue 9* and *Starcruiser*) to American networks. Freiberger subsequently went on to be story editor on the third season of *Quincy ME* for a period of time in 1977 before moving on to produce the final season of *The Six Million Dollar Man*.

Johnny Byrne's involvement with Year Two had been reduced to scripting three episodes, so there is no reason to assume that by late June of 1977 he would have had any involvement with a potential spin-off series.

But clearly there was a potential spin-off! The key details are clear:

- A reference to the year 1999 would either be included in the title, or in the opening narrative of the show.
- The series would be set on 'a Moonbase built by earth people on the moon which is itself traveling through space having broken away from orbit.'
- Maya ('an alien being capable of changing its form but represented by a human female') was to be 'the principle or major continuing character.'

Considering that the series was going to be set on Moonbase Alpha (as is clear from the description, even though it isn't named) it sounds more like an evolution than a spin-off. Presumably Martin Landau and Barbara Bain would not have been in the cast, leaving Maya elevated to the main principal role, and a new group of supporting characters would have been assembled that may have included actors like Nick Tate and Tony Anholt, as Catherine Schell speculated.

Whether the planning proceeded any further than this documentation is unknown, but obviously the required level of interest failed to materialize, and the spin-off series was never produced. These documents, however, provide another glimpse into the lost universe of *Space: 1999*.

APPENDICES

SPACE: 1999
Year One Live-Action Shooting Schedule

By David Hirsch

The first series was shot over a period of 14 months from December 1973 through March 1975 (though visual effects started a month earlier). ITC originally hoped to have *Space: 1999* on air in September 1974, but the eventual delay afforded the production time to go back and reshoot scenes later.

(NOTE: These dates were reconciled from Martin Landau's document collection of the On-day Call Sheets. Missing dates were reconciled from earlier Shooting Schedules (presented in *italic*), which may have been revised at the time of shooting and therefore incorrect. Filming locations are presented in the order they were scheduled to be shot.)

'BREAKAWAY' (Episode 1)

Monday, December 3, 1973
Nuclear Waste Disposal Area 2 - Stage M

Tuesday, December 4, 1973 – Tuesday, December 11, 1973
Main Mission / Koenig's Office - Stage L

Wednesday, December 12, 1973
Nuclear Waste Disposal Area 2 & Corridor - Stage M

Thursday, December 13, 1973
Eagle Passenger Module & Travel Tube - Stage M
Diagnostic & Medical Center - Stage L

Friday, December 14, 1973
Corridor Reception - Stage H
Technical Section - Projection Tunnel

Monday, December 17, 1973
Main Mission & Koenig's Office (Breakaway sequence) - Stage L
Eagle Passenger Module (Simmonds), Travel Tube (Koenig & Simmonds Arrival) - Stage M

Tuesday, December 18, 1973
Eagle Command Module, Moon Surface - Stage M
Helena's Office - Stage L

Wednesday, December 19, 1973 — Thursday, January 10, 1974
NO SHOOTING INFORMATION AVAILABLE

Monday, January 7, 1974
Helena's Office, Diagnostic Unit & Medical Center - Stage L

Tuesday, January 8, 1974
Technical Section - Projection Tunnel

Wednesday, January 9, 1974
Intensive Care Unit - Stage H
Ext. Moon Surface (Crashed Moon Buggy called for) - Stage M

Friday, January 11, 1974
Intensive Care Unit, Standard Series Title Sequence, NDA 2 Depot Inserts,
Man Mission Monitor Insert, Helena's Office Insert, Passenger Module Insert
- Stage H

'MATTER OF LIFE AND DEATH' (Episode 2)

Monday, January 14, 1974
Eagle Command Module, Travel Tube - Stage M

Tuesday, January 15, 1974
Main Mission, Koenig's Office - Stage L

Wednesday, January 16, 1974
Care Unit - Stage L

Thursday, January 17, 1974 — Monday, January 21, 1974
Main Mission & Koenig's Office - Stage L

Tuesday, January 22, 1974
Main Mission & Koenig's Office - Stage L

Wednesday, January 23, 1974
Interior Eagle & Planet - Stage M

Thursday, January 24, 1974
Exterior Planet Surface (with Practical Pond & Live Birds) - Stage M

Friday, January 25, 1974
Exterior Planet Surface - Stage M

Monday, January 28, 1974
Helena's Quarters & Bergman's Lab - Stage L

Tuesday, January 27, 1974 — Wednesday, February 13, 1974
NO SHOOTING INFORMATION AVAILABLE

'BLACK SUN' (Episode 3)

Thursday, February 14, 1974
Main Mission & Koenig's Office, Smitty's Quarters, Morrow's Quarters,
Main Mission Caption Inserts - Stage L

Friday, February 15, 1974 & Monday, February 18, 1974
NO SHOOTING INFORMATION AVAILABLE

Tuesday, February 19, 1974
Moon Surface & **MAIN TITLE** shoot - Stage M
Interior Corridor - Stage H
Interior Main Power Unit & Interior Intensive Care Unit - Stage L

Wednesday, February 20, 1974 — Thursday March 14, 1974
NO SHOOTING INFORMATION AVAILABLE

'RING AROUND THE MOON' (Episode 4)

NO SHOOTING INFORMATION AVAILABLE

'EARTHBOUND' (Episode 5)

Friday, March 15, 1974
Interior Corridor, Travel Tube - Stage H
Interior Diagnostic Unit - Stage L

Monday, March 18, 1974
Interior Diagnostic Unit, Power Station - Stage L
Interior Kaldorian Ship - Stage M

Tuesday, March 19, 1974
NO SHOOTING INFORMATION AVAILABLE

<u>Wednesday, March 20, 1974</u>
Interior Kaldorian Ship - Stage M

<u>Thursday, March 21, 1974</u>
Interior Kaldorian Ship, Crash Unit & Vacuum Chamber, Eagle Command
Module
- Stage M

<u>Friday, March 22. 1974</u>
Eagle Command Module & Interior Kaldorian Ship - Stage M

<u>Monday, March 25, 1974</u>
Main Mission - Stage L
Eagle Passenger Module Pick-Ups (for **'BLACK SUN')** - Stage M

<u>Tuesday, March 26, 1974</u>
NO SHOOTING INFORMATION AVAILABLE

<u>Wednesday, March 27, 1974 — Thursday, March 28, 1974</u>
Main Mission & Koenig's Office - Stage L

<u>Friday, March 29, 1974</u>
NO SHOOTING INFORMATION AVAILABLE

<u>Monday, April 1, 1974</u>
Main Mission & Koenig's Office - Stage L

'ANOTHER TIME, ANOTHER PLACE' (Episode 6)

<u>Tuesday, April 2, 1974</u>
Main Mission - Stage L

<u>Wednesday, April 3, 1974</u>
Main Mission & Koenig's Office - Stage L

<u>Thursday, April 4, 1974</u>
Main Mission & Koenig's Office - Stage L

<u>Friday, April 5, 1974 — Monday, April 8, 1974</u>
Main Mission & Koenig's Office - Stage L

<u>Tuesday, April 9, 1974</u>
Koenig's Office & Main Mission / Diagnostic Unit - Stage L

Wednesday, April 10, 1974
Diagnostic Unit & Autopsy Room / Deserted Main Mission - Stage L

Thursday, April 11, 1974
Diagnostic Unit - Stage L
Interior Eagle Modules - Stage M
Corridor - Stage H

Friday, April 12, 1974 – Monday, April 15, 1974
EASTER HOLIDAY

Tuesday, April 16, 1974
Interior Corridor - Stage H
Eagle Command Module / Passenger Module & Crashed Eagle, Exterior
Earth Surface & Tower Section, Exterior Earth Surface Settlement - Stage M

Wednesday, April 17, 1974
Exterior Earth Surface Settlement & Garden - Stage M

Thursday, April 18, 1974
NO SHOOTING INFORMATION AVAILABLE

Friday, April 19, 1974
Exterior Settlement Outside Bergman's Unit - Stage M

Monday, April 22, 1974
Living Unit, Black Velvet (Diagnostic Unit & Main Mission)
'B' Unit Shoot - North Tunnel

Tuesday, April 23, 1974
Black Velvet & Computer Screen (Main Mission)
Second Unit - North Tunnel

'MISSING LINK' (Episode 7)

Wednesday, April 24, 1974
Zenno (Orange Void) - Stage L

Thursday, April 25, 1974
Zenno (Orange Void) - Stage L
'ANOTHER TIME, ANOTHER PLACE' 'B' Unit: Black Velvet (Main
Mission VFX), Diagnostic Unit (VFX), Inserts - North Tunnel

<u>Friday, April 26, 1974</u>
Zenno (Orange Void) - Stage L
Corridor & Travel Tube - Stage H
Rescue Eagle - Stage M

<u>Monday, April 29, 1974</u>
Zenno (Green Void) - Stage L
Corridor & Travel Tube - Stage H
Rescue Eagle, Interior Diagnostic & Corridor Section - Stage M

<u>Tuesday, April 30, 1974</u>
Rescue Eagle, Diagnostic Unit & Corridor - Stage M

<u>Wednesday, May 1, 1974</u>
Diagnostic Unit & Corridor, Rescue Eagle - Stage M
Main Mission (including '**Ring Around the Moon'** pickups) - Stage L
Eagle Command Module - Stage M (Standby Set)

<u>Thursday, May 2, 1974</u>
Main Mission (including '**Ring Around the Moon'** pickups) - Stage L
Eagle Command Module - Stage M

<u>Friday, May 3, 1974</u>
Eagle Command Module & Passenger Module - Stage M
Zenno (Koenig's Quarters) - Stage M

<u>Monday, May 6, 1974</u>
Zenno (Koenig's Quarters) - Stage M

<u>Tuesday, May 7, 1974</u>
Zenno (Koenig's Quarters) - Stage M
Eagle Command Module (Carter '**BREAKAWAY'** pickups, '**GUARDIAN OF PIRI'** start)
- North Tunnel

'GUARDIAN OF PIRI' (Episode 8)

<u>Wednesday, May 8, 1974</u>
Eagle Command Module - North Tunnel

<u>Thursday, May 9, 1974</u>
Eagle Command Module - North Tunnel
Corridor & Travel Tube, Koenig's Quarters - Stage M

<u>Friday, May 10, 1974</u>
Interior Corridor & Travel Tube, Koenig's Quarters - Stage M

<u>Monday, May 13, 1974</u>
Main Mission - Stage L

<u>Tuesday, May 14, 1974 — Wednesday, May 15, 1974</u>
Main Mission & Balcony - Stage L

<u>Thursday, May 16, 1974 — Friday, May 17, 1974</u>
Main Mission & Koenig's Office, Diagnostic Unit - Stage L

<u>Monday, May 20, 1974</u>
Diagnostic Unit - Stage L
Exterior Piri Planet Surface - Stage M

<u>Tuesday, May 21, 1974</u>
Exterior Paradise Garden with Eagle Section - Stage M

<u>Wednesday, May 22, 1974 — Thursday, May 23, 1974</u>
Exterior Paradise Garden & Guardian Exterior - Stage M

<u>Friday, May 24, 1974</u>
Exterior Guardian, Exterior Planet with Eagle, Exterior Planet - Stage M
Interior Command Module, Main Mission Inserts - North Tunnel

'FORCE OF LIFE' (Episode 9)

<u>*Monday, May 27, 1974*</u>
NO SHOOTING INFORMATION AVAILABLE

<u>Tuesday, May 28, 1974 — Wednesday, May 29, 1974</u>
Interior Corridors - Stage H

<u>Thursday, May 30, 1974</u>
Interior Corridors - Stage H
Medical Center & Corridor - Stage L

<u>Friday, May 31, 1974 — Monday, June 3, 1974</u>
Medical Center & Corridor, Solarium - Stage L

<u>Tuesday, June 4, 1974</u>
Solarium, Married Quarters - Stage H

<u>Wednesday, June 5, 1974</u>
Married Quarters - Stage H
Nuclear Generating Area - Stage M

<u>Thursday, June 6, 1974</u>
Married Quarters - Stage H
Nuclear Generating Area & Corridor - Stage M

<u>Friday, June 7, 1974</u>
Nuclear Generating Area - Stage M

<u>*Monday, June 10, 1974 — Friday, June 28, 1974*</u>
NO SHOOTING INFORMATION AVAILABLE

<u>Monday, July 1, 1974</u>
Nuclear Generating Area - Stage M

<u>Tuesday, July 2, 1974</u>
Nuclear Generating Area - Stage M
Koenig's Office & Main Mission - Stage L

<u>Wednesday, July 3, 1974</u>
Main Mission & Koenig's Office - Stage L

<u>Thursday, July 4, 1974</u>
Main Mission, Koenig's Office, Corridor (Standby Set) - Stage L

<u>Friday, July 5, 1974</u>
Corridor - Stage H
Medical Center - Stage L
Nuclear Generating Area ('**ALPHA CHILD'** start) - Stage M

'ALPHA CHILD' (Episode 10)

<u>Monday, July 8, 1974</u>
Bergman's Quarters, Main Mission & Koenig's Office - Stage L
'ANOTHER TIME, ANOTHER PLACE' visual effects pickups - Bray
Studios

<u>Tuesday, July 9, 1974 — Friday, July 12, 1974</u>
Main Mission & Koenig's Office - Stage L

<u>Monday, July 15, 1974</u>
Main Mission & Koenig's Office, Medical Department, Main Mission Inserts
(including '**GUARDIAN OF PIRI**' gauntlet FX), Diagnostic Unit insert
('**GUARDIAN OF PIRI**' Kano head plug), Barry Morse **MAIN TITLE**
sequence - Stage L

<u>Tuesday, July 16, 1974</u> — <u>Wednesday, July 17, 1974</u>
Medical Department - Stage L

<u>Thursday, July 18, 1974</u>
Medical Department - Stage L
Interior Corridor - Stage H

<u>Friday, July 19, 1974</u>
Interior Corridor - Stage H
Interior Command Module - Stage M

<u>Monday, July 22, 1974</u>
Explorer Command Module, Explorer Passenger Module, Exterior Lunar
Surface & Airlock, Monitor Insert (additional shooting for '**MISSING
LINK**'), Medical Department Insert (for '**ALPHA CHILD**') - Stage M

'THE LAST SUNSET' (Episode 11)

<u>Tuesday, July 23, 1974</u>
Interior Command Module, Interior Passenger Module - Stage M

<u>Wednesday, July 24, 1974</u>
Main Mission & Koenig's Office (Night Backing) - Stage L

<u>Thursday, July 25, 1974</u>
Main Mission & Koenig's Office (Day Backing) - Stage L

<u>Friday, July 26, 1974</u>
Main Mission & Koenig's Office (Storm FX) - Stage L

<u>Monday, July 29, 1974</u>
Main Mission - Stage L
Interior Crashed Passenger Module - Stage M

<u>Tuesday, July 30, 1974</u>
Interior Crashed Passenger Module - Stage M

Wednesday, July 31, 1974
Interior Crashed Passenger Module, Exterior Moon Surface & Morrow's Shack
- Stage M

Thursday, August 1, 1974
Exterior Moon Surface & Morrow's Shack - Stage M

Friday, August 2, 1974
Exterior / Interior Planet Surface - Stage M

Monday, August 5, 1974
Interior Technical Section & Corridor - Stage L

Tuesday, August 6, 1974
Exterior Planet Surface & Interior Airlock - Stage M

'VOYAGER'S RETURN' (Episode 12)

Wednesday, August 7, 1974
Koenig's Office & Main Mission - Stage L
('**LAST SUNSET**' pickups) Exterior Moon Surface (Zienia Merton fight reaction), Interior Hut, Technical Center, Main Mission, Koenig's Office, Exterior Moon Surface - Stage H

Thursday, August 8, 1974 -- Monday, August 12, 1974
Koenig's Office & Main Mission - Stage L

Tuesday, August 13, 1974
Main Mission & Koenig's Office - Stage L
Corridor, Intersection, Travel Tube - Stage H
Medical Department - Stage L

Wednesday, August 14, 1974
Medical Department, Eagle One & Two, Archon Background, Main Mission & Koenig Office Inserts - Stage L

Thursday, August 15, 1974
Interior Voyager One & Boarding Tube - Stage M

Friday, August 16, 1974
Interior Voyager One (Sidon POV), Archon Background - Stage M

Monday, August 19, 1974 — Tuesday, August 20, 1974
Interior Experimental Center Lab - Stage M

Wednesday, August 21, 1974
Interior Experimental Center Lab - Stage M
Main Mission Inserts (Countdown Clock & Lunar Chart) - Stage L
Exterior Moon Surface ('**LAST SUNSET**' Second Unit) - Lot
Technical Section Corridor (Air Mortar Blast), Ext./Int. Morrow Hut,
Technical Section Corridor, Ext. Moon Surface - Stage H

'COLLISION COURSE' (Episode 13)

Thursday, August 22, 1974
Interior Passenger Module, Airlock, Travel Tube - Stage M
Interior Command Module, Eagle Two Rescue Eagle, Reconnaissance Eagle -
Stage L

Friday, August 23, 1974
Interior Eagle - Stage L
Interior Corridor - Stage H
Interior Medical Department - Stage L

Monday, August 26, 1974
BANK HOLIDAY

Tuesday, August 27, 1974
Medical Department, Koenig's Office - Stage L

Wednesday, August 28, 1974
Interior Spaceship Chamber & Passenger Module - Stage M

Thursday, August 29, 1974
Interior Spaceship Chamber - Stage M
Koenig's Office & Main Mission - Stage L

Friday, August 30, 1974 — Thursday, September 5, 1974
Main Mission & Koenig's Office - Stage L

Friday, September 6, 1974
Main Mission & Koenig's Office, Koenig's Quarters & Corridor - Stage L

'DEATH'S OTHER DOMINION' (Episode 14)

Monday, September 9, 1974
Main Mission & Koenig's Office - Stage L

Tuesday, September 10, 1974
Main Mission & Koenig's Office - Stage L
Interior Command Module - Stage H
Exterior Ice Planet Surface (Day/Dusk/Night) - Stage L

Wednesday, September 11, 1974
Exterior Ice Planet Surface - Stage L

Thursday, September 12, 1974
Exterior Ice Planet Surface - Stage L
Int./Ext. Passenger Module - Stage H

Friday, September 13, 1974
Int./Ext. Passenger Module - Stage H
Interior Ice Planet - Stage M

Monday, September 16, 1974
Interior Ice Palace - Stage M

Tuesday, September 17, 1974 — Friday, September 20, 1974
Interior Ice Palace, Lab, Communications Center - Stage M

Monday, September 23, 1974
Interior Ice Palace, Shipyard Balcony, Cave of the Revered - Stage M

'THE FULL CIRCLE' (Episode 15)

Tuesday, September 24, 1973
Interior Command Module, Passenger Module - Stage H

Wednesday, September 25, 1974
Interior Passenger Module - Stage H
Main Mission & Koenig's Office - Stage L

Thursday, September 26, 1974
Interior Medical Department - Stage L

Friday, September 27, 1974 — Monday, September 30, 1974
Ext. Area One Retha Forest, Ext. Area Two Retha Forest, Ext. Retha Forest
Clearing, Ext. Clearing, Ext. Landing/Passenger Module - Lot

Tuesday, October 1, 1974
Ext. Mist Are One, Ext. Clearing, Ext. Mist Area Two - Lot

Wednesday, October 2, 1974
Ext. Mist Area Two, Int. Caves - Stage M

Thursday, October 3, 1974 — Tuesday, October 8, 1974
Interior Caves - Stage M

'END OF ETERNITY' (Episode 16)

Wednesday, October 9, 1974
Main Mission & Koenig's Office - Stage L

Thursday, October 10, 1974
Koenig's Office - Stage L
('**FULL CIRCLE**' Second Unit) Ext. Pit / Int. Pit Retha Forest - Lot

Friday, October 11, 1974 — Monday, October 14, 1974
Main Mission & Koenig's Office - Stage L

Tuesday, October 15, 1974
Main Mission & Koenig's Office, Autopsy & Intensive Care Unit - Stage L

Wednesday, October 16, 1974
Intensive Care Unit, Baxter's Quarters - Stage L

Thursday, October 17, 1974
Intensive Care Unit, Baxter's Quarters, Medical Center - Stage L

Friday, October 18, 1974
Medical Department - Stage L
Corridor & Travel Tube - Stage H

Monday, October 21, 1974
Corridor - Stage H
Corridor & Airlock - Stage M

<u>Tuesday, October 22, 1974</u>
Corridor & Airlock, Eagle Passenger Module, Ext. Asteroid Surface - Stage M

<u>Wednesday, October 23, 1974</u>
Main Mission & Koenig's Office - Stage L
Ext. Asteroid Surface & Int. Tunnel - Stage M

'WAR GAMES' (Episode 17)

<u>Thursday, October 24, 1974</u>
Main Mission - Stage L

<u>Friday, October 25, 1974</u>
Main Mission & Koenig's Office - Stage L

<u>Monday, October 28, 1974</u>
Main Mission & Koenig's Office - Stage L
Second Unit pickups:
Interior Tilting Airlock (**'END OF ETERNITY'**), Interior Corridor (**'WAR GAMES'**) - Stage M
Main Mission inserts to be shot between 1:00 pm and 2:00 pm (**'END OF ETERNITY'** and **'COLLISION COURSE'**), Koenig's Office inserts (**'END OF ETERNITY'**) - Stage L

<u>Tuesday, October 29, 1974</u>
Main Mission & Koenig's Office - Stage L

<u>Wednesday, October 30, 1974</u>
Koenig's Office, Medical Center & Corridor - Stage L

<u>Thursday, October 31, 1974</u>
Medical Center & Corridor - Stage L
Corridors - stage H
Eagle Passenger Module - Stage M

<u>Friday, November 1, 1974</u>
Eagle Reconnaissance Module, Command Module - Stage M

<u>Monday, November 4, 1974</u>
Eagle Module, Int. Planet Control Center - Stage M

Tuesday, November 5, 1974 — Wednesday, November 6, 1974
Interior Planet Control Center - Stage M

Thursday, November 7, 1974
Interior Planet Control Center, Exterior Space - Stage M

'THE LAST ENEMY' (Episode 18)

Friday, November 8, 1974
Corridor & Travel Tube - Stage H
Command Module, Main Mission & Koenig's Office - Stage L
Second Unit pickups:
Exterior Space ('**WAR GAMES'**) - Stage M
Main Mission 'Hand' inserts to be shot between 1:00 pm and 2:00 pm ('**WAR GAMES'**) - Stage L
Diagnostic Unit Kano 'head plug-in' ('**GUARDIAN OF PIRI'**) - Stage M

Monday, November 11, 1974 — Friday, November 15, 1974
Main Mission & Koenig's Office - Stage L

Monday, November 18, 1974
Main Mission & Koenig's Office - Stage L
Interior Travel Tube & Connecting Airlock - Stage M

Tuesday, November 19, 1974
Int. Alien Control Center (Dione's Ready Room), Int. Alien Background (Alien burn-in), Int. Alien Backing (Theia burn-ins), Int. Alien Backing (Talos burn-ins) - Stage M

'THE TROUBLED SPIRIT' (Episode 19)

Wednesday, November 20, 1974
Main Mission, Koenig's Office - Stage L

Thursday, November 21, 1974
Koenig's Office, Music Room - Stage L
Corridor & Travel Tube - Stage H

Friday, November 22, 1974
Corridor - Stage H
Medical Department - Stage L

Monday, November 25, 1974 — Tuesday, November 26, 1974
Medical Department - Stage L

Wednesday, November 27, 1974
Medical Department - Stage L
Hydroponic Unit - Stage M

Thursday, November 28, 1974 — Wednesday, December 4, 1974
Hydroponic Unit - Stage M
('**FULL CIRCLE**' Second Unit pickups) Int. Cave (Barbara Bain Cavewife
C.U.), Int. Mist Area (Koenig C.U.) - Stage L

'SPACE BRAIN' (Episode 20)

Thursday, December 5, 1974
Main Mission & Koenig's Office - Stage L
Second Unit pickups:
Hydroponic Unit ('**THE TROUBLED SPIRIT**'- CS Warren) & Unit
Laboratory ('**THE TROUBLED SPIRIT**' - CS Hands Round Table), Medical
Center / Isolation Area ('**THE TROUBLED SPIRIT**' - Spirit Body Leaves
Mateo), Medical Center ('**END OF ETERNITY**' - Baxter Exits Through Door)
- Stage M

Friday, December 6, 1974 — Monday, December 9, 1974
Main Mission & Koenig's Office - Stage L

Tuesday, December 10, 1974
Main Mission & Koenig's Office - Stage L

Wednesday, December 11, 1974
Main Mission & Koenig's Office - Stage L
Command Module - Eagle 7 (Stand-by Set) - North Tunnel

Thursday, December 12, 1974
Eagle Passenger & Command Module, Ext. Space - North Tunnel

Friday, December 13, 1974 — Monday, December 16, 1974
Medical Center & Intensive Care Unit - Stage L

Tuesday, December 17, 1974
Medical & Intensive Care Unit - Stage L

Wednesday, December 18, 1974
Medical & Intensive Care Unit, Melita's Quarters - Stage L
Corridors - Stage H
Computer Room (Stand-by Set) - Stage M

Thursday, December 19, 1974
Computer Room & Corridor, Technical Department - Stage M

'THE INFERNAL MACHINE' (Episode 21)

Friday, December 20, 1974
Koenig's Quarters, Main Mission - Stage L
Second Unit pickups:
Ext. Space, Int. Command Module (Koenig Re-Take), Command Module
(Monitor with Heartbeat Pattern), Main Mission (CS Koenig's Commlock
Picture), Computer Room (CS Kelly's Hands On Buttons) - North Tunnel

Monday, December 23, 1974
Main Mission - Stage L

Tuesday, December 24, 1974
Main Mission - Stage L
Command Module, Passenger Module & Connecting Tube - North Tunnel
Corridor - Stage H

Wednesday, December 25, 1974 — Friday, December 27, 1974
CHRISTMAS HOLIDAY

Monday, December 30, 1974
Corridor - Stage H
Machine Lift / Corridor & Machine Chamber - Stage M

Tuesday, December 31, 1974
Machine Room & Corridor - Stage M

Wednesday, January 1, 1975
NEW YEAR HOLIDAY

Thursday, January 2, 1975 — Wednesday, January 8, 1975
Machine Room & Corridor - Stage M

Thursday, January 9, 1975
Machine Room & Corridor - Stage M
Machine Room (Rostrum Coffin Shot) - Stage L

'MISSION OF THE DARIANS' (Episode 22)

Friday, January 10, 1975
Main Mission - Stage L
Eagle Command Module - North Tunnel

Monday, January 13, 1975
Passenger Module, Airlock & Corridor Section - North Tunnel

Tuesday, January 14, 1975
Int. Airlock & Corridor Section - North Tunnel
Corridor 1, Corridor 2 - Stage H

Wednesday, January 15, 1975
Corridor One, Corridor Two (Daria) - Stage H
Rest Room (Daria) - Stage L

Thursday, January 16, 1975
Rest Room, Transplant Room - Stage L

Friday, January 17, 1975
Transplant Room - Stage L
Settlement Corridor / Area & Undergrowth, Settlement Area - Stage M

Monday, January 18, 1975
Settlement Area - Stage M

Tuesday, January 19, 1975
Settlement Corridor / Gantry & Undergrowth, Settlement Area - Stage M

Wednesday, January 20, 1975
Settlement Area - Stage M
Darian Command Center - Stage L

Thursday, January 21, 1975
Darian Command Center - Stage L
Corridor Complex - Stage H
Gantry Entrance & Airlock - Stage M

Friday, January 22, 1975
Darian Command Center - Stage L
Corridor Complex - Stage H
Gantry Entrance & Airlock, Gantry Backing, Gantry Exit / Airlock &
Corridor, Matte Shot - Stage M

'DRAGON'S DOMAIN' (Episode 23)

Monday, January 27, 1975
Main Mission, Medical Center - Stage L

Tuesday, January 28, 1975
Medical Center - Stage L

Wednesday, January 29, 1975
Medical Center, Cellini's Quarters & Corridor - Stage L

Thursday, January 30, 1975
Cellini's Quarters & Corridor - Stage L
Commissioner Dixon's Office (Earth) - Stage M
Technical Department - Stage L

Friday, January 31, 1975
Commissioner Dixon's Office (Earth) - Stage M
Technical Department, Helena's Quarters - Stage L

Monday, February 3, 1975
Int. Earth Hospital & Corridor, Command Module Stand-By Eagle / Eagle
One / Eagle Two - Stage M

Tuesday, February 4, 1975
Command Module Stand-By Eagle / Eagle One / Eagle Two, Passenger
Module - Stage M

Wednesday, February 5, 1975
Passenger Module - Stage M
Corridor & Airlock, Corridor, Boarding Tube - Stage H

Thursday, February 6, 1975
NO SHOOTING INFORMATION AVAILABLE

Friday, February 7, 1975
Probeship Command Module, Probeship Passenger Module - Stage M

Monday, February 10, 1975
Eagle & Passenger Probeship, Eagle Passenger Module, Probeship Passenger Module - Stage M

'THE TESTAMENT OF ARKADIA' (Episode 24)

Tuesday, February 11, 1975
Main Mission - Stage L
'DRAGON'S DOMAIN' Second Unit pickups:
Eagle Section & Probeship, Passenger Section Probeship, Command Module Probeship, Passenger Section Probeship (Montage) - Stage M

Wednesday, February 12, 1975
Main Mission - Stage L
'DRAGON'S DOMAIN' Second Unit pickups:
Passenger Section Probeship, Command Module Probeship, Passenger Section Probeship (Montage) - Stage M

Thursday, February 13, 1975
Main Mission - Stage L
'DRAGON'S DOMAIN' Second Unit pickups:
Passenger Module, Passenger Section Probeship, Command Module Probeship, - Stage M

Friday, February 14, 1975
Main Mission, Koenig's Office - Stage L

Monday, February 17, 1975
Koenig's Office & Main Mission, Reference Library, Recreation Room - Stage L

Tuesday, February 18, 1975
Corridor (Blue Filter), Corridor (White Filter), Corridor & Protein Room (Green Filter), Corridor 4 (Orange Filter), Corridor & Travel Tube (Red Filter) - Stage H
Int. Eagle 2 & Boarding Tube, Int. Eagle 4 & Boarding Tube - North Tunnel

Wednesday, February 19, 1975
Int. Eagle 4 & Boarding Tube, Passenger Module (R-L) Eagle (4), Passenger Module (R-L) Eagle (1) - North Tunnel
Reference Library (Re-Take), Recreation Room - Stage L

Ext. Planet Surface & Base Camp - Stage M

Thursday, February 20, 1975
Passenger Module (R-L) Eagle (1), Command Module (R-L) Eagle (4),
Command Module (R-L) Eagle (2), Command Module (L-R) Eagle (2),
Command Module (L-R) Eagle (1) - North Tunnel

Friday, February 21, 1975
Ext. Planet Surface - Tree Area (Day), Ext. Planet Surface - Base Camp
(Sunset), Ext. Planet Surface (Day), Ext. Planet Surface - Ext. Cave, Int. Cave
(Day) - Stage M

Monday, February 24, 1975
Ext. Planet Surface & Ext. Cave Entrance, Int. Cave (Day) - Stage M

Tuesday, February 25, 1975
Int. Cave (Sunset), Ext. Cave Entrance (Sunset) - Stage M
'B' Unit Burn-in pickups:
Talos and Theia Backgrounds, Main Mission (Big Screen, Towards Koenig's
Office, Observation Platform Windows, Balcony Stairs From Koenig's
Office), Ext. Lunar Surface (Black Drapes) ('**THE LAST ENEMY'**) - Stage L
Int. Eagles ('**SPACE BRAIN'**) - North Tunnel

Wednesday, February 26, 1975
Main Mission (pickups), Koenig's Office ('**THE LAST ENEMY'**) - Stage L

Thursday, February 27, 1975
Main Mission, Koenig's Office ('**THE LAST ENEMY'**), Main Mission
('**SPACE BRAIN'**) - Stage L

Friday, February 28, 1975
Int. Command Center Ship ('**THE LAST ENEMY'**) - Stage H
Lunar Surface (Black Drape for '**THE LAST ENEMY'** Helmet Shots),
Corridor Wall ('**THE TESTAMENT OF ARKADIA'**) - North Tunnel

YEAR ONE ARTISTES

By David Hirsch

The following lists have been culled from Martin Landau's incomplete collection of Call Sheets. Some names may be incorrectly spelled or missing entirely and we have retained these errors for historical accuracy. Note how various background performers are moved around as needed, sometimes eventually given names (eg Suzanne Roquette initially listed as 'Operative (5)' in the call sheets, probably because her line of dialogue, where she introduces herself to Koenig, was not in the script).

1. 'BREAKAWAY'

Series Regular Performers

Martin Landau	Koenig
Barbara Bain	Helena
Barry Morse	Bergman
Prentis Hancock	Morrow
Zienia Merton	Sandra
Nick Tate	Carter
Anton Philips	Mathias

Guest & Background Performers

Lon Satton	Ouma
Roy Dotrice	Simmonds
Shane Rimmer	Newscaster
Alf Joint	Steiner
Roy Scammel	Nordstrom
Colin Skeaping	Ellis
Nik Zaran	Jackson
Robin Scott	Eric
David Rhys Anderson	Frank
Christopher Matthews	Operative (1)
Loftus Burton	Operative (2)
Michael Zorba	Operative (3)
Paul Weston	Operative (4)
Suzanne Roquette	Operative (5)
Chai Lee	Operative (6)
Valerie Van Ost	Operator A
Norma West	Operator B

Stand Ins

John Clifford	Koenig
Suzanne Heimer	Helena
Tony Allen	Bergman
Bill Westley	Simmonds

Stunts

Alf Joint	Balcony Fall
Paul Weston	Jerk Fall, Koenig Stunt Double

2. 'MATTER OF LIFE AND DEATH'

Series Regular Performers

Martin Landau	Koenig
Barbara Bain	Helena
Barry Morse	Bergman
Prentis Hancock	Morrow
Zienia Merton	Sandra
Nick Tate	Carter
Clifton Jones	Kano
Anton Philips	Mathias

Guest & Background Performers

Richard Johnson	Russell

Tony Allyn	1st Security Guard
Quentin Pierre	2nd Security Guard
Christopher Matthews	Operative (1)
Loftus Burton	Operative (2)
Jeremy Anthony	Operative (3)
Andy Dempsey	Operative (4)
Suzanne Roquette	Operative (5)
Chai Lee	Operative (6)

Stand Ins

John Clifford	Koenig
Suzanne Heimer	Helena
Alan Meacham	Bergman
Tony Allyn	Russell
Jane Henley	Sandra

Stunts

Alf Joint	
Paul Weston	Koenig Stunt Double
Dorothy Ford	Helena Stunt Double

3. 'BLACK SUN'

Series Regular Performers

Martin Landau	Koenig
Barbara Bain	Helena
Barry Morse	Bergman
Prentis Hancock	Morrow
Zienia Merton	Sandra
Nick Tate	Carter
Clifton Jones	Kano
Anton Philips	Mathias
Suzanne Roquette	Tanya

Guest & Background Performers

Paul Jones	Mike
Jon Laurimore	Smitty
Jack McKenzie	1st Engineer
Richard Eden	2nd Engineer
Philip Clifton	3rd Engineer

Jan Harvey	Operator
Ronald Chenery	Osgood
Vincent Wong	Fujita
Corinne Skinner-Carter	Robinson
Loftus Burton	Operative (1)
Andy Dempsey	Operative (2)
Chai Lee	Operative (3)
David Robb	Operative (4)
Marc Zuber	Operative (5)
Tony Goldwyn	1st Guard
Guy Groen	Technician

Stand Ins

John Clifford	Koenig
Suzanne Heimer	Helena
Alan Meacham	Bergman
Tony Allyn	Russell
Jane Henley	Sandra

Stunts

No Stunt Credits

4. 'RING AROUND THE MOON'
(No Call Sheets Available)

Series Regular Performers

Martin Landau	Koenig
Barbara Bain	Helena
Barry Morse	Bergman
Prentis Hancock	Morrow
Zienia Merton	Sandra
Nick Tate	Carter
Clifton Jones	Kano
Anton Philips	Mathias
Suzanne Roquette	Tanya

Guest & Background Performers

No Performer Credits

Stand Ins

No Stand In Credits

Stunts

No Stunt Credits

5. 'EARTHBOUND'

Series Regular Performers

Martin Landau	Koenig
Barbara Bain	Helena
Barry Morse	Bergman
Prentis Hancock	Morrow
Zienia Merton	Sandra
Nick Tate	Carter
Clifton Jones	Kano
Anton Philips	Mathias
Suzanne Roquette	Tanya

Guest & Background Performers

Christopher Lee	Zantor
Roy Dotrice	Simmonds
Tony Allwyn	1st Guard
Steve Paterson	3rd Guard
John Aston	4th Guard
Peter Wear	Kaldorian 1
Michael Montgomery	Kaldorian 2
Angela Staines	Kaldorian 3
Christine Hewitt	Kaldorian 4
Rhonda Parker	Kaldorian 5
Loftus Burton	Main Mission Operative 1
Andy Dempsey	Main Mission Operative 2
Robert Philips	Main Mission Operative 3
June Bolton	Main Mission Operative 4
Joy Harrison	Main Mission Operative 5
Richard Eden	2nd Technician
Guy Groen	3rd Technician
Jack McKenzie	1st Technician
Roy Everson	Security Guard
Quentin Pierre	2nd Security Guard
Norton Clarke	Security Guard
John Lee Barber	Co-Pilot

Stand Ins

Alan Meacham	Koenig
Suzanne Heimer	Helena
Tony Allyn	Bergman
Bill Westley	Simmonds (March 15 only)
Mike Stevens	Simmonds (March 8 — on)
Frank Harper	Zantor

Stunts

Lesley Stamps	Helena Stunt Double (March 20 only)
Eileen Harvey	Helena Stunt Double (March 21 — on)

6. 'ANOTHER TIME, ANOTHER PLACE'

Series Regular Performers

Martin Landau	Koenig
Barbara Bain	Helena / Earth Helena
Barry Morse	Bergman / Earth Bergman
Prentis Hancock	Morrow / Earth Morrow
Zienia Merton	Sandra / Earth Sandra
Nick Tate	Carter
Clifton Jones	Kano / Earth Kano
Anton Philips	Mathias
Suzanne Roquette	Tanya

Guest & Background Performers

Judy Geeson	Regina
Andy Dempsey	Main Mission Operative 1
Loftus Burton	Main Mission Operative 2
Robert Philips	Main Mission

	Operative 3
June Bolton	Main Mission
	Operative 4
Joy Harrison	Main Mission
	Operative 5
Alan Harris	Main Mission
Mike Stevens	Main Mission
Lesley Stamps	Main Mission
Chris Williams	Orderly 1
Saad Ghazi	Orderly 2
Fran Hunter	Medical
Alan Gibson	Child
Barbara Speaks	Child
Claire McLellan	Child
Corona[42]	Child
Valerie Summers	Voice Over - Post
Barbara Kelly	Voice Over - Post

Stand Ins

Alan Meacham	Koenig
Mike Stevens	Koenig (April 16 only)
Suzanne Heimer	Helena
Tony Allyn	Bergman
Jane Henley	Regina
Pamela Rose	Regina (April 25 only)

Stunts

Alan Meacham	Koenig Double
Harry Van Engel	Carter Double
Pamela Rose	Regina Double
Colin Skeeping	Technician

7. 'MISSING LINK'

Series Regular Performers

Martin Landau	Koenig
Barbara Bain	Helena
Barry Morse	Bergman
Prentis Hancock	Morrow
Zienia Merton	Sandra
Nick Tate	Carter
Clifton Jones	Kano
Anton Philips	Mathias
Suzanne Roquette	Tanya

Guest & Background Performers

Peter Cushing	Raan
Joanna Dunham	Vana
Oliver MacGreevy	Creature 1
Norman McGlenn	Creature 2
Robert Bridges	Creature 3
Jill Damas	Orderly 2
Chris Williams	Orderly 1
Tony Allyn	1st Guard
Val Musetti	2nd Guard

Stand Ins

Alan Meacham	Koenig
Suzanne Heimer	Helena
Ron Watkins	Bergman
George Holdcroft	Raan
Lesley Stamps	Vana

Stunts

George Leech	Bergman
Sadie Bien	Sandra
Paul Weston	Mathias

8. 'GUARDIAN OF PIRI'

Series Regular Performers

Martin Landau	Koenig
Barbara Bain	Helena
Barry Morse	Bergman
Prentis Hancock	Morrow
Zienia Merton	Sandra
Nick Tate	Carter
Clifton Jones	Kano
Anton Philips	Mathias
Suzanne Roquette	Tanya

---

[42] This most likely refers to the Corona acting school from where extras were hired.

Guest & Background Performers

Catherine Schell	Pirian Girl
Gareth Hunt	Irving (May 7 shoot)
Michael Culver	Irving (May 20 shoot − on)
John Lee Barber	David (May 7 shoot)
John Gleeson	Davis (May 20 shoot − on)
James Fagan	Johnson
June Bolton	Operative 1
Christine Donna	Operative 2
Raymond Harris	Operative 3
Loftus Burton	Operative 4
Andy Dempsey	Operative 5
Tony Allyn	First Guard
Trevor Ainsley	Technical Head
Anne Hanson	Sarah Graham
Willow	Nurse 1
Juliet King	Nurse 2
Jodi Sherwood	Nurse 3
Tony Goodall	Alpha Staff

Stand Ins

Alan Meacham	Koenig
Suzanne Heimer	Helena
Ron Watkins	Bergman
Carolyn Paul	Pirian Girl

Stunts

Marc Boyle	Koenig
Joe Dunne	Carter
Dorothy Ford	Pirian Girl
Terry Walsh	Morrow
Alf Joint	Stunt Arranger

9. 'FORCE OF LIFE'

Series Regular Performers

Martin Landau	Koenig
Barbara Bain	Helena
Barry Morse	Bergman
Prentis Hancock	Morrow
Zienia Merton	Sandra
Nick Tate	Carter
Clifton Jones	Kano
Anton Philips	Mathias
Suzanne Roquette	Tanya

Guest & Background Performers

Ian McShane	Anton Zoref
Gay Hamilton	Eva
John Hamill	Dominix
Lea Dregorn	Girl
Eva Rueber-Staier	Jane
Tony Goodall	Alphan 1
Jill Damas	Alphan 2
David Beck	Alphan 3
Alan Harris	Alphan 4
Chris Williams	Orderly 1
Vincent Wong	Orderly 2
Tony Allyn	1st Guard
Quentin Pierre	2nd Guard
John Starbutt	3rd Guard
Clive Hornby	4th Guard
Jack Shepherd	5th Guard
Maureen Tan	Nurse 1
Jodi Sherwood	Nurse 2
Leon Burton	Bather 1
John Repsch	Bather 2
Hazel Wilson	Bather 3
June Bolton	Operative 1
Sarah Bullen	Operative 2
Raymond Harris	Operative 3
Loftus Burton	Operative 4
Andy Dempsey	Operative 5
Norton Clark	Security Guard
David McNally	Patient

Stand Ins

Alan Meacham	Koenig
Suzanne Heimer	Helena
Ron Watkins	Bergman
Mike Stevens	Zoref
Bill Risley	Zoref (July 2 only)
Christine Spooner	Eva

Stunts

Alf Joint	Stunt Arranger

10. 'ALPHA CHILD'

Series Regular Performers

Martin Landau	Koenig
Barbara Bain	Helena
Barry Morse	Bergman
Prentis Hancock	Morrow
Zienia Merton	Sandra
Nick Tate	Carter
Clifton Jones	Kano
Anton Philips	Mathias
Suzanne Roquette	Tanya

Guest & Background Performers

Wayne Brooks	Jackie
Julian Glover	Jarak
Cyd Hayman	Rena / Cynthia
Rula Lenska	Joan Conway
June Bolton	Operative 1 (July 8 shoot)
Maureen Tan	Operative 1 (July 9 shoot — on)
Sarah Bullen	Operative 2
Raymond Harris	Operative 3
Loftus Burton	Operative 4
Andy Dempsey	Operative 5
Andrea Allen	Nurse Paula
Tony Allyn	1st Guard
Quentin Pierre	2nd Guard
Gerry Crampton	3rd Guard
David Brandon	4th Guard
Linda Westover	Nurse (2)
Jodi Sherwood	Nurse (3)
Anita West	Alphan 1
Bina Williams	Baby

Stand Ins

Mike Stevens	Koenig (July 5 shoot)
Alan Meacham	Koenig

Suzanne Heimer	Helena
Ron Watkins	Bergman
Harry Van Engel	Carter
Richard Sheekey	Jarak
Christine Spooner	Rena

Stunts

Alf Joint	Stunt Arranger

11. 'THE LAST SUNSET'

Series Regular Performers

Martin Landau	Koenig
Barbara Bain	Helena
Barry Morse	Bergman
Prentis Hancock	Morrow
Zienia Merton	Sandra
Nick Tate	Carter
Clifton Jones	Kano
Anton Philips	Mathias
Suzanne Roquette	Tanya

Guest & Background Performers

Robert Arnold	Johnson
Paul Grist	First Pilot
Maureen Tan	Operative 1
Sarah Bullen	Operative 2
Robert Phillips	Operative 3
Loftus Burton	Operative 4
Andy Dempsey	Operative 5
Janet Allen	Alphan 1
Penny Stevenson	Alphan 2
Linzy Scott	Alphan 3
Sally Osborne	Alphan 4
Linda Westover	Alphan 5
Venita Witty	Alphan 6
Jodi Sherwood	Alphan 7
Quentin Pierre	Alphan 8
Jack McKenzie	Tech 1
Ricard Adams	Tech 2
Anita West	Tech 3
Guy Francois Groen	Tech 4
Alf Joint	Tech 5
Romo Gorrara	Tech 6
Tony Allyn	First Guard

Mike Stevens	Alpha Staff
Anita West	Tech (1)
Laurie Davis	Tech (2)

Stand Ins

| Alan Harris | Alpha Staff / Tech (3) |

Alan Meacham	Koenig
Suzanne Heimer	Helena
Al Flemyng	Tech (4)
Eileen Harvey	Helena (July 25 shoot)

Stand Ins

| Ron Watkins | Bergman |

| Alan Meacham | Koenig |
| Suzanne Heimer | Helena |

Stunts

| Ron Watkins | Bergman |
| Max Craig | Bergman (August 19 shoot) |

Alf Joint	Stunt Arranger
Terry Walsh	Morrow
Terry Maidment	Carter
Brian Towns	Linden
Sadie Eden	Sandra
Mike Stevens	Archon
Dorothy Ford	Helena
Eddie Stacy	Koenig

Stunts

12. 'VOYAGER'S RETURN'

| Alf Joint | Stunt Arranger |

Series Regular Performers

13. 'COLLISION COURSE'

| Martin Landau | Koenig |
| Barbara Bain | Helena |

Series Regular Performers

Barry Morse	Bergman
Prentis Hancock	Morrow
Martin Landau	Koenig
Zienia Merton	Sandra
Barbara Bain	Helena
Nick Tate	Carter
Barry Morse	Bergman
Clifton Jones	Kano
Prentis Hancock	Morrow
Anton Philips	Mathias
Zienia Merton	Sandra
Suzanne Roquette	Tanya
Nick Tate	Carter
		Clifton Jones	Kano
		Anton Philips	Mathias
		Suzanne Roquette	Tanya

Guest & Background Performers

Jeremy Kemp	Linden
Alex Scott	Archon
Barry Stokes	Haines

Guest & Background Performers

Lawrence Trimble	Abrams
Ricard Gardner	Pilot 1
Margaret Leighton	Arra
Robert Swales	Pilot 2
Richard Gardner	Pilot
Sarah Bullen	Operative 1
Merdel Jordine	Nurse (1)
Linda Westover	Operative 2
Cary Lee	Nurse (2)
Loftus Burton	Operative 3
Tony Haines	Orderly
Robert Phillips	Operative 4
Sarah Bullen	Operative 1
Andy Dempsey	Operative 5
Anne Lambert	Operative 2
Chris Williams	Operative 6
Loftus Burton	Operative 3
Mike Stevens	Main Mission
Andy Dempsey	Operative 4
		Robert Burton	Operative 5

Robert Phillips	Operative 5 (September 5 shoot)	Jack Shepherd	Thulian (1)
		Laurie Davis	Thulian (2)
		Eddy Nedar	Thulian (3)
Mary Berleigh	Main Mission	Tony Houghton	Thulian (4)
Lynn Morrison	Main Mission	John Lee-Barber	Thulian (5)
Cathy Gilfrin	Main Mission	Suzanne St. Clair	Thulian (6)
Allan Harris	Main Mission	Barbara Bermel	Thulian (7)
Mike Stevens	Main Mission	Jenny Devenish	Thulian (8)
Romo Gorrara	1st Guard	Carolyn Hudson	Thulian (9)
Lee Crawford	2nd Guard	Valerie Leon	Thulian (10)
		Glenda Allan	Thulian (11)

Stand Ins

		Dave Murphy	Thulian (12)
		Mike Ryan	Thulian (13)
Alan Meacham	Koenig	Anette Linden	Thulian (14)
Suzanne Heimer	Helena	Ellen Sheean	Revered (1)
Max Craig	Bergman	Adrien Burgess	Revered (2)
Bunny Sieman	Arra	Margaret Lawley	Revered (3)
		Terry Rendle	Revered (4)
		Ian Ruskin	Revered (5)
		Robert Driscoll	Revered (6)

Stunts

		Lesley Collet	Revered (7)
Romo Gorrara	Stunt Arranger	Sarah Bullen	Operative 1
Eddie Stacey	Koenig	Anne Lambert	Operative 2
George Leech	Bergman	Leon Burton	Operative 3
Tim Condron	Carter	Andy Dempsey	Operative 4
Terry Walsh	Morrow	Robert Phillips	Operative 5
Vic Armstrong	Fighter		
Peter Pocock	Jumper		

Stand Ins

Alan Meacham	Koenig
Suzanne Heimer	Helena
Ron Watkins	Bergman
Max Craig	Rowland
E Cogiell	Tanner

14. 'DEATH'S OTHER DOMINION'

Series Regular Performers

Martin Landau	Koenig
Barbara Bain	Helena
Barry Morse	Bergman
Prentis Hancock	Morrow
Zienia Merton	Sandra
Nick Tate	Carter
Clifton Jones	Kano
Anton Philips	Mathias
Suzanne Roquette	Tanya

Stunts

Eddie Stacey	Stunt Thulian
Joe Dunne	Stunt Thulian

15. 'THE FULL CIRCLE'

Guest & Background Performers

Series Regular Performers

Brian Blessed	Rowland
John Shrapnel	Tanner
David Ellison	Ted
Mary Miller	Frieda

Martin Landau	Koenig
Barbara Bain	Helena / Cavewife
Barry Morse	Bergman

Prentis Hancock — Morrow
Zienia Merton — Sandra
Nick Tate — Carter
Clifton Jones — Kano
Anton Philips — Mathias
Suzanne Roquette — Tanya

Guest & Background Performers

Oliver Cotton — Spearman
Tony Allyn — Caveman / 1st Guard
Alan Meacham — Caveman
Tony Boyd — Caveman
Anthony Powell — Caveman
Jeffery Taylor — Caveman
Andy Dempsey — Main Mission / Caveman
Sarah Bullen — Main Mission / Cavewoman
Lynda Westover — Main Mission / Cavewoman
Lisa Woods — Cavewoman
Jaqueline Blackmore — Cavewoman
Anne Lambert — Operative (1)
Yocki — Operative (2)
Loftus Burton — Operative (3)
Robert Phillips — Operative (4)
Colin Rix — Co-Pilot
Kathy Mallory — Nurse (A)
Glenda Allen — Nurse (B)
Fran Hunter — Nurse (B - October 1 shoot)
Chai Lee — Nurse (C)
Chris Williams — Orderly

Stand Ins

Alan Meacham — Koenig
Suzanne Heimer — Helena
Eileen Harvey — Helena (September 27 shoot)
Ron Watkins — Bergman

Stunts

Alf Joint — Stunt Arranger / Koenig / Caveman
Eddie Stacey — Spearman
Tim Condren — Carter
Quentin Pierre — Kano Double

16. 'END OF ETERNITY'

Series Regular Performers

Martin Landau — Koenig
Barbara Bain — Helena
Barry Morse — Bergman
Prentis Hancock — Morrow
Zienia Merton — Sandra
Nick Tate — Carter
Clifton Jones — Kano
Anton Philips — Mathias
Suzanne Roquette — Tanya

Guest & Background Performers

Peter Bowles — Balor
Jim Smillie — Baxter
Vincent Wong — Dr Fujita
Jan Rennison — Mission Operative (1)
Binu Balini — Mission Operative (2)
Raymond Harris — Mission Operative (3)
Andy Dempsey — Mission Operative (4)
Laurie Davis — Main Mission
Tony Allyn — Security Guard
Quentin Pierre — Security Guard
Judith Hepburn — Nurse (A)
Kathy Mallory — Nurse (B)
Chris Williams — Orderly (A)
Paul Kirby — Orderly (B)
Alan Harris — Patient
Robert Atiko — Alphan
Anthony Scott — Alphan (1)
Uffe Neuman — Alphan (2)
Mike Stevens — Man

Laraine Humphreys	Information Girl

Stand Ins

Alan Meacham	Koenig
Suzanne Heimer	Helena
Ron Watkins	Bergman
Lew Morgan	Balor

Stunts

Alf Joint	Stunt Arranger / Balor / Alpha (1)
Eddie Stacey	Koenig / Security Guard
Joe Dunne	Bergman
Colin Skeaping	Baxter / Security Guard
Chris Webb	Alphan (2)
Paul Weston	Guard (1)
Martin Grace	Guard (2)

17. 'WAR GAMES'

Series Regular Performers

Martin Landau	Koenig
Barbara Bain	Helena
Barry Morse	Bergman
Prentis Hancock	Morrow
Zienia Merton	Sandra
Nick Tate	Carter
Clifton Jones	Kano
Anton Philips	Mathias
Suzanne Roquette	Tanya

Guest & Background Performers

Anthony Valentine	Male Alien
Isla Blair	Female Alien
Robert Arnold	Johnson (Carter Co-Pilot)
Sarah Bullen	Operative (1)
Binu Balini	Operative (2)
Andy Dempsey	Operative (3)
Raymond Harris	Operative (4)
Laurie Davis	Operative (5)
Paul Weston	Technician (3)
Colin Skeaping	Technician (4)
Martin Grace	1st Guard
Lee Crawford	Security Guard
Judith Hepburn	Nurse (A)
Kathy Mallory	Nurse (B)
Jenny Galston	Nurse (C)
Carol Dee	Casualty (1)
Ricard Adams	Casualty (2)
Tony Goodall	First Alphan
Robert Atiko	Second Alphan
Ron Watson	Passenger

Stand Ins

Alan Meacham	Koenig
Suzanne Heimer	Helena
Ron Watkins	Bergman / Male Alien
Eileen Harvey	Female Alien (November 4 shoot)
Jane Henley	Female Alien (November 5 — on)

Stunts

Alf Joint	Stunt Arranger
Eddie Stacey	Koenig
Dorothy Ford	Helena
Tim Condren	Carter
Paul Weston	Mathias
Martin Grace	Casualty

18. 'THE LAST ENEMY'

Series Regular Performers

Martin Landau	Koenig
Barbara Bain	Helena
Barry Morse	Bergman
Prentis Hancock	Morrow
Zienia Merton	Sandra
Nick Tate	Carter
Clifton Jones	Kano
Anton Philips	Mathias
Suzanne Roquette	Tanya

Guest & Background Performers

Caroline Mortimer	Dione
Maxine Audley	Thea
Kevin Stoney	Talos
Caroline Courage	1st Girl (Command Ship)
Linda Brooks	2nd Girl (Command Ship)
Tara Faraday	3rd Girl (Command Ship)
Sarah Bullen	Operative (1)
Clair Lutter	Operative (2) (November 11 only)
Ann Maj-Britt	Operative (2) (February 26 — on)
Andy Sutcliffe	Operative (3) (November 11 only) Main Mission (February 26 — on)
Loftus Burton	Operative (3) (February 26 — on)
Andy Dempsey	Operative (4)
Laurie Davis	Operative (5)
Andy Sutcliffe	Alpha Staff
Tony Allyn	1st Guard
Quentin Pierre	2nd Guard
Robert Case	3rd Guard
John Lee-Barber	Pilot
Alan Bennion	Alien

Stand Ins

Alan Meacham	Koenig
Bill Westley	Koenig Inside Space Suit
Suzanne Heimer	Helena
Ron Watkins	Bergman
Renee Heimer	Dione

Stunts

No Stunt Credits

19. 'THE TROUBLED SPIRIT'

Series Regular Performers

Martin Landau	Koenig
Barbara Bain	Helena
Barry Morse	Bergman
Prentis Hancock	Morrow
Zienia Merton	Sandra
Nick Tate	Carter
Clifton Jones	Kano
Anton Philips	Mathias
Suzanne Roquette	Tanya

Guest & Background Performers

Giancarlo Prete	Mateo
Val Musetti	Spirit Mateo
Hilary Dwyer	Laura
Anthony Nicholls	Warren
Jim Sullivan	Sitar Player
Sarah Bullen	Operative (1)
Binu Balini	Operative (2)
Loftus Burton	Operative (3)
Andy Dempsey	Operative (4)
Xanthi Gardner	Alphan (1)
Vernon Morris	Alphan (2)
Robert Atiko	Alphan
Eddy Nedari	Alphan
Richard Shore	Main Mission
Laurie Davis	Main Mission
Judith Hepburn	Nurse (A)
Jenni Galston	Nurse (B)
Jan Hennison	Nurse (C)
Chris Williams	Orderly (1)
Tony Allyn	1st Guard
Quentin Pierre	2nd Guard

Stand Ins

Alan Meacham	Koenig
Suzanne Heimer	Helena
Ron Watkins	Bergman

Mike Stevens	Mateo
Fran Hunter	Laura
Bill Westley	Warren / Mateo
	Hand Double

Stunts

No Stunt Credits

20. 'SPACE BRAIN'

Series Regular Performers

Martin Landau	Koenig
Barbara Bain	Helena
Barry Morse	Bergman
Prentis Hancock	Morrow
Zienia Merton	Sandra
Nick Tate	Carter
Clifton Jones	Kano
Anton Philips	Mathias
Suzanne Roquette	Tanya

Guest & Background Performers

Shane Rimmer	Kelly
Carla Romanelli	Melita
Sarah Bullen	Operative (1)
Jacqueline Delhaye	Operative (2)
Andy Dempsey	Operative (2) (February 27)
Loftus Burton	Operative (3)
Andy Dempsey	Operative (4)
Ann Maj-Britt	Operative (4) (February 27)
Laurie Davis	Operative (5)
Tony Allyn	1st Guard
Quentin Pierre	2nd Guard
Robert Atiko	Technician (A)
Michael Sirett	Technician (B)

Stand Ins

Alan Meacham	Koenig
Mike Stevens	Koenig (December 20 re-take)
Norton Clark	Koenig Hand

	Double
Suzanne Heimer	Helena
Ron Watkins	Bergman
Lew Hooper	Kelley
Lynn Morrison	Melita
Laurie Davis	(February 27)
Mike Stevens	(February 27)

Stunts

Eddie Stacey	Stunt Arranger
Tim Condron	Carter
Joe Dunne	Kelly

21. 'THE INFERNAL MACHINE'

Series Regular Performers

Martin Landau	Koenig
Barbara Bain	Helena
Barry Morse	Bergman
Zienia Merton	Sandra
Nick Tate	Carter
Clifton Jones	Kano
Anton Philips	Mathias
Suzanne Roquette	Tanya

Guest & Background Performers

Leo McKern	Companion / Gwent
Gary Waldhorn	Winters
Sarah Bullen	Operative (1)
Jan Rennison	Operative (2)
Erica Stevens	Operative (3)
Loftus Burton	Operative (4)
Andy Dempsey	Operative (5)
Andy Sutcliffe	Operative (6)
Mike Stevens	Main Mission Staff
Alan Harris	Main Mission Staff
Paul Kirby	Main Mission Staff
Remy Dussek	Main Mission Staff
Lesley Stamps	Main Mission Staff

Al Flemyng — Alphan
Tony Allyn — 1st Guard
Quentin Pierre — 2nd Guard
James Clayton — 3rd Guard
Ricard Shore — Supplies

Stand Ins

Alan Meacham — Koenig
Suzanne Heimer — Helena
Ron Watkins — Bergman
Len Piper — Companion

Stunts

Eileen Harvey — Helena

22. 'MISSION OF THE DARIANS'

Series Regular Performers

Martin Landau — Koenig
Barbara Bain — Helena
Barry Morse — Bergman
Prentis Hancock — Morrow
Zienia Merton — Sandra
Nick Tate — Carter
Clifton Jones — Kano
Anton Philips — Mathias
Suzanne Roquette — Tanya

Guest & Background Performers

Joan Collins — Kara
Dennis Burgess — Neman
Robert Russell — Hadin
Paul Antrim — Lowry
Aubrey Morris — Old Man
Gerald Stadden — Male Mute
Jackie Horton — Female Mute
Sarah Bullen — Operative (1)
Ann Maj-Britt — Operative (2)
Andy Dempsey — Operative (3)
Loftus Burton — Operative (4)
Andy Sutcliffe — Operative (5)
Cam — Operative (6)
Joe Dunne — Survivor (1)

Bill Hemmings — Survivor (2)
Ron Tarr — Survivor (3)
Trevor Lawrence — Survivor (4)
Jacky Clair — Survivor (4)
Allan Travell — Survivor (5)
James Muir — Survivor (6)
Maxwell Alford — Survivor (7)
Warren Black — Survivor (7 / 9) (January 17 — on)
Tony Waldern — Survivor (8)
Laurie Davis — Survivor (10)
Mel Warner — Survivor (11)
Robin Hopwood — Survivor (12)
Michael Dilks — Survivor (13)
Dan Long — Survivor (B)
Jennifer Guy — Survivor Female (1)
Theo Hayman — Survivor Female (2)
Nina Kitchen — Survivor Female (3)
Rosalind Bailey — Survivor Female (5)
Valerie Phillips — Survivor Female (6)
Jennie Creswell — Survivor Female (7)
Michael Boothe — Darian (1)
Alan Meacham — Darian (2)
Chris Hodge — Darian (3)
Richard Smith — Darian (4)
Sean Hopwood — Darian (5) Guard
Tara Farady — Darian (6)
Linda Hooks — Darian (7)
Carl Bohum — Darian (9)
Jeremy Ranchev — Darian (10)
Paul Kirby — Dead Body
John Clements — Dead Body
Peter Simpson — Dead Body
Linda Hooks — Dead Body
Erica Simmonds — Dead Body
Mercedes Berleigh — Survivor - Dead

Stand Ins

Alan Meacham — Koenig

280

Mike Stevens	Koenig (January 15)	Erica Svenson	Nurse (C)
Suzanne Heimer	Helena	Jacqueline Thompson	Nurse (D)
Ron Watkins	Bergman	David Valentine	Orderly (A)
Julie Helm	Kara	Paul Kirby	Orderly (B)
Frank Harper	Neman	Bob Sherman	Announcer
		Iain Smith	Technician (1)
		Graham Simpson	Technician (2)
		Ricard Adams	Technician (3)
		Al Flemyng	Technician (4)

Stunts

Joe Dunne	Stunt Arranger	Roy Everson	Technician (4) (February 12 Second Unit shoot)
Terry Walsh	Morrow		
Tim Condron	Carter		
Dinny Powell	Lowry		
Marc Boyle	Neman	Arden Harrington	Technician (5)
Eddie Stacey	Misc. Darians	John Bryant	Technician (February 12 Second Unit shoot)
Terry Plumber	Fight Survivor		
Nick Hobbs	Fight Survivor		
Les Crawford	Fight Darian (Spacesuit)	Gypsie Kemp	Earth Nurse
		Robert Arnold	Pilot

23. 'DRAGON'S DOMAIN'

		Tony Allyn	1st Guard
		Quentin Pierre	2nd Guard

Series Regular Performers

Stand Ins

Martin Landau	Koenig		
Barbara Bain	Helena	Alan Meacham	Koenig
Barry Morse	Bergman	Suzanne Heimer	Helena
Prentis Hancock	Morrow	Ron Watkins	Bergman
Zienia Merton	Sandra	Mike Stevens	Cellini
Nick Tate	Carter	Alan Bennett	Cellini (February 12 Second Unit shoot)
Clifton Jones	Kano		
Anton Philips	Mathias		
Suzanne Roquette	Tanya		
		Aiden Harrington	Dixon

Guest & Background Performers

Stunts

Gianni Garko	Cellini		
Douglas Wilmer	Dixon	Eddie Stacey	Stunt Arranger
Michael Sheard	King	Jacquie Thompson	Helena Hand Double
Susan Jameson	Mackie		
Barbara Kellerman	Vishenskya	Martin Grace	Cellini
Loftus Burton	Operative (1)	Roberta Gibbs	Mackie (February 5 rehearsal only)
Andy Dempsey	Operative (2)		
Sarah Bullen	Operative (3)		
Ann Maj-Britt	Operative (4)		
Andy Sutcliffe	Operative (5)	Sue Crosland	Vishenskya (February 7 — on)
Cam	Nurse (A)		
Laraine Humphrys	Nurse (B)		

Dorothy Ford	Vishenskya (February 5 rehearsal only)Mackie (February 7 — on)	Ann Maj-Britt	Operative (2)
		Andy Dempsey	Operative (3)
		Loftus Burton	Operative (4)
		Mike Stevens	Main Mission
		Andy Sutcliffe	Main Mission
		Tony Allyn	Irwin
Reg Dent	King	Quentin Pierre	N'Doe
		Clive Hornby	3rd Guard

24. 'THE TESTAMENT OF ARKADIA'

Norton Clarke — 4th Guard

Series Regular Performers

Martin Landau	Koenig
Barbara Bain	Helena
Barry Morse	Bergman
Prentis Hancock	Morrow
Zienia Merton	Sandra Carter
Nick Tate	
Clifton Jones	Kano
Anton Philips	Mathias
Suzanne Roquette	Tanya

Guest & Background Performers

Orso Maria Guerrini	Luke
Lisa Harrow	Anna
Sarah Bullen	Operative (1)

Stand Ins

Alan Meacham	Koenig
Suzanne Heimer	Helena
Ron Watkins	Bergman
Aiden Harrington	Luke
Fran Hunter	Anna

Stunts

| Eddie Stacey | Stunt Arranger / Koenig (Kendo sequence) |
| Gerry Crampton | Luke (Kendo sequence) |

GROUP THREE PRODUCTION LTD.   "SPACE 1999" T.V. SERIES

                          CALL SHEET NO.1.   EPISODE NO.1. "BREAKAWAY"

DIRECTOR: LEE KATZIN   STAGE: 'M'

DATE: MONDAY, 3rd December, 1973.   UNIT CALL: 8.30a.m.

ARTISTE   CHARACTER   D/ROOM   MAKE UP   SET CALL

EXT. NUCLEAR DISPOSAL AREA.   Sc.Nos. 2.6.10.12. (3.7.9. Prefilm)
                              33.34.35.39. (36.38.38A. Prefilm)

ALF JOINT   STEINER   325   7.45a.m.   8.30a.m.
RCY SCAMMEL   NORDSTROM   326   7.30a.m.   8.30a.m.
COLIN SKEAPING   ELLIS   324   on stand by till 1.00p.m.
NIK ZARAN   JACKSON   321   on stand by till 1.00p.m.

Art Dept: Names to be printed on helmets of spacemen.

Props: Cracked visor, commlocks, radiation counters, key to cap, box of tools,
            radiation probes, dummy.

Action vehicle: Moon buggy to be on set at   8.00a.m.

Wardrobe: Jerk jacket to be used on Nordstrom.
                Pluggshott to be available for uniform fitting from 7.30a.m.

Electronics: Video cameras to stand by for recording close ups on Spacemen.

Sp.Fx: Moon dust fx, (Sc.39).
                Eagle model required for reflection shot and matte shot Sc. 34

Construction: Black drapes required for matte shot Sc.34.

Camera: High speed Mitchell required.

Make Up: Contact lenses for Roy Scammel.
                Mr. Aujla required to help fit lenses from 9.30a.m.

Fire Dept: To reset smoke alarm equipment on M Stage.

Stunt Arranger: To supervise all trampoline and stunt equipment.

Electrical: Laser posts lights to be practical.

CATERING: a.m. and p.m. breaks for 75 people , i.e. 10.00a.m. and 3.30p.m.

RUSHES: Theatre 4 at 1.00p.m.

                                         KEN BAKER,
                                         Assistant Director.

EPISODE 3: "BLACK SUN"

CALL SHEET NO. 11

DIRECTOR: LEE KATZIN   STAGE: L

DATE: THURSDAY, 14th February, 1974.   UNIT CALL: 8.30a.m.

ARTISTE	CHARACTER	D/ROOM	MAKE UP CALL	SET CALL

1. INT. MAIN MISSION/KOENIG'S OFFICE. Sc.Nos. 118 to complete.
   125,127pt.(pre-ageing),130.

MARTIN LANDAU	KOENIG	321	7.30a.m.	8.30a.m.
BARRY MORSE	BERGMAN	32g	8.00a.m.	8.30a.m.
PRENTIS HANCOCK	MORROW	335	7.45a.m.	8.30a.m.

Stand Ins:
John Clifford	for	Mr. Landau	8.00a.m.	8.30a.m.
Alan Meacham	for	Mr. Morse	8.00a.m.	8.30a.m.

Props: Bergman's case, brandy bottle and repeats, glasses, cigars, matches, reports.

M/Up/Wardrobe: Sc.118. Stage 4. Sc.125. Stage 5. Sc.127pt. Stage 6 pre-ageing.
Sc.130. Stage 7. Bergman, Koenig in spacesuits.

Camera Dept: Velocilator, tracks, anamorphic lens, diopters, Moyhead, and standard
Mitchell for lock-off shot, camera jacks, rotating star filters,
Pologon lens piece, 400mm lens.

Sp.Fx. Dept: Frost and breath fxs.

Art Dept: Black drapes & white backing required. Transparent computer piece for
Sc.127pt. Curtain and mirror board fxs.

Drapes: 2 Drapes to stand by.

Electrical: Sc.118. Auxiliary/Reflected. Sc.125. Auxiliary/Reflected.
Sc.127pt. Yellow light fx + light change: No shadows.
Sc.130. Yellow light.

2. COVER SET:
INT. SMITTY'S QUARTERS. Sc.No.122.

JON LAURIMORE	SMITTY	336	8.00a.m.	9.00a.m.
JACK McKENZIE	1ST ENGINEER	326	8.00a.m.	9.00a.m.
RICHARD EDEN	2ND ENGINEER	327	7.45a.m.	9.00a.m.
PHILIP CLIFTON	3RD ENGINEER	328	7.45a.m.	9.00a.m.

Extra Artistes:
1 Engineer			8.30a.m.	9.00a.m.
1 Man			8.30a.m.	9.00a.m.
2 Women			8.30a.m.	9.00a.m.

Props: Cards, betting chips.

M/Up/Wardrobe: Stage 5. Extra clothing. Caps for crowd.

Electrical: Auxiliary lighting.

Construction: Rostrum required.

3. COVER SET:
INT. MORROW'S QUARTERS. Sc.No. 124.

PRENTIS HANCOCK	MORROW	335	from above	
SUZANNE ROQUETTE	TANYA	325	9.00a.m.	10.00a.m.

Props: Guitar.
M/Up/Wardrobe: Stage 5. Morrow in spacesuit.

4. COVER SHOTS - INSERTS OF CAPTIONS FOR Sc.61.

5. INT. MAIN MISSION. Sc.127pt. (Ageing sequence)

MARTIN LANDAU	KOENIG	321	from above	
BARRY MORSE	BERGMAN	324	from above	

Stand Ins: from above.

/Continued.......

"BLACK SUN"
CALL SHEET NO.11. CONT'D.   Page 2.
FOR: THURSDAY, 14.2.74.

Art Dept: Black drapes and white backing from above.
M/Up/Hair: 3 Stages of Ageing - Koenig's hand.
           Ageing of Koenig & Bergman.
W/Robe: White robes or spacesuits to be decided.
Camera: from above.

CATERING: a.m. and p.m. breaks on L Stage for 65 people.

RUSHES: Theatre 7 at 5.30p.m.

TRANSPORT: Joe Himpfen to collect Mr. Landau at 6.45a.m.
           Unit Car (Mac) to collect Mr. Morse at 7.15a.m.

PRODUCTION NOTE: A B.B.C. Unit will be in attendance during the day to cover various
                 sequences for "SCREEN TEST".

                                          KEN BAKER,
                                          Assistant Director.

GROUP THREE PRODUCTIONS LTD.　　　　"SPACE 1999" TELEVISION SERIES
　　　　　　　　　　　　　　　　　　EPISODE 6 "ANOTHER TIME,
　　　　　　　　　　　　　　　　　　　　　　　ANOTHER PLACE"

CALL SHEET NO: 1

DIRECTOR: DAVID TOMBLIN　　　　　　STAGE:　L

DATE:　　TUESDAY 2ND APRIL, 1974　　UNIT CALL: 8.30 a.m.

ARTISTE	CHARACTER		D/ROOM	M/U CALL	SET CALL
INT. MAIN MISSION SC: NOS: 1A.　3.5.7.　9.　11.　79.					
MARTIN LANDAU	KOENIG		321	9.00am	10.00am
BARBARA BAIN	HELENA		322	8.30am	10.00am
BARRY MORSE	BERGMAN		324	9.30am	10.00am
JUDY GEESON	REGINA		325	7.15am	8.30am
PRENTIS HANCOCK	MORROW		336	7.45am	8.30am
ZIENIA MERTON	SANDRA		328	7.30am	8.30am
NICK TATE	CARTER		326	7.30am	8.30am
CLIFTON JONES	KANO		327	8.00am	8.30am
SUZANNE ROQUETTE	TANYA	'I'	181	7.30am	8.30am
ANDY DEMPSEY	OPERATIVE 1	'I'	180	7.45am	8.30am
LOFTUS BURTON	OPERATIVE 2	'I'	182	8.00am	8.30am
ROBERT PHILIPS	OPERATIVE 3	'I'	195	7.45am	8.30am
JUNE BOLTON	OPERATIVE 4	'I'	196	7.30am	8.30am
JOY HARRISON	OPERATIVE 5	'I'	197	7.30am	8.30am
STAND-INS:					
A.N. Other　　　for	Mr. Landau			8.00am	8.30am
Suzanne Heimer for	Miss Bain			8.00am	8.30am
Tony Allen　　　for	Mr. Morse			8.00am	8.30am
Jane Henley　　 for	Miss Geeson			8.00am	8.30am
EXTRA ARTISTES:					
Alan Harris	Main Mission			8.00am	8.30am
Mike Stevens	Main Mission			8.00am	8.30am
Lesley Stamps	Main Mission			8.00am	8.30am
Pamela Rose	Double for Miss Geeson			8.00am	8.30am
STUNT ARTIST					
Colin Skeaping	Technician			8.00am	8.30am

PROPS:　Mattresses, boxes, trolleys, dressing to spill over, bunch of
　　　　flowers.

ELECTRONIC:　Sc: 1A (A) Radar (B) Pulsator (C) Moonbase (D) Eagle.
　　　　　　　Sc: 3　(A) Radar with dot. (B) (C) (D) as 1A.
　　　　　　　Sc: 5　(A) Radar with dot - vt noise over.
　　　　　　　　　　 (B) (C) (D) as 1A.
　　　　　　　Sc: 7　as 5　-　all monitors die during action.
　　　　　　　Sc: 79 (A) High speed pulsator (B) Moon. Earth. Moon.
　　　　　　　　　　 (C) Moonbase (D) Eagle.

CAMERA DEPT:　Condenser 9.8 for Arriflex. 15mm for R.35. High speed
　　　　　　　 R.35. Wild Arriflex. Star filters. Padding for camera
　　　　　　　 (stunt shot).

ELECTRICAL:　Light fx. on windows from Sc: 7. Coloured light fx.
　　　　　　　Light change. Lights fail Sc: 7. Mirror board fx.
　　　　　　　required. White out fx. Sc: 11.

SPECIAL FX:　Sparks and smoke fx. from Sc: 3. Trolleys on jerk wires -
　　　　　　　2-way. 2 Moles fans for window fx. Glitter fx.

continued............./

EP: 6 "ANOTHER TIME, ANOTHER PLACE"   TUESDAY 2ND APRIL, 1974

CALL SHEET NO: 1

FIRE DEPT: Smoke alarms to be removed on L Stage.

ART DEPT: Matt cover for B.P. screen from Sc: 3.
               Black velvet to stand-by from Sc: 7.

DRAPES DEPT: Drapes to stand-by on L Stage from 8.30am.

TRANSPORT: (1) Ray Atkins to collect Miss Bain at 7.45am
               (2) Unit car to collect Mr. Landau at 8.15am
               (3) Unit car to collect Mr. Morse at 8.45am
               (4) Unit car to collect Miss Geeson at 6.30am

CATERING: A.M. and P.M. break for 75 on L Stage.

SCHEDULE FOR: Tues. 2/4   Int. Main Mission/Koenig's Office
                           Sc: Nos: 1A.3.5.7.9.11.79.
               Wed. 3/4   Int. Main Mission/Koenig's Office
                           Sc: Nos: 21.15.18.22.
               Thur. 4/4   Int. Main Mission/Koenig's Office
                           Sc: Nos: 24.25.27.29.32pt.

                           KEN BAKER
                           Assistant Director

SPECIAL NOTE:

          Pictures numers One and Two have had a tremendous
          reception in the States and Sir Lew Grade has
          especially asked that his thanks and appreciation
          be passed on to all members of the Unit.

                           GERRY ANDERSON

YEAR TWO PROVISIONAL SCHEDULES

By Robert E Wood

The following Provisional Schedules lay out proposed timelines for the production of *Space: 1999*'s second series. Dated 1st October 1975 it is clear the producers knew they were going to run into problems with their shooting schedule and delivery dates for completed episodes.

GERRY ANDERSON PRODUCTIONS LIMITED
SPACE: 1999 SERIES II
PROVISIONAL SCHEDULE No. 1 FOR DISCUSSION

1st October 1975

NOTES:
1. Assume start date to be November 17th, 1975.
2. Based on a normal UK working day of 8 hours.
3. Allowing an average of 11 shooting days per episode (88 hours).
4. Allowing a post-production period of 56 working days per episode up to date of delivery of the 16mm CRI[43] to USA
5. No allowance made for a two week hiatus in middle of production.

It will be observed that 18 CRI's can be delivered to USA no less than four weeks prior to the estimated transmission times. Episodes 19 and 20 would be delivered dangerously near to estimated transmission time. Episodes 22, 23 and 24 are problems.

EP	SHOOTING PERIOD	DELIVERY OF CRI TO USA	ESTIMATED TRANSMISSION IN USA
1.	Nov 17 – Dec 1 (1975)	Feb 23 (1976)	Sept 18 (1976)
2.	Dec 2 – Dec 16	Mar 10	Sept 25
3.	Dec 17 – Jan 5 (76)	Mar 26	Oct 2
4.	Jan 6 – Jan 20	Apr 13	Oct 9

---

[43] CRI: Colour Reversal Intermediate. A Reversal is created by a film process that produces a positive image directly using two developer stages. A Colour Reversal Intermediate is a reversal element containing a positive image or negative masked stock.

5.	Jan 21 – Feb 4	May 3	Oct 16
6.	Feb 5 – Feb 19	May 19	Oct 23
7.	Feb 20 – Mar 5	June 7	Oct 30
8.	Mar 8 – Mar 22	June 23	Nov 6
9.	Mar 23 – Apr 6	July 9	Nov 13
10.	Apr 7 – Apr 23	July 27	Nov 20
11.	Apr 26 – May 10	Aug 12	Nov 27
12.	May 11 – May 25	Aug 31	Dec 4
13.	May 26 – June 10	Sept 16	Dec 11
14.	June 11 – June 25	Oct 4	Dec 18
15.	June 28 – July 12	Oct 20	Dec 25
16.	July 13 – July 27	Nov 5	Jan 1 (1977)
17.	July 28 – Aug 11	Nov 23	Jan 8
18.	Aug 12 – Aug 26	Dec 9	Jan 15
19.	Aug 27 – Sept 13	Dec 28	Jan 22
20.	Sept 14 – Sept 28	Jan 13 (1977)	Jan 29
21.	Sept 29 – Oct 13	Jan 31	Feb 5
22.	Oct 14 – Oct 28	Feb 16	Feb 12
23.	Oct 29 – Nov 12	Mar 4	Feb 19
24.	Nov 15 – Nov 29	Mar 22	Feb 26

PROVISIONAL SCHEDULE No. 2 FOR DISCUSSION

1st October 1975

NOTES:

1. Assume start date to be November 17th, 1975.
2. Based on a negotiated UK working day of 10 hours.
3. Allowing an average of 9 shooting days per episode (90 hours).
4. Allowing a post-production period of 56 working days per episode up to date of delivery to USA of the 16mm CRI.
5. Allowing for a two week hiatus in middle of production.

It will be observed that 24 CRI's can be delivered to USA no less than four weeks prior to the estimated transmission dates.

EP	SHOOTING PERIOD	DELIVERY OF CRI TO USA	ESTIMATED TRANSMISSION IN USA
1.	Nov 17 – Nov 27 (1975)	Feb 19 (1976)	Sept 18 (1976)
2.	Nov 28 – Dec 10 (1975)	Mar 4 (1976)	Sept 25
3.	Dec 11 – Dec 23 (1975)	Mar 18	Oct 2
4.	Dec 24 1975 – Jan 8 1976	Apr 1	Oct 9
5.	Jan 9 – Jan 21	Apr 29	Oct 16
6.	Jan 22 – Feb 3	May 13	Oct 23

7.	Feb 4 – Feb 16	May 27	Oct 30
8.	Feb 17 – Feb 27	June 11	Nov 6
9.	Mar 1 – Mar 11	June 25	Nov 13
10.	Mar 12 – Mar 24	July 9	Nov 20
11.	Mar 25 – April 6	July 23	Nov 27

TWO WEEK HIATUS – APRIL 7th – APRIL 20th

12.	Apr 21 – May 3	Aug 6	Dec 4
13.	May 4 – May 14	Aug 20	Dec 11
14.	May 17 – May 27	Sept 6	Dec 18
15.	May 28 – June 10	Sept 20	Dec 25
16.	June 11 – June 23	Oct 4	Jan 1 (1977)
17.	June 24 – July 6	Oct 18	Jan 8
18.	July 7 – July 19	Nov 1	Jan 15
19.	July 20 – July 30	Nov 15	Jan 22
20.	Aug 2 – Aug 12	Nov 29	Jan 29
21.	Aug 13 – Aug 25	Dec 13	Feb 5
22.	Aug 26 – Sept 8	Dec 28	Feb 12
23.	Sept 9 – Sept 20	Jan 11 (1977)	Feb 19
24.	Sept 21 – Oct 1	Jan 25	Feb 26

Proposed postproduction schedule of 56 working days for each episode after completion of main unit and S/FX shooting, and up to delivery of 16mm CRI to America.

GERRY ANDERSON PRODUCTIONS LIMITED at PINEWOOD STUDIOS
Post-Production – Working Days

10 days to Fine Cut
11 days to Track Lay and Dub
5 days to Neg Cut
5 days to First Married Print

Total: 31 working days

ITC AND DENHAM LABORATORIES
ESTIMATED POST-PRODUCTION SCHEDULE

25 days from First Married Print to 35 mm CRI and Print – to 16mm CRI and Print and delivery of 16mm CRI to USA.

Total: 56 working days
In the end, filming on episode one, 'The Metamorph', didn't begin until

26th January 1976 – over two months later than these provisional schedules anticipated – and episode 24, 'The Dorcons', wrapped on 23rd December 1976, a full month later than the latest predicted completion date in these schedules. Predictably, American broadcast dates fell behind by equal measure. This, despite the fact that the production implemented four sets of 'double-up' episodes filmed simultaneously (dividing the cast and crew in two units, with either Landau or Bain taking the lead in each episode) in order to speed up production; the first being 'The Rules of Luton' and 'The Mark of Archanon', filmed in May 1976, the second being 'The Catacombs of the Moon' and 'The AB Chrysalis', filmed in June/July 1976, the third being 'Space Warp' and 'A Matter of Balance', filmed in August 1976, and the fourth being 'Dorzak' and 'Devil's Planet', filmed in November 1976.

The two-week hiatus did not occur, but Fred Freiberger wrote 'The Beta Cloud' episode to require minimal participation from Martin Landau and Barbara Bain in order to enable them to go on holiday, as stipulated in their contract.

The final episode, 'The Dorcons', aired in the major US markets of San Francisco (KRON-TV) on April 2, 1977, and in New York City (WPIX-TV) on May 7, 1977, closing out the season's broadcasts substantially later than the Feburary 26, 1977 air date projected in these provisional schedules.

Among the problems associated with late delivery of episodes to television stations is the fact that the stations must air more repeats and running repeats instead of first-run broadcasts typically results in lower ratings.

MARTIN LANDAU'S SHOOTING SCHEDULES

By Robert E Wood

Martin Landau kept track of various details throughout the shooting of both seasons of *Space: 1999*. These included filming dates, directors, and guest stars, but of primary importance from his point-of-view was the number of days worked, and the overtime, because that affected how much he and Barbara Bain would be paid.

In a column running down the left side of these pages, Landau tracked the number of weeks spent filming. For formatting reasons, we are not including those in the transcribed text here. Please refer to the photographic reproductions also included in this book.

These documents will be of interest to fans for the historical details of the filming of the series, as well as occasional side notes that Landau included. In a few instances minor edits have been made to Martin Landau's notes for consistency of presentation.

YEAR ONE

Arrived London Monday Oct. 22nd 1973 – Grosvenor House – Moved into 31 Maida Av. W2 Nov. 1st 1973

No. 1 Show – "BREAKAWAY"
Dir: Lee Katzin
Guest: Roy Dotrice
Rehearsal week (Nov. 26th – Nov. 30 1973)
Shooting (Dec. 3rd 1973 Monday – Jan. 11th 1974 Friday)
(1 week rehearsal) (6 weeks shooting)
(Christmas + New Years – 4 days)
Shooting total: 30 days (Overtime 21 days + 4 days below) **2[44]

---

[44] The double star and number 2 here signify that two shooting days involved working late nights, as becomes apparent with Landau's notes on the extra scenes shot for 'Breakaway' after episode three, 'Black Sun', was completed. Landau also noted (circled in the top right corner of this first page) that the stars signified a late night.

No. 2 – "MATTER OF LIFE AND DEATH"
Dir: Chas. Crichton
Guest: Richard Johnson
(Jan. 14th 1974 Monday – Jan. 30th 1974 Wednesday)
Shooting total: 13 days (Overtime 4 days) *3

No. 3 – "BLACK SUN"
Dir: Lee Katzin
(Jan. 31st 1974 Thursday – Feb. 21st 1974 Thursday AM)
(Overtime 6 days)

No. 1 – "BREAKAWAY" Added Scenes
Dir: Lee Katzin[45]
(Feb. 21st 74 (PM) – Feb. 26 1974 8:30 PM)
(Overtime 4 days) *2-26 Late Night to 8:20 *4th Late Night

No. 4 – "RING AROUND THE MOON"
Dir: Ray Austin
(Feb. 27 74 Wed. – Mar. 14 74 Thurs.)
(Overtime 4 ½ days) * Late Nights 3-7, 3-12

No. 5 – "EARTHBOUND"
Dir: Chas. Crichton
Guests: Christopher Lee, Roy Dotrice
(March 15 74 Friday – April 1 74 Monday)
(Overtime 3 days) *Late Nights 3-21, 3-27

No. 6 – "ANOTHER TIME, ANOTHER PLACE"
Dir: David Tomblin
Guest: Judy Geeson
(April 2 74 Tuesday – April 19 74 Friday)
(Easter (Fri. 4-12 – Mon. 4-15 Off)
(Overtime 3 days) *4-10, **4-18 til 7 PM
2nd Unit to finish Monday 4-22

---

[45] Note that Martin Landau credits Lee Katzin with directing the added scenes for 'Breakaway', which contradicts Gerry Anderson's story that he directed the scenes. The only other pick-ups shot for 'Breakaway' were on May 7 1974, featuring Carter in the Eagle Command Module (which Gerry Anderson could have directed). See the CORRESPONDENCE 'Going Theatrical & Network' section of this book for additional discussion of this subject.

No. 7 – "MISSING LINK"
Dir: Ray Austin
Guests: Joanna Dunham, Peter Cushing
(April 22 74 Mon. – May 7 74 Tues.)
(Overtime 3 days) *One extended day

No. 8 – "GUARDIAN OF PIRI"
Dir: Chas. Crichton
Guest: Catherine Schell
(May 7 74 Tues. – May 24 74 Fri)
(Overtime 5 days) *Wed. May 22 extended day til 7 PM

No. 9 – "FORCE OF LIFE"
Dir: David Tomblin
Guest: Ian McShane
(Tues. May 28 74 Tues. – June 7 74 Fri.)
*One late day Thurs. Jun. 6

HIATUS FOR 3 WEEKS
Amsterdam, Knokke, Bruges, Paris with Julie + BB
Biarritz with BB
Susie in States[46]

No. 9 – "FORCE OF LIFE" RESUMED
(Mon. July 1 74 – Fri. July 5 (AM))
(4 ½ days Over)

No. 10 – "ALPHA CHILD"
Dir. Ray Austin
Guests: Julian Glover, Syd Hayman, Wayne (Boy)
(Fri. July 5 (PM) – Mon. July 22)
(2 days Over)

No. 11 – "THE LAST SUNSET"
Dir. Chas. Crichton
(Tues. July 23 74 – Tues. Aug. 6 74)
(2 days Over)
Elinor 7-27 No Guests[47]

---

[46] Martin Landau and Barbara Bain went on holiday with their daughter Julie (actress Juliet Landau) to Holland, Belgium, and Paris, France. Landau and Bain then continued their holiday to Biarritz, France. Meanwhile, their daughter Susie went to the United States.

[47] Elinor was one of Martin Landau's sisters. She lived in New York and evidently came over to England for a holiday from July 7 – 27, without guests.

No. 12 – "VOYAGER'S RETURN"
Dir: Robt. Kellett
Guest: Jeremy Kemp
(Wed. Aug 7 – Wed. Aug. 21 74)
(2 days Over)

No. 13 – "COLLISION COURSE"
Dir: Ray Austin
Guest Star: Margaret Leighton
(Thurs. Aug. 22 74 – Fri. Sept. 6 74)
(3 days Over)

No. 14 – "DEATH'S OTHER DOMINION"
Dir: Chas. Crichton
Guests: Brian Blessed, John Shrapnel
(Mon. Sept. 9 74 – Mon. Sept. 23 74)
(2 days Over) 1 hour over Wed. 11, Thurs. 12

No. 15 – "THE FULL CIRCLE"
Dir: Bob Kellett
Guest: Oliver Cotton
(Tues. Sept. 24 74 – Tues. Oct. 8 74)
(2 days Over)

No. 16 – "END OF ETERNITY"
Dir: Ray Austin
Guest: Peter Bowles
(Wed. Oct. 9 74 – Wed. Oct. 23 74)
(2 days Over) 2 hours over – final day + day before

No. 17 – "WAR GAMES"
Dir: Chas. Crichton
Guests: Isla Blair, Anthony Valentine
(Thurs. Oct. 24 74 – Fri. Nov. 8 74) 12 days
(3 days Over) Thurs 11-7 – Late Night 3 hours

No. 18 – "THE LAST ENEMY" (CROSSFIRE?)[48]
Dir: Bob Kellett
Guest: Caroline Mortimer

---

[48] Twice in this document Landau notes 'Crossfire' as an alternate title for 'The Last Enemy'. It isn't clear whether it was a suggestion he was making, or whether the possibility of changing the episode title was coming from elsewhere. Judging by the plot of the episode, 'Crossfire' would have probably been a more fitting title.

(Fri. Nov. 8 74 (Overlap)[49] – Tues. Nov. 19 74)
12 days (1 day Under) (Added scenes Feb. 25 – 28 1975)

No. 19 – "THE TROUBLED SPIRIT"
Dir: Ray Austin
Guests: Giancarlo Prete, Hillary Dwyer
(Wed. Nov. 20 74 – Wed. Dec. 4 74)
(2 days Over) 1 late 8:30

No. 20 – "SPACE BRAIN"
Dir: Chas. Crichton
Guest: Carla Romanelli
(Thurs. Dec. 5 74 – Thurs. Dec. 19 74)
(Added scenes Feb 25 – 28 75)
(2 days Over) 2 late days 8:30; Thurs. 12-12, Wed. 12-28

No. 21 – "THE INFERNAL MACHINE"
Dir: David Tomblin
Guest: Leo McKern
(Fri. Dec. 20 74 – Thurs. Jan. 9 75)
(3 days off X-Mas; 1 day New Years)
(2 days Over) 1 late day 3 hrs.

No. 22 – "MISSION OF THE DARIANS"
Dir: Ray Austin
Guest: Joan Collins
(Fri. Jan. 10 75 – Fri. Jan 24 75)
(2 days Over) 2 late days

No. 23 – "DRAGON'S DOMAIN"
Dir: Charles Crichton
Guest: Gianni Garko
(Mon. Jan. 27 75 – Feb. 10 75)
(2 days Over)

No. 24 – "THE TESTAMENT OF ARKADIA"
Dir: David Tomblin
Guests: Lisa Harrow, Orso Maria Guerrini
(Tues. Deb. 11 75 – Tues. Feb. 25 75)
(2 days Over)

---

[49] Landau's 'Overlap' note included an arrow pointing at the 'Late Night 3 hours' notation from 'War Games'.

Added scenes for 2 shows ("SPACE BRAIN" + "THE LAST ENEMY" (CROSSFIRE) starting Tues. Feb. 25, Wed. Feb. 26 – Feb 28 (WRAP PARTY)

3 ½ DAYS ON PICK-UPS

FIN 2-28-75

Dubbed Monday March 3 (DARIANS)

YEAR TWO

Arrived Tues. Jan. 13 1976 – Claridges – Moved to 49 Chester Sq. SW1 Sun. Jan. 18 1976

No. 1 Show – "THE METAMORPH"
Dir: Chas. Crichton
Guest: Brian Blessed
(Mon. Jan. 26 76 – Mon. Feb. 16 76)
(Total 16 days)
Late night – 3 hrs – Thursday 1-29-76 – Worked extra hour 2-4-76

No. 2 – "THE EXILES"
Dir: Ray Austin
Guests: Stacy Dorning, Peter Duncan
(Tues. Feb. 17 76 – Wed. March 3 76)
(Total 13 days)
Worked late 2-17-76 Finishing #1
Worked late 2-18-76 on show #2
Wed. night party – BB and me

No. 3 – "ONE SECOND OF HUMANITY"[50]
Dir: Chas. Crichton
Guests: Billie Whitelaw, Leigh Lawson
(Thurs. March 4 76 – Wed. March 17 76)
(Total 10 days)
Late night 3-11-76

No. 4 – "ALL THAT GLISTERS"
Dir. Ray Austin

---

[50] Later changed to 'One Moment of Humanity'

Guest: Patrick Mower
(Thurs. March 18 76 – Wed. March 31 76)

No. 5 – "JOURNEY TO WHERE"
Dir: Tom Clegg
Guests: Freddie Jones, Isla Blair, Roger Bizley
(Thurs. April 1 76 – Thurs. April 15 76)

No. 6 – "THE TAYBOR"
Dir: Bob Brooks
Guest: Willoughby Goddard
(Fri. April 16 76 – Fri. April 30 76)
(Good Friday off – Easter Monday off)

No. 7 – "THE RULES OF LUTON" (DOUBLE-UP SHOOTING) (ML)
Dir: Val Guest
(Mon. May 3 76 – Fri. May 14 76)

No. 8 – "THE MARK OF ARCHANON" (DOUBLE-UP SHOOTING) (BB)
Dir: Chas. Crichton
Guests: John Standing, Michael Gallagher
(Tues. May 4 76 – Mon. May 17 76)

No. 9 – "BRIAN THE BRAIN"
Dir: Kevin Connor
Guest: Bernard Cribbins
(Tues. May 18 76 – Wed. June 2 76 (AM))
(Mon. May 31 – Whitson holiday off)

No. 10 – "NEW ADAM, NEW EVE"
Dir: Chas. Crichton
Guest: Guy Rolfe
(Wed. June 2 76 (PM) – Fri. June 18 76)
(12 ½ days)

No. 11 – "THE AB CHRYSALIS" (DOUBLE-UP SHOOTING) (ML)
Dir: Val Guest
(Fri. June 18 76 – Tues. July 6 76)

No. 12 – "THE CATACOMBS OF THE MOON" (DOUBLE-UP SHOOTING)
(BB)
Dir: Robt. Lynn
Guests: Jas. Laurenson, Pamela Stephenson

(Mon. June 21 76 – Tues. July 6 76)
(Heat wave – Wimbledon) Robbie + Penny[51]

No. 13 – "SEED OF DESTRUCTION" (Mirror Show)
Dir: Kevin Connor
(Wed. July 7 76 – Mon. July 19 76)
Worked Saturday July 17th 1976 (Martha Nairn)

No. 14 – "THE BETA CLOUD"*
Dir: Robt. Lynn
(Tues. July 20 76 – Wed. Aug. 4 76)
* Vacation Show – Barbara and Martin

No. 15 – "A MATTER OF BALANCE" (DOUBLE-UP) (ML)
Dir: Chas. Crichton
Guest: Lynne Frederick
(Thurs. Aug 5 76 – Mon. Aug. 23 76)

No. 16 – "SPACE WARP" (DOUBLE-UP) (BB)
Dir: Peter Medak
(Thurs. Aug. 5 76 – Tues. Aug. 24 76)

No. 17 / No. 18 (2-Parter) – "THE BRINGERS OF WONDER"
Dir: Tom Clegg
Guests: Stuart Damon, Jeff Kissoon, Toby Robins, etc.
(Wed. Aug. 25 76 – Tues. Sept. 28 76)
No. 19 – "THE LAMBDA FACTOR"
Dir: Chas. Crichton
Guest: Deborah Fallender
(Wed. Sept. 29 76 – Fri. Oct. 15 76)

No. 20 – "THE SÉANCE SPECTRE" (Formerly "THE MUTINY")
Dir: Peter Medak
Guests: Ken Hutchinson, Carolyn Seymour (Medak's wife)
(Mon. Oct. 18 76 – Mon. Nov. 1 76)
(Worked Saturday Oct. 30th 1976)

No. 21 – "DORZAK" (DOUBLE-UP) (BB)
Dir: Val Guest
Guests: Lee Montague, Jill Townsend, Kathryn Leigh Scott

---

[51] 'Robbie + Penny' refers to Rob Reiner and Penny Marshall, who were married at the time and were friends with Martin Landau and Barbara Bain.

(Tues. Nov 2, 76 – Thurs. Nov. 18 76)

No. 22 – "DEVIL'S MOON" ("DEVIL'S PLANET") (DOUBLE-UP) (ML)
Dir: Tom Clegg
Guest: Hildegarde Neil and the Girls in Red
(Tues. Nov. 2 76 – Wed. Nov. 17 76)

No. 23 – "THE IMMUNITY SYNDROME"
Dir: Bob Brooks
Guest: Karl Held
(Mon. Nov. 22 76 – Mon. Dec. 6 76)

No. 24 – "THE DORCONS"
Dir: Tom Clegg
Guest: Ann Firbank
(Tues. Dec. 7 76 – Thurs. Dec. 23 76)

Left-margin week count / dates:

1 OCT 22 MON
2 OCT 29
3 NOV 5
4 NOV 12
5 NOV 19
6 NOV 26
7 DEC 3 *
8 DEC 10
9 DEC 17 40
10 DEC 24
11 DEC 31
12 JAN 7
13 JAN 14 80
14 JAN 21
15 JAN 28
16 FEB 4
17 FEB 11 120
18 FEB 18
19 FEB 25
20 MAR 4
21 MAR 11
22 3/18 160
23 3/25
24 4-1
25 4-8 56
26 4-15 200
27 4-22
28 4-29
29-5-6
30-5-13 240
31-5-20
32-5-27
33-6-3 280
34-6-11
35-6-18
36-6-24
37-7-1
38-7-8 320
39-7-15
40-7-22
41-7-29
42-8-5 360
43-8-12
44-8-19
45-8-26
46-9-2
47-9-9 400
48-9-16
49-9-23
50-9-30
51-10-7 440
52-10-14
53-10-21
54 10-28
55 11-4 480
56 11-11
57 11-18
58 11-25

ARRIVED London MONDAY OCT 22ND 1973 — MOVED INTO 31 MAIDA AV. W2
GROSVENOR HOUSE   NOV. 1ST 1973

NO. 1 SHOW — "BREAKAWAY" REHEARSAL WEEK (NOV 26TH — NOV 30 1973)
(1 WEEK REHEARSAL) DIR: LEE KATZIN   SHOOTING (DEC. 3RD 1973 — JAN. 11TH 1974)
(6 WEEKS SHOOTING)   MONDAY   FRIDAY
SHOOTING TOTAL   (CHRISTMAS + NEW YEARS - 4 DAYS)
30 DAYS - (OVERTIME 21 DAYS)   GUEST: ROY DOTRICE
             4 DAYS BELOW

NO. 2 - "MATTER OF LIFE AND DEATH"
DIR: CHAS. CRICHTON   JAN. 14TH 1974 — JAN. 30TH 1974
GUEST: RICHARD JOHNSON   MONDAY   WEDNESDAY
SHOOTING TOTAL
13 DAYS (OVERTIME 4 DAYS) GUEST: RICHARD JOHNSON

NO. 3 "BLACK SUN"
DIR: LEE KATZIN   JAN. 31ST 1974 — FEB 21ST 1974
(OVERTIME 6 DAYS)   THURSDAY   THURSDAY A.M.

ADDED #1 "BREAKAWAY"   THURSDAY   TUESDAY
SCENES DIR. LEE KATZIN FEB 21ST 74 — FEB 26 1974
LATE NIGHT (4 DAYS OVERTIME) (P.M.) 8:30 PM

NO. 4 "RING AROUND THE MOON" FEB. 27 '74 — THURS MAR 14TH '74
DIR. RAY AUSTIN   WED.
(4½ DAYS OVER)

NO. 5 "EARTHBOUND"   MARCH 15 '74 — APRIL 1ST '74
DIR. CHAS. CRICHTON   FRIDAY   MONDAY
GUESTS. CHRISTOPHER LEE / ROY DOTRICE
                             OVERTIME - 3 DAYS

NO. 6 "ANOTHER TIME, ANOTHER PLACE" APRIL 2ND 74 — APRIL 18 '74
DIR. DAVID TOMBLIN   TUESDAY   FRIDAY
GUEST: JUDY GEESON   (OVERTIME - 3 DAYS)
EASTER GOOD (FRI. 4-12 - MONY 4-15 OFF) 2ND UNIT MONDAY 4-22 TO FINISH

NO. 7 "MISSING LINK"
DIR. RAY AUSTIN   APRIL 22 '74 — MAY 7 '74
GUESTS: JOANNA DUNHAM   MONDAY   MONDAY TUES
        PETER CUSHING   (overtime 3 DAYS)   ONE EXTENDED DAY

NO. 8 "GUARDIAN OF PIRI"   MAY 7TH 74 — MAY 24 74
DIR. CHAS. CRICHTON   TUES   FRI
GUEST: CATHERINE SCHELL   (overtime 5 DAYS)   WED MAY 22 EXTENDED DAY 'TIL 7 PM

NO. 9 "FORCE OF LIFE"   (MON, HOLIDAY)
DIR. DAVID TOMBLIN   TUES MAY 28 74 — FRI JUNE 7 '74
GUEST: IAN McSHANE   TUES   ONE LATE DAY THURS JUNE 6

HIATUS FOR 3 WEEKS AMSTERDAM PARIS WITH JULIE + BB   SUSIE IN STATES
                    KNOKKE   BIARRITZ WITH BB
                    BRUGGE

NO. 9 "FORCE OF LIFE" RESUMED (MON JULY 1 — FRI JULY 5 (AM) 4½ DAYS OVER

NO. 10 "ALPHA CHILD"   (FRI JULY 5 (PM) — MON JULY 22)
DIR. RAY AUSTIN
GUESTS: JULIAN GLOVER

NO. 11 "THE LAST SUNSET"   TUES JULY 23 — TUES AUG 6 74   2 DAYS OVER
DIR. CHAS. CRICHTON

NO. 12 "VOYAGER'S RETURN"   WED. AUG 7 1974 — WED. AUG 21 1974   2 DAYS OVER
DIR. ROBT. KELLETT

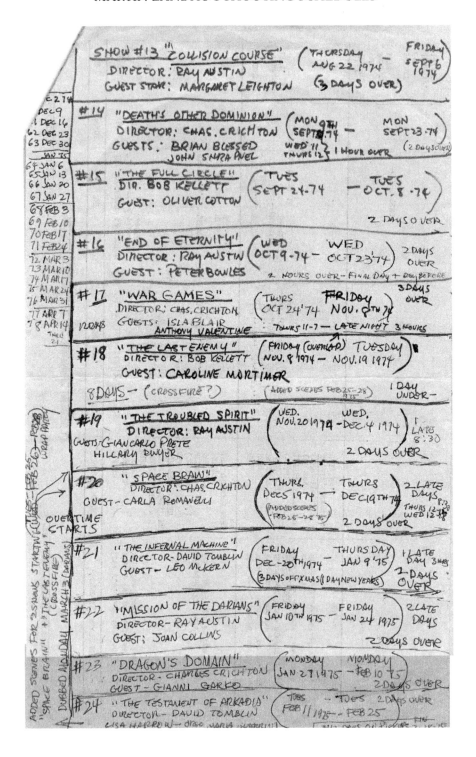

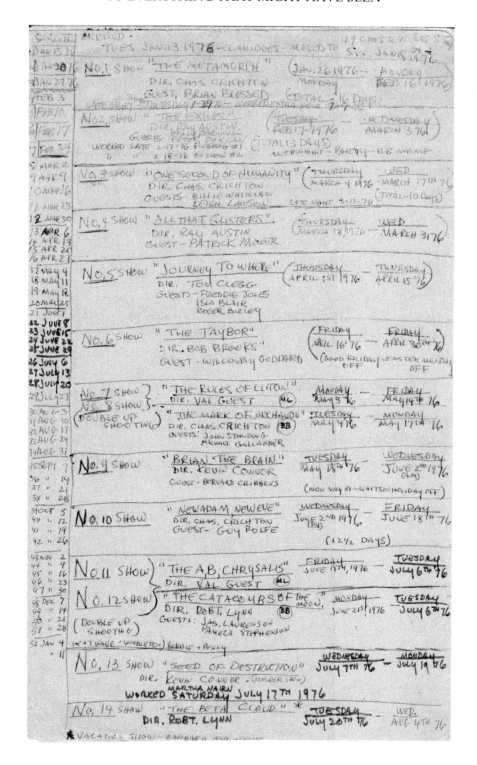

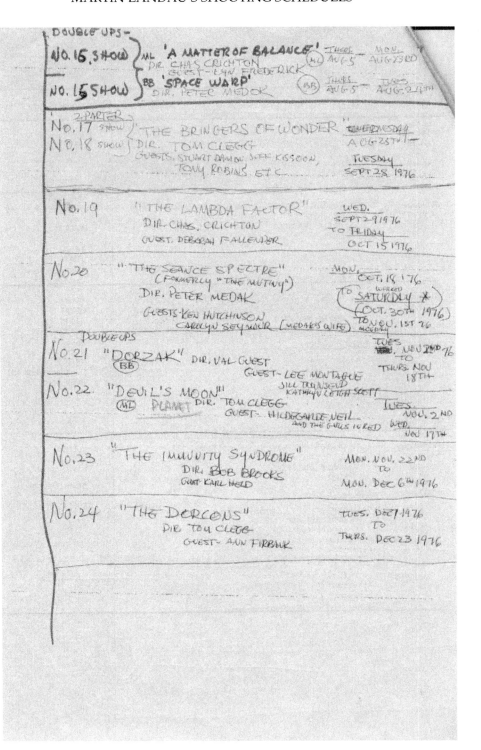

DOUBLE UPS—

NO. 16 SHOW ⎱ ML 'A MATTER OF BALANCE' THURS. MON.
DIR. CHAS CRICHTON (ML) AUG 5 — AUG 23RD
GUEST— LYN FREDERICK

NO. 15 SHOW ⎰ BB 'SPACE WARP' THURS. TUES
DIR. PETER MEDAK (BB) AUG 5 — AUG 24TH

2-PARTER
No. 17 SHOW ⎱ "THE BRINGERS OF WONDER" WEDNESDAY
No. 18 SHOW ⎰ DIR. TOM CLEGG AUG 25TH —
GUESTS. STUART DAMON, JEFF KISSOON,
TONY ROBINS ETC...... TUESDAY
SEPT 28 1976

No. 19 "THE LAMBDA FACTOR" WED.
DIR. CHAS. CRICHTON SEPT 29 1976
GUEST. DEBORAH FALLENDER TO FRIDAY
OCT 15 1976

No. 20 "THE SEANCE SPECTRE" MON.
(FORMERLY "THE MUTINY") OCT. 19 '76
DIR. PETER MEDAK WORKED
TO SATURDAY ✷
GUESTS- KEN HUTCHINSON (OCT. 30TH 1976)
CAROLYN SEYMOUR (MEDAK'S WIFE) TO NOV. 1ST 76
MONDAY

DOUBLE UPS TUES, NOV 2ND 76
No. 21 "DORZAK" DIR. VAL GUEST TO
(BB) THURS. NOV
GUEST- LEE MONTAGUE 18TH

JILL TOWNSEND
No. 22. "DEVIL'S MOON" KATHRYN LEIGH SCOTT
(ML) PLANET DIR. TOM CLEGG TUES
GUEST- HILDEGARDE NEIL NOV. 2ND
AND THE GIRLS IN RED WED.
NOV 17TH

No. 23 "THE IMMUNITY SYNDROME" MON. NOV. 22ND
DIR. BOB BROOKS TO
GUEST KARL HELD MON. DEC 6TH 1976

No. 24 "THE DORCONS" TUES. DEC 7 1976
DIR. TOM CLEGG TO
GUEST- ANN FIRBANK THURS. DEC 23 1976

SPACE: 1999 NEW YORK BROADCASTS

By Robert E Wood

Martin Landau maintained detailed notes on the broadcasts of *Space: 1999* in the key New York City market on WPIX-TV as the number of broadcasts likely affected how much he would be paid. Here are his notes:

"N.Y.C."		SERIES I SPACE: 1999

SPACE: 1999 – SEPT/ 21, 1975 – APRIL 15, 1978
62 RUNS BEYOND 2nd

	1ST RUN	2ND RUN	3RD RUN	4TH RUN	5TH RUN
1. BREAKAWAY					
	9-21-75	1-24-76 (PM)	5-29-76 (AM)		
2. MATTER OF LIFE AND DEATH					
	12-14-75	3-13-76 (PM)	9-4-76	12-3-77 (AM)	
3. BLACK SUN					
	11-23-75	2-14-76 (PM)	6-6-76 (PM)	7-31-76	9-4-76 (NH[52])
4. RING AROUND THE MOON					
	4-3-76 (AM)				
5. EARTHBOUND					
	2-28-76 (PM)	6-20-76 (PM)	8-21-76		
6. ANOTHER TIME, ANOTHER PLACE					
	2-8-76 (PM)	3-27-76 (PM)	8-28-76 (NH)		
7. MISSING LINK					
	2-29-76 (PM)	4-17-76 (AM)	10-15-77 (AM)		
8. GUARDIAN OF PIRI					
	11-2-75	1-25-76 (PM)	5-16-76 (PM)	7-10-76	7-31-76 (NH)
9. FORCE OF LIFE					
	1-11-76	5-2-76 (PM)	6-26-76 (PM)		
10. ALPHA CHILD					
	10-26-75	1-18-76	5-9-76 (PM)	8-14-76	
11. THE LAST SUNSET					
	3-7-76 (PM)	4-24-76 (AM)	10-22-77 (AM)		
12. VOYAGER'S RETURN					
	12-7-75	3-6-76 (PM)	8-28-76		
13. COLLISION COURSE					
	10-12-75	1-4-76	4-18-76 (PM)	6-19-76 (AM)	

---

[52] NH stands for New Haven, Connecticut.

14. DEATH'S OTHER DOMINION
        10-5-75   12-28-75   4-11-76 (PM)   4-25-76 (PM)   6-12-76 (AM)

15. THE FULL CIRCLE
        2-22-76 (PM)   4-10-76 (AM)   10-1-77 (AM)

16. END OF ETERNITY
        10-19-75   11-30-75   2-21-76 (PM)   6-13-76 (PM)   8-7-76[53]

17. WAR GAMES
        11-9-75   1-31-76 (PM)   5-23-76 (PM)   7-17-76

18. THE LAST ENEMY
        4-4-76 (PM)   5-22-76 (AM)   11-19-77 (PM)

19. THE TROUBLED SPIRIT
        3-21-76 (PM)   5-8-76 (PM)   7-3-76 (NH)   11-5-77 (AM)

20. SPACE BRAIN
        2-15-76 (PM)   3-14-76 (PM)   5-1-76 (AM)   10-8-77 (AM)   10-29-77 (AM)

21. THE INFERNAL MACHINE
        2-1-76 (PM)   3-20-76 (PM)   9-11-76

22. MISSION OF THE DARIANS
        11-16-75   2-7-76 (PM)   5-30-76 (PM)   7-24-76

23. DRAGON'S DOMAIN
        9-28-75   12-21-75   6-5-76 (AM)   8-7-76

24. THE TESTAMENT OF ARKADIA
        5-15-76 (AM)   7-10-76 (NH)

"N.Y.C."   SERIES II   SPACE: 1999
1ST RUN   2ND RUN   3RD RUN   4TH RUN

1. THE METAMORPH
        9-26-76   12-18-76   10-1-77 (PM)

2. THE EXILES
        10-3-76   10-10-76[54]   4-23-77   11-5-77 (PM)

3. ONE MOMENT OF HUMANITY
        12-11-76   5-21-77   10-29-77 (PM)

4. ALL THAT GLISTERS
        3-5-77   9-24-77   2-18-78

5. JOURNEY TO WHERE
        1-1-77   10-8-77 (PM)

6. THE TAYBOR
        10-17-76   6-11-77   11-19-77 (PM)

7. THE RULES OF LUTON
        11-14-76   5-28-77   11-12-77 (PM)

8. THE MARK OF ARCHANON
        10-31-76   1-22-77   20-22-77 (PM)

9. BRIAN THE BRAIN
        11-7-76   4-30-77   11-26-77 (PM)

10. NEW ADAM, NEW EVE
        10-24-76   1-15-77   10-15-77 (PM)

11. THE AB CHRYSALIS
        10-10-76   6-25-77   12-24-77

---

[53] The entry for 'End of Eternity' includes a note for a 6th Run: 8-4-76 NH

[54] Martin Landau flagged this date because he also has the first broadcast of 'The AB Chrysalis' noted as airing on the same date. The first broadcast of 'The AB Chrysalis' is the correct episode for this date.

12. THE CATACOMBS OF THE MOON
        11-27-76   6-18-77   12-3-77 (PM
13. SEED OF DESTRUCTION
        12-4-76   7-2-77   12-31-77
14. THE BETA CLOUD
        2-19-77   7-30-77   1-28-78
15. SPACE WARP
        2-5-77   7-16-77   1-7-78
16. A MATTER OF BALANCE
        2-12-77   7-23-77   2-11-78
17. THE BRINGERS OF WONDER (PT. 1)
        3-19-77   8-20-77   2-4-78
18. THE BRINGERS OF WONDER (PT. 2)
        3-26-77   8-27-77   2-18-78
19. THE LAMBDA FACTOR
        2-26-77   8-6-77   1-21-78
20. THE SÉANCE SPECTRE
        3-12-77   8-13-77   2-4-78
21. DORZAK
        6-4-77   12-17-77 (PM)
22. DEVIL'S PLANET
        4-16-77   9-10-77   4-8-78
23. THE IMMUNITY SYNDROME
        4-9-77   9-3-77   4-1-78   3-25-78
24. THE DORCONS
        5-7-77   9-17-77   4-15-78

Landau noted that on both Saturday Nov. 12 1977 at 11AM and Saturday Sept. 10 1977 at 7PM, 'NAME OF SHOW NOT LISTED IN TV GUIDE BUT *SPACE* PLAYED AND IT <u>MUST</u> BE A 3RD RUN AS ALL SHOWS HAVE PLAYED AT LEAST TWICE.'

"N.Y.C." SERIES I "SPACE: 1999" ①

SPACE: 1999 — SEPT-21-1975 —— APRIL 15-1978

	1ST RUN	2ND RUN	3RD RUN	4TH RUN	5TH RUN
1. BREAKAWAY 62 RUNS BEYOND 2ND	9-21-75	1-34 76 (AM)	5-29 76 (AM)		
2. MATTER OF LIFE AND DEATH	12-14-75	3-13 76 (PM)	9-4-76	12-3-77 (AM)	
3. BLACK SUN	11-23 75	2-14 76 (PM)	6-6 76 (PM)	7-31 76	9-4 76 NEW HAVEN
4. RING AROUND THE MOON	4-3-76 (AM)				
5. EARTH BOUND	2-28 76 (PM)	6-30 76 (PM)	8-21 76		
6. ANOTHER TIME, ANOTHER PLACE	2-8 76 (PM)	3-27 76 (PM)	8-28 76 NEW HAVEN	9-18 76	
7. MISSING LINK	2-29 76 (PM)	4-17 76 (AM)	10-15-77 (AM)		
8. GUARDIAN OF PIRI	11-2-75	1-25 76 (PM)	5-16 76 (PM)	7-10 76	7-31 76 NEW HAVEN
9. FORCE OF LIFE	1-11 76	5-2 76 (PM)	6-26 76 (PM)		
10. ALPHA CHILD	10-26-75	1-18-76	5-9 76 (PM)	8-14 76	
11. THE LAST SUNSET	3-7 76 (PM)	4-24 76 (AM)	10-22-77 (AM)		
12. VOYAGER'S RETURN	12-7-75	3-6 76 (PM)	8-28 76		

308

SPACE:1999 **N.Y.C.**   SERIES I   "SPACE:1999"   ②

	1ST RUN	2ND RUN	3RD RUN	4TH RUN	5TH RUN
13. COLLISION COURSE	10-12 75	1-4 76	4-18 76 (PM)	6-19 76 (AM)	
14. DEATH'S OTHER DOMINION	10-5 75	12-28 75	4-11 76 (PM)	4-25 76 (AM)	6-12 76 (AM)
15. THE FULL CIRCLE	2-22 76 (PM)	4-10 76 (AM)	10-1 77 (AM)		
16. END OF ETERNITY	10-19 75	11-30 75	2-21 76 (AM)	6-13 76 (PM)	8-7 76 3-4 76
17. WAR GAMES	11-9 75	1-31 76 (PM)	5-23 76 (PM)	7-17 76	
18. THE LAST ENEMY	4-4 76 (PM)	5-22 76 (AM)	11-19 77 (PM)		
19. THE TROUBLED SPIRIT	3-21 76 (PM)	5-8 76 (AM)	7-3 76 NEW HAVEN	11-5 77 (AM)	
20. SPACE BRAIN	2-15 76 (PM	3-14 76 (PM)	5-1 76 (AM)	10-8 77 (AM)	10-29 77 (AM)
21. THE INTERNAL MACHINE	2-1 76 (PA)	3-20 76 (PM)	9-11 76		
22. MISSION OF THE DARIANS	11-16 75	2-7 76 (PM)	5-30 76 (PM)	7-24 76	
23. DRAGON'S DOMAIN	9-28 75	12-21 75	6-5 76 (PM)	8-7 76	8-7 76
24. THE TESTAMENT OF ARCADIA	5-15 76 (AM)	8-10 76 NEW HAVEN			

N.Y.C. SERIES II   "SPACE:1999"   ③

	1ST RUN	2ND	3RD	4TH	5T.
1. THE METAMORPH	9:25 76	12:8 76	10:1 77 (PM)		
2. THE EXILES	10:3 76	10:10 76	4:23 77	11:5 77 (PM)	
3. ONE SECOND OF HUMANITY	12-11-76	5:21 77	10:29 77 (PM)		
4. ALL THAT GLISTERS	3:5 77	9:24 77	2-18 78		
5. JOURNEY TO WHERE	1-1 77	10:8 77 (PM)			
6. THE TAYBOR	10:17 76	6:11 77	11 19 77(PM)		
7. THE RULES OF LUTON	4:14 76	5:28 77	11:12 77 (PM)		
8. THE MARK OF ARCHANON	10:31 76	1-22 77	10:22 77 (PM)		
9. BRIAN THE BRAIN	11:7 76	4:30 77	11:26 77(PM)		
10. NEW ADAM, NEW EVE	10:24 76	1:15 77	10:15 77 (CPM)		
11. A,B, CHRYSALIS	? 10:10 76	6:25 77	12:24 77		
12. THE CATACOMBS OF THE MOON	NOV. 27 1976	6:18 77	12:3 77 (PM)		

Sat Nov 12 77 11 AM {NAME OF SHOW NOT LISTED IN TV GUIDE
Sat Sept 10 77 7PM {BUT "SPACE" PLAYED AND IT MUST BE A 3RD RUN.
AS ALL SHOWS HAVE PLAYED AT LEAST TWICE

N.Y.C. SERIES II "SPACE: 1999" (4)

		1st Run	2nd Run	3rd Run	4th Run	5"
13.	SEED OF DESTRUCTION	12·4·76	7·2·77	12·5·77		
14.	THE BETA CLOUD	2·19·77	9·30·77	1·24·78		
15.	SPACE WARP	2·5·77	7·16·77	1·7·78		
16.	A MATTER OF BALANCE	2·12·77	7·23·77	2·11·78		
17.	THE BRINGERS OF WONDER (PT. 1)	3·19·77	8·20·77	2·4·78		
18.	THE BRINGERS OF WONDER (PT. 2)	3·26·77	8·27·77	2·11·78		
19.	THE LAMBDA FACTOR	2·26·77	9·6·77	1·21·78		
20.	THE SEANCE SPECTRE	3·12·77	9·13·77	2·4·78		
21.	DORZAK	6·4·77	12·17·77 (PM)			
22.	DEVIL'S MOON	4·16·77	9·10·77	4·8·78		
23.	THE IMMUNITY SYNDROME	4·9·77	9·3·77	4·1·78	3·25·78	
24.	THE DORCONS	5·7·77	9·17·77	4·15·78		

MOONBASE ALPHA PLANS AND PRODUCTION DRAWINGS

Reproduced here are a number of production drawings created for *Space: 1999*.

ALPHA MOONBASE

Moonbase Alpha 1975 exterior plan by Brian Johnson.

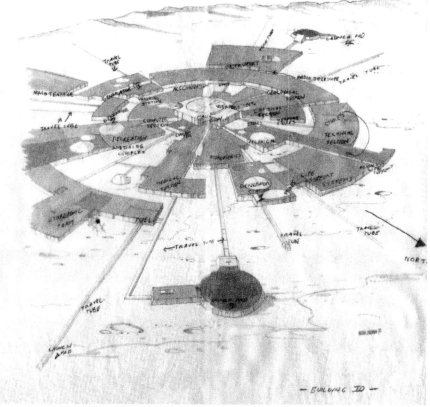

Moonbase Alpha 1975 building ID plan by Brian Johnson.

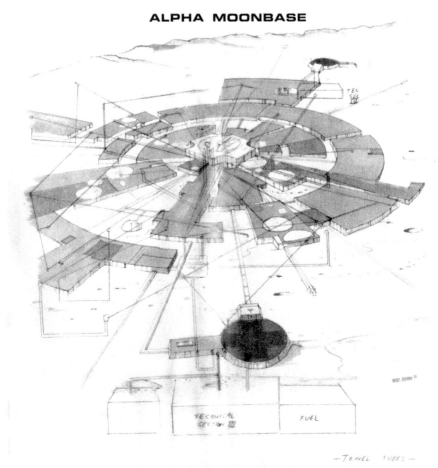

Moonbase Alpha 1975 Travel Tube network plan by Brian Johnson.

The original Moonbase Alpha model.

The Moonbase backdrop.

'The Bringers of Wonder' Alien design. By Keith Wilson.

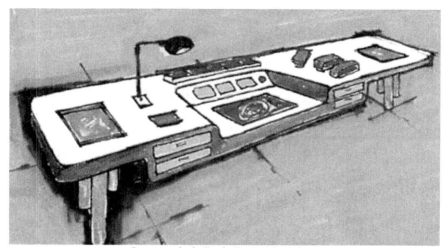

Commander's Desk. By Keith Wilson.

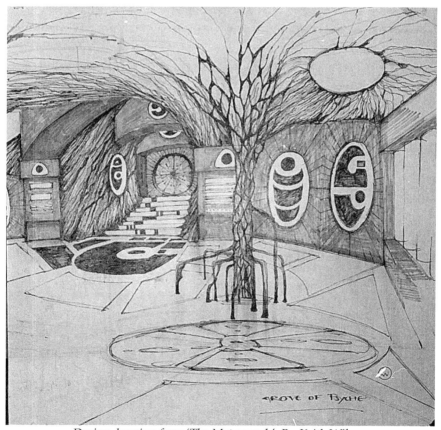

Design drawing from 'The Metamorph'. By Keith Wilson.

Commpost. By Keith Wilson.

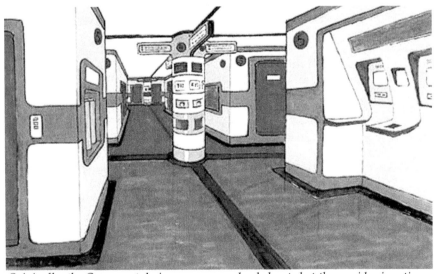

Originally, the Commpost design was a round pole located at the corridor junctions. Realistically, the four-sided final design was more cost effective to construct. By Keith Wilson.

First day shooting slates from VFX unit (top) and live-action (bottom).

INDEX

ABOUT THE AUTHORS

DAVID HIRSCH

Born in 1957, David grew up watching the many TV series created by Gerry and Sylvia Anderson. During his first year of college, he elected to write a paper for a film study class on their work, but with little research material available in the pre-internet era, he was forced to make a daring attempt to secure information from the company that distributed their programs in America, ITC.

A fortuitous meeting with Robert Mandell, son of company president Abe Mandell, eventually led to an introduction to Kerry O'Quinn and Norman Jacobs, publishers of *Starlog* Magazine. A brief summer internship in 1977 led to a long association with the magazine where he worked his way up from contributor (Issue #7) to Associate Editor.

Among his work for the magazine, he edited *Moonbase Alpha Technical Notebook: Official Edition* (1977), 'Gerry Anderson's Space Report' column and several popular titles in the *Starlog Guidebook* series. These included *Fantastic Worlds* (1978), *Science Fiction Weapons* (1979), *Spaceships* (Revised & Expanded 1980), *Special Effects, Vol. 2* (1980), *Science Fiction Heroes* (1980), *Science Fiction Villians* (1980), *TV Episode Guides, Vol. 1* (1981) and *TV Episode Guides, Vol. 2* (1982).

Though he left his full-time position after Issue #71 (1983), David continued as a free-lance writer, now specializing in film and TV music with his AudioLog column (#201, 1994 through 252, 1998) and interviewed many composers such as David Arnold (*Independence Day*), Leonard Rosenman (*RoboCop 2*) and, for their *Star Trek* Magazines, Dennis McCarthy, Ron Jones and Jay Chattaway.

This passion has also led to work on several soundtrack albums as a consultant, producer and writing liner notes. Titles include *Star Trek Volume 2: Doomsday Machine & Amok Time* (Sol Kaplan & Gerald Fried, GNP Crescendo Records 1992), *Space: 1999* (Year 2, Derek Wadsworth, Composer Promo 1995), *Godzilla* (50th Anniversary Edition, Akira Ifukube, La-La Land Records 2004), *Thunderbird 6* (Barry Gray, MGM Music 2005), *King Kong vs. Godzilla* (Akira Ifukube, La-La Land Records 2006) and the 1998 American *Godzilla* (David Arnold, BSX Records 2012).

He has contributed to several books including *The Star Trek Encyclopedia* (Michael and Denise Okuda, Simon & Shuster 1997 edition), *Videohound's Soundtracks* (Didier C Deutsch, Visible Ink 1998), the *Space: 1999* novel 'The Whispering Sea' (John Kenneth Muir, Powys Media, 2014) and *Martin Bower's World of Models* (Shaun McClure & Martin Bower 2019).

More recently, David has achieved a life-long dream to write for a Gerry

Anderson production when son Jamie Anderson invited him to write scripts for the audio drama revival *Terrahawks volume 2 ~ 'Lights, Camera, Disaster'* (Big Finish 2016) and *Terrahawks volume 3 ~ 'Set Sail for Mis-Adventure'* and *'You Foe'* (Big Finish 2017).

Currently, he is consulting on an update of his first book, the *Moonbase Alpha Technical Operations Manual* (Chris Thompson & Andrew Clements, Anderson Entertainment, 2021) and producing a series of albums for the Japanese *a cappella* group Bukimisha (*Godzilla vs Rodan*, BSX Records 2021).

ROBERT E WOOD

Born in 1971, Robert's love of *Space: 1999* has been nearly life-long and has led him to numerous extraordinary experiences, not least of which was a fifteen-year friendship and working relationship with series star Barry Morse, during which they produced (as a triumvirate with Anthony Wynn) a television movie version of Morse's one-man stage show *Merely Players* (2000), TV specials *Spotlight on Barry Morse* and *Spotlight on 1999* (both 2002), the *Space: 1999* audio book *Resurrection* performed by Barry Morse (released by Powys Media in 2010), the audio drama *Rogues and Vagabonds: A Theatrical Scrapbook* (released on CD in 2013), and stage plays including multiple performances of *Merely Players* in the United States, Canada, and England, and a 1999 Los Angeles production of *Love Letters* which reunited Morse with his *Space: 1999* co-star Barbara Bain.

Robert also worked with Barry Morse and Anthony Wynn on numerous books including *Merely Players: The Scripts* (2003), Morse's autobiography *Remember with Advantages* (2006), *Stories of the Theatre* (2006), and following Morse's passing Robert continued to collaborate with Wynn to memorialize Morse in additional books *Such Stuff as Dreams ...* (2009), *Valiant for Truth: Barry Morse and his Lifelong Association with Bernard Shaw* (2012), and *The Wit and Wisdom of Barry Morse* (2013).

Robert's friendship with *Space: 1999* actress Zienia Merton also led him to edit her autobiography, *Anecdotes & Armadillos* (2005).

Throughout 2020 and 2021, while writing this book *To Everything That Might Have Been*, Robert has also been editing the soon-to-be-announced autobiography of another *Space: 1999* star.

As an authority on *Space: 1999* Robert has appeared on numerous television programs, radio talk shows, and podcasts and has been published in magazines such as *Filmfax* (issues 116 and 117, 2008). His book *Destination: Moonbase Alpha – The Unofficial and Unauthorised Guide to Space: 1999* (2010) is the most comprehensive guide to the series ever published.

Since 2012 Robert has been working closely with writer and script editor Christopher Penfold and writing partner Steve Warnek developing concepts and writing screenplays for television and film projects.

CHRISTOPHER PENFOLD

Christopher Penfold has been both writer and script editor in British film and television for over forty years during which he has either written or script edited over 300 hours of prime-time TV including single plays and several feature films. Christopher was story consultant and lead writer for the first season of Gerry Anderson's cult series *Space: 1999*, which starred Martin Landau and Barbara Bain, and wrote the second season of *The Tripods* for the BBC. He script-edited and wrote for the immensely popular BBC series *All Creatures Great And Small* and he either wrote or script-edited over 100 episodes of ITV's long-running hit show *The Bill*. For ten years he taught on the Carlton Screenwriters Course, which produced some of the most successful writers in UK television today. In 1998 he set up his own script production company, ScriptWorks, through which he assisted in the script development of Saul Metzstein's first feature film, *Late Night Shopping* (a prizewinner at Berlin in 2000); John Deery's first feature film, *Conspiracy Of Silence* (winner of the Hartley-Merrill International Screenwriting Award at Cannes in 2001); Kevin Sampson's *Awaydays*; Jonathan Glazer's second feature film *Birth*, which starred Nicole Kidman and Lauren Bacall, and his 2013 feature *Under The Skin*, which starred Scarlett Johansson. Most recently he has assisted in the development of Nicholas Martin's screenplays for *Florence Foster Jenkins*, which was directed by Stephen Frears and starred Meryl Streep and Hugh Grant. From 1999 Christopher was series editor for 78 episodes of ITV's *Midsomer Murders*, which has been possibly the most successful long-form drama series in the history of television, with 128 feature-length episodes produced to date and which is sold in 186 countries.

Printed in Great Britain
by Amazon

84416515R00190